CAPRICORN
RHYMING DICTIONARY

Capricorn
Rhyming Dictionary
(AID TO RHYME)

by
Bessie G. Redfield

CAPRICORN BOOKS
NEW YORK

CAPRICORN BOOKS EDITION, 1965

Fourth Impression

by
Bessie G. Redfield
──────────
Copyright, 1938
by
Bessie G. Redfield

To

WILLIAM THOMPSON REDFIELD

MADE IN THE UNITED STATES OF AMERICA

HOW TO USE THIS BOOK

The reader will notice the carefully arranged groupings of the words, and their endings, which are specifically placed for his convenience. For instance, the endings of each group of words are in the left column, and the references are in the right-hand column in smaller type under *see,* with suffixes which are added to make plurals, or different tenses of verbs. Thus any word with *ly* refers to **E** group of words, and *en* to those ending in **EN**; also that words with the same endings, but pronounced differently are starred thus *. When pronounced more than one way, the star is repeated, as, for example, in **OUGH**, which has five different pronunciations.

CAPRICORN
RHYMING DICTIONARY

A SOUNDS

Appliqué, attaché, au fait, ballet, **A***
bébé, béret, bouquet, buffet, cabriolet, *see*
cachet, café, chalet, cliché, consommé, AY
coryphée, coupé, crochet, croquet, curé, EIGH
décolleté, déplumé, distrait, épée, ex- EY*
tempore, fiancée, foyer, glacé, gourmet, UAY
lettre de cachet, Madame de Sévigné, UET**
maté, matinée, mauvais, mêlée, métier, S-AISE
moiré, naïveté, narghile, née, névé,
O.K., padre, papiermâché, passé, per
se, Pompeii, protégée, purée, quai, re-
poussé, requiescat in pace, résumé, re-
troussé, réveillé, risqué, roué, sachet,
sesame, soirée, sujet, toupet, ukulele,
visé

Addenda, Ætna, Agra, Agrippa, **A****
Ahura Mazda, akasha, Alaska, alfalfa, *see*
Alhambra, Amalthæa, amoeba, am- ABRA
pulla, anaconda, anathema, Androm- ACA
eda, apocrypha, aqua, aqua vitæ, ADA
Aquila, arietta, Atahualpa, Atlanta, AGA
Attila, Ayesha, Ba, Barbarossa, Beer- AH
sheba, Bermuda, bertha, beta, biretta, ALA
Bogota, bonanza, Borsippa, Brahma, ALPHA
Buddha, Burma, Calcutta, calla, Ca- AMA

4

nova, Caracalla, caramba, Casabianca,	**A**
Casanova, cascara, Cassandra, catal-	ANA
pa, Catawba, Cleopatra, Clytemnestra,	ANDA
cobra, comma, contra, copra, Cordova,	ANNA
corolla, Cuba, delta, deva, dharma, di-	ANZA
gamma, dilemma, dogma, Durga, éclat,	ARA
Electra, eureka, Europa, ex cathedra,	ATA
extra, farina, fauna, felucca, fra,	AVA
Frigga, Gæa, gamma, Ganesa, Garuda,	AWAY
geisha, Geneva, Golgotha, grandpa,	AY
hacienda, hagiographa, ha-ha, Hecuba,	AYA
Hiawatha, Hybla, impedimenta, Inca,	EA
Indra, infanta, influenza, infra, jinrick-	EBRA
sha, Joppa, Judæa, Ka, Kaaba, kalpa,	EDDA
Kamchatka, kappa, Karma, kibla,	ELLA
Krishna, Lady Godiva, larva, Laura,	EMA
Leda, Lhassa, Libra, Lyra, ma, Ma-	ENA
deira, magenta, Magna Charta, Ma-	ENNA
hadeva, mahatma, malacca, Malta,	ERA
mama, Manila, mantra, marimba,	ESTA
Marpessa, Mazeppa, mazurka, mea	IA
culpa, Mecca, mesa, miasma, Minerva,	ICA
Minnehaha, Mona Lisa, Mount Shasta,	IGMA
Mylitta, naphtha, Nova Zembla,	IKA
Odessa, okra, Omaha, omega, operetta,	ILLA
orchestra, Ouida, ouija, pa, Padua,	IMA
pagoda, palestra, Palmyra, pampa,	INA
papa, pasha, peseta, piazza, Pietà,	IRA
Pisa, polka, puma, pupa, Pyrrha, Ra,	ISTA
regatta, Rig-Veda, rotunda, savanna,	ITA
Scylla, Seneca, seta, Sheba, Shiva,	OA
sierra, Smyrna, soda, sofa, spa, Sparta,	ODA
Spinoza, Sumatra, sura, syringa, taf-	OGA
feta, Tampa, tapioca, ta-ta, terra	OLA
firma, St. Theresa, Topeka, tuba,	OMA
tundra, ultra, umbra, Ursa, Valhalla,	ONA
Vega, vendetta, Venezuela, veranda,	ONDA

vice-versa, viva, vodka, Volga, Voluspa, **A****
yucca, Zarathustra

ONNA
ORA
OSA
OTA
ULA
UMBRA
USA
YA
YDRA

Baal, kraal, kursaal, Transvaal **AAL**
see
AL

Ab, Ahab, blab, cab, confab, crab, **AB***
dab, drab, gab, grab, hissing-crab, jab, *see*
Moab, nab, Punjab, Queen Mab, Ra- ARAB
hab, sand-dab, scab, slab, stab, tab,
taxi-cab

Squab, swab **AB****
see
OB

Babble, dabble, gabble, grabble, **ABBLE**
rabble, scrabble, squabble *see*
EL
LE

Cabby, drabby, flabby, scabby, tabby **ABBY**
see
E**

Astrolabe **ABE**
see

Abel, Babel, label

ABEL
see
EL
LE

Able, adorable, affable, allowable,
amicable, answerable, arable, assess-
able, available, breakable, cable, cal-
culable, capable, censurable, commend-
able, commensurable, comparable, con-
ceivable, consolable, constable, de-
lectable, demonstrable, deplorable,
desirable, despicable, detachable, dis-
able, disputable, durable, enable, es-
capable, estimable, evaporable, exe-
crable, explicable, fable, formidable,
friable, gable, get-at-able, hall-table,
immeasurable, immutable, impassable,
impeccable, impenetrable, imperish-
able, implacable, impracticable, im-
pregnable, improbable, inalienable, in-
applicable, incalculable, incapable, in-
commensurable, incomparable, incon-
solable, incontestable, indefatigable,
indefinable, indemonstrable, indescrib-
able, indispensable, indisputable, in-
effable, ineradicable, inexcusable, in-
exorable, inflammable, inscrutable, in-
separable, insurmountable, intermin-
able, invaluable, inviolable, invulnerable, irrefragable, irrefutable, irrevoc-
able, jumpable, knowable, laudable,
likable, lovable, memorable, mono-
syllable, mutable, navigable, notable,
palatable, palpable, parable, pardon-
able, passable, peccable, perishable,
pleasurable, polysyllable, portable,

ABLE
see
EABLE
EL
ERABLE
IABLE
ITABLE
LE
UABLE
y-ABLY

practicable, pregnable, presentable, **ABLE**
printable, probable, punishable, ques-
tionable, readable, reasonable, recep-
table, redoubtable, refutable, regret-
table, removable, resolvable, retable,
Round Table, revocable, sable, scruta-
ble, seasonable, spankable, stable, sur-
mountable, syllable, table, tarnishable,
taxable, teachable, tenable, terminable,
time-table, tractable, unable, unassail-
able, unavoidable, unbearable, unbe-
lievable, undiminishable, unfathom-
able, unmentionable, unprintable, un-
seasonable, unshakable, unspeakable,
unstable, unstridable, unsurpassable,
unwarrantable, usable, vegetable, voc-
able, vulnerable, warrantable

Ably, adorably, amicably, favorably, **ABLY**
inevitably, irrevocably, irritably, justi-   *see*
fiably, preferably, presumably, un-   E**
speakably   ABLE-*y*

Baboo, bugaboo, taboo   **ABOO**
   see
   OO

Abracadabra, candelabra   **ABRA**
   see
   A**

Danse macabre   **ABRE**
   see

Almanac, Armagnac, Balzac, biv-   **AC**
ouac, bric-à-brac, cognac, cul-de-sac,   *see*
ipecac, lac, lilac, Pachamac, Potomac,   ACH*

sandarac, Saranac, shellac, sumac, tabac

AC
ACK
AK
IAC

Alpaca, cloaca, paca, portulaca, Titicaca

ACA
see
A**

Ace, Alsace, anchoring-place, apace, beardless-face, birthplace, brace, chimney-place, commonplace, deface, disgrace, displace, dough-face, dwellingplace, efface, embrace, face, furnace, gold-lace, grace, grimace, hiding-place, Horace, interlace, interspace, lace, mace, macrimé lace, marketplace, menace, misplace, necklace, open-face, pace, palace, place, point lace, pokerface, populace, preface, Queen Anne's lace, race, refuge-place, replace, resting-place, retrace, Samothrace, scapegrace, shame-face, solace, space, surface, tailrace, terrace, trace, trystingplace, unlace, wheyface

ACE
see
ASE*
ed-AIST
   ASTE-*d*
s-IS**
   IZ

Adjacent, complacent

ACENT
see
ENT

Bach, Bel-Merodach, Meshach, Shadrach, stomach, sumach

ACH*
see
AC
ACK

Detach, spinach

ACH**
see
ATCH*

Apache, cache, moustache, pistache   **ACHE***
see
ASH*

Ache, head-ache, heart-ache   **ACHE****
see
AKE

Drachm   **ACHM**
see
AM

Steam-yacht, yacht   **ACHT**
see
OT

Audacious, contumacious, curvacious, edacious, efficacious, fumacious, gracious, loquacious, mendacious, mordacious, perspicacious, pertinacious, predacious, pugnacious, rapacious, sagacious, sequacious, spacious, veracious, vivacious, voracious   **ACIOUS**
see
IOUS
OUS

Capacity, mendacity, opacity, perspicacity, pertinacity, pugnacity, rapacity, sagacity, tenacity, veracity, vivacity, voracity   **ACITY**
see
E**
ITY

Aback, Adirondack, alack, applejack, attack, back, bareback, black, bookrack, bookstack, bootblack, bootjack, canvasback, clack, come-back, Cossack, crack, cracker-jack, dirttrack, drawback, flapjack, flashback, full back, gimcrack, greenback, gripsack, gunnysack, hack, hackmatack,   **ACK**
see
AC
ACH*
AK

hardtack, hat-rack, haversack, hay-rack, high-low-jack, hi-jack, horseback, hunchback, Jack, knack, knapsack, knick-knack, lack, lampblack, leather-back, lumberjack, pack, paddywhack, pickaback, pitch-black, quack, quarter-back, rack, ransack, razorback, rick-rack, sack, setback, shack, shoe-black, sidetrack, slack, slap jack, smack, smoke-stack, snack, spur-track, squir-rel-track, stack, steeple-jack, switch-back, tack, tamarack, thumb-tack, thwack, toast-rack, track, tricktrack, Union Jack, unpack, whack, wisecrack, wrack, zwieback

ACK

Blacken, bracken, slacken

ACKEN
see
EN

Backer, blacker, cannon-cracker, cracker, Georgia cracker, hi-jacker, nutcracker, slacker

ACKER
see
ER

Blue-jacket, bracket, jacket, mon-key-jacket, packet, pea-jacket, racket, strait-jacket

ACKET
see
ET

Cackle, crackle, grackle, ramshackle, shackle, tackle

ACKLE
see
EL
LE

Barracks

ACKS
see
ACK-*s*

Barnacle, binnacle, debacle, manacle, miracle, obstacle, oracle, pinnacle, receptacle, spectacle, tabernacle, tentacle

ACLE
see
EL
LE

Acre, God's acre, massacre, nacre, simulacre, wiseacre

ACRE
see
ER

Abstract, act, attract, bract, cataract, compact, contract, counteract, detract, distract, enact, exact, extract, fact, impact, inexact, intact, interact, matter-of-fact, pact, protract, react, refract, retract, riot-act, Stamp Act, subtract, tact, tract, transact

ACT
see
ACK-*ed*
ed-EAD*
ED
S-AC-*s*
ACH*-*s*
ACK-*s*
AX

Didactic, lactic, prophylactic, tactic

ACTIC
see
IC

Actor, chiropractor, detractor, extractor, factor, tractor

ACTOR
see
OR

Accuracy, adequacy, advocacy, aristocracy, celibacy, confederacy, contumacy, democracy, diplomacy, effeminacy, fallacy, gynecocracy, illiteracy, intimacy, lacy, legacy, literacy, lunacy, obstinacy, papacy, pharmacy, plutocracy, privacy, racy, supremacy, theocracy

ACY
see
E**
ICACY
IRACY

Accad, ad., bad, Bagdad, ballad, brad, cad, Carlsbad, clad, dad, doodad, egad, fad, farad, footpad, forbad, gad, Galahad, glad, had, ironclad, Jehad, lad, lily-pad, mad, mail-clad, monad, olive-clad, pad, sad, salad, shad, Sinbad, snowclad, stark-mad, steel-clad, tetrad, Trinidad, Upanishad, velvet-clad

AD*
see
ADE**
AID***
IAD
YAD

Wad

AD**
see
OD

Armada, Canada, cicada, Granada, Haggada, posada, Torquemada

ADA
see
A**

Add

ADD
see
AD

Addle, paddle, saddle, skedaddle, staddle, straddle, swaddle, twaddle, waddle

ADDLE
see
EL
LE

Abrade, accolade, ambuscade, arcade, balustrade, barricade, blade, blockade, brigade, brocade, cannonade, cascade, cavalcade, centigrade, charade, cockade, colonnade, crusade, deadly nightshade, decade, degrade, escalade, escapade, esplanade, evade, everglade, facade, fade, free-trade, fusillade, glade, harlequinade, homemade, invade, jade, lade, lampshade,

ADE*
see
AID
ENADE
UADE
S-ADES**

lemonade, marmalade, masquerade, **ADE***
nightshade, orangeade, palisade, pa-
rade, pasquinade, pervade, pomade,
readymade, renegade, retrograde, rho-
domantade, shade, shoulder-blade,
spade, stockade, sunshade, tirade,
trade, wade, well-made

   Comrade, Scheherazade **ADE****
                   see
                   AD

   Crusader, masquerader, trader **ADER**
                   see
                   ER

   Alcibiades, Cyclades, Hades, Hippo- **ADES***
tades, Miltiades, Pleiades   *see*
                   EA*-*s*
                   EASE

   Crusades, palisades **ADES****
                   see
                   ADE*-*s*

   Badge, cadge, Madge **ADGE**
                   see

   Monadic, nomadic, sporadic **ADIC**
                   see
                   IC

   Avocado, bastinado, bravado, Colo- **ADO**
rado, comerado, crusado, desperado,   *see*
El Dorado, mikado, prado, renegado,   O*
stoccado, tornado

Ambassador, conquistador, depre- **ADOR**
dator, Ecuador, Labrador, matador, *see*
picador, San Salvador, toreador OR

Arcady, lady, landlady, malady, **ADY**
milady, shady *see*
E**

Algæ, antennæ, arbor-vitæ, brae, **Æ**
Danæ, dies iræ, dramatis personæ, *see*
horæ, lapus linguæ, larvæ, lingnum E*
vitæ, minutiæ, Mycenæ, Parcæ, sundæ,
Thermopylæ

Azrael, Ishmael, Israel, Jael, **AEL**
Michael, Raphael *see*
EL
LE

Chafe, safe, unsafe, vouchsafe **AFE***
see
AIF

Carafe **AFE****
see
AFF

Chaff, distaff, draff, Falstaff, flag- **AFF**
staff, gaff, pikestaff, pilgrim staff, riff- *see*
raff, sclaff, shandy gaff, staff, working- AFE**
staff AFFE
ALF
APH

Giraffe **AFFE**
see
AFE**

Abaft, aft, aircraft, anti-aircraft, craft, daft, draft, fore and aft, graft, haft, handicraft, kingcraft, priestcraft, quaft, shaft, statecraft, waft, witch-craft

AFT
see
APH-*ed*
AUGHT**

After, hereafter, rafter, thereafter

AFTER
see
ER

Bag, beanbag, black flag, blueflag, brag, brain-fag, button-bag, carpet-bag, crag, ditty-bag, drag, dufflebag, fag, flag, gag, hag, handbag, jutting-crag, lag, mailbag, money-bag, nag, rag, ragtag, saddlebag, sag, saltbag, sandbag, scallawag, scrag, shag, slag, sleeping-bag, snag, stag, starry flag, tag, wag, water-bag, wig-wag, zigzag

AG
see

Malaga, Naga, rutabaga, saga

AGA
see
A**

Adage, advantage, age, anchorage, appendage, assemblage, baggage, ban-dage, birdcage, bondage, boscage, cabbage, cage, Carthage, cartilage, classic-age, cleavage, coinage, cold-storage, cordage, cottage, courage, cribbage, damage, dangerous age, dis-courage, disparage, dosage, drainage, encourage, enrage, ensilage, equipage, espionage, flowering sage, forage, frontage, fruitage, fuselage, garbage, Golden Age, greengage, Greenwich Vil-lage, herbage, heritage, homage, hos-

AGE*
see
AUGE
EAGE
EDGE
EGE
ERAGE
IAGE
ORAGE
OTAGE
UAGE
S-ES*

tage, image, leafage, leakage, luggage, **AGE***
manage, middle age, mismanage, mort-
gage, mucilage, nonage, orphanage,
ossifrage, outrage, package, page, par-
entage, parsonage, pasturage, patron-
age, percentage, pilgrimage, pillage,
plumage, portage, postage, pottage,
presage, rage, rampage, ravage, rum-
mage, sabotage, sage, salvage, sausage,
savage, saxifrage, scrimmage, scrum-
mage, scutage, seepage, sewage, short-
age, shrinkage, silage, skunkcabbage,
smallage, spoilage, stage, steerage,
stone age, stoppage, storage, suffrage,
tallage, tankage, tillage, title-page,
tutelage, umbrage, upstage, usage,
vantage, vassalage, vicarage, village,
vintage, visage, voyage, wage, wolfish-
rage, wreckage

Appanage, badinage, bon voyage, **AGE****
boscage, camouflage, entourage, es- *see*
pionage, feuillage, garage, massage,
ménage, mirage, persiflage, personage

Agent, press-agent **AGENT**
see
ENT

Dowager, lager, manager, old stager, **AGER**
onager, tanager, wager *see*
ER

Diaphragm **AGM**
see
AM

Champagne, Charlemagne, Bretagne **AGNE**
see
AIN

Ago, archipelago, dago, farrago, **AGO**
Iago, lumbago, plumbago, sago, solid-   *see*
ago, virago, years-ago   O*

Aragon, Dagon, dragon, flagon, **AGON**
hexagon, octagon, paragon, pentagon,   *see*
snapdragon, tarragon, tetragon, wagon,   AN**
waterwagon   ON

Anagram, diagram, pentagram **AGRAM**
see
AM

Hague, plague, Prague, vague **AGUE***
see
EG

Colleague, league **AGUE****
see
UE**

Ague, argue **AGUE*****
see
U*

Asparagus, sarcophagus, Tagus **AGUS**
see
US

Abdullah, ah, amah, bah, Beulah, **AH**
bismillah, blah, cheetah, dahabeeyah,   *see*
Deborah, fellah, Gomorrah, howdah,   A**
hurrah, huzzah, Jehovah, Jonah, jub-   IAH

bah, Judah, kiblah, maharajah, Ma-   **AH**
nassah, Menephtah, Methuselah,
Micah, Mizpah, mullah, Noah, pah,
Pisgah, Ptah, purdah, rajah, Rizpah,
Rosh Hashanah, Selah, shah, Shah-
Namah, Shekinah, Shenandoah, shil-
lelah, sirrah, Terah, Torah, yeah

Adonai, caravanserai, El Shaddai,   **AI**
Mordecai, Shanghai, Sinai   *see*
                                    I*

Aramaic, archaic, Hebraic, laic,   **AIC**
Lamaic, mosaic, prosaic, Romaic, vol-   *see*
taic   IC

Afraid, aid, air-raid, bondmaid,   **AID***
braid, handmaid, inlaid, laid, maid,   *see*
mermaid, milkmaid, overpaid, paid,   ADE*
plaid, poorly-paid, raid, repaid, sea-   AY-*ed*
maid, shepherd's plaid, staid, unpaid,
upbraid, waylaid

Aforesaid, said, Thebaid, unsaid   **AID****
                                    see
                                    EAD*

Naif, waif   **AIF**
                                    see
                                    AFE*

Arraign, campaign   **AIGN**
                                    see
                                    AIN

Straight   **AIGHT**
                                    see
                                    ATE

Haik

AIK
see
IKE

Ail, assail, avail, bail, bewail, black-mail, bobtail, cat-tail, cocktail, curtail, derail, detail, dinner-pail, dovetail, draggle-tail, entail, fail, fan-mail, fan-tail, flail, foxtail, frail, grail, hail, hand-rail, hangnail, hobnail, jail, mail, main-sail, mare's tail, monorail, nail, oxtail, pail, pigtail, pintail, prevail, quail, rail, remail, retail, ringtail, sail, silver nail, slaptail, snail, stay-sail, swallow-tail, taffrail, tail, tattered-sail, thumbnail, trail, travail, vail, wagtail, wail, wassail

AIL
see
ALE
EIL

Blackmailer, trailer

AILER
see
ER

Acclaim, aim, claim, declaim, dis-claim, Ephraim, exclaim, maim, Miz-raim, proclaim, quitclaim, reclaim

AIM
see
AME*

Abstain, again, amain, appertain, at-tain, bargain, blain, boatswain, brain, Cain, captain, certain, chain, chamber-lain, chaplain, chieftain, chilblain, come-again, complain, constrain, con-tain, coxswain, cross-grain, curtain, detain, disdain, domain, drain, drop curtain, enchain, endless-chain, enter-tain, explain, fain, foreordain, foun-tain, gain, grain, ingrain, legerdemain, main, maintain, Mark Twain, moun-tain, obtain, ordain, pain, pattering-

AIN
see
AGNE
AIGN
AINE
ANE
EIGN
EIN

rain, plain, plantain, porcelain, pre-
ordain, purslain, quatrain, rain, rattle-
brain, refrain, regain, remain, restrain,
retain, sea-captain, simple-swain, soda-
fountain, Spain, Spanish Main, stain,
St. Germain, strain, sustain, suzerain,
swain, tent-curtain, terrain, train,
twain, vain, vervain, villain, weather
stain

AIN

Aquitaine, chatelaine, cocaine, Lor-
raine, migraine, moraine, ptomaine

AINE
see
AIN

Aint, aquaint, complaint, constraint,
faint, liveries-quaint, paint, patron
saint, plaint, quaint, restraint, saint,
self-restraint, taint, warpaint

AINT
see
EINT
ly-E**

Affair, air, armchair, backstair, bath
chair, camel's hair, campchair, chair,
Corsair, debonair, éclair, fair, flair,
hair, horsehair, impair, kinky hair,
lair, maidenhair, Mayfair, mid air,
mohair, open-air, pair, repair, rocking-
chair, sedan-chair, stair, study-chair,
unfair, Vanity Fair, Windsor chair

AIR
see
AIRE
ARE*
EAR**
EIR*

Brumaire, debonaire, doctrinaire,
Frimaire, legionnaire, millionaire, mul-
timillionaire, questionnaire, savoir
faire, secretaire, solitaire, Vendemaire,
vin ordinaire, Voltaire

AIRE
see
AIR

Bairn, cairn, Pitcairn

AIRN
see

Airy, dairy, fairy, hairy **AIRY**
see
E**

Dais, Sais **AIS***
see
IS*

Calais, Rabelais **AIS****
see
A*

Braise, chaise, malaise, Marseillaise, **AISE**
mayonnaise, Père-la-Chaise, polonaise, *see*
postchaise, praise, raise, self-praise AISSE
A*-*s*
AIZE
ASE**
AY-*s*
EIGH-*s*

Archaism, Hebraism, Judaism, La- **AISM**
maism *see*
ISM

Bouillabaisse, caisse **AISSE**
see
AISE

Waist, wasp-waist **AIST**
see
ASTE

Bait, bull bait, fishbait, gait, plait, **AIT**
portrait, strait, wait, whitebait *see*
ATE

Bull baiter, congress gaiter, gaiter, waiter

AITER
see
ER

Faith, water-wraith, wraith

AITH*
see

Saith

AITH**
see
ETH

Glaive, naive, waive

AIVE
see
AVE*

Baize, maize

AIZE
see
AISE

Al Borak, Barak, Irak, Karnak, kodak, yak, yashmak

AK
see
AC
ACH*
ACK

Air-brake, bake, betake, brake, cake, canebrake, clambake, coasterbrake, cornflake, drake, earthquake, fake, flake, forsake, gartersnake, give and take, griddlecake, handshake, intake, keepsake, kittiwake, lake, make, mandrake, mercy-sake, mistake, namesake, overtake, pancake, partake, quake, rake, rattlesnake, retake, saffron cake, sake, sea-snake, shake, sheep-bake, sheldrake, shortcake, snake, snowflake,

AKE
see
ACHE**
AQUE**
EAK**

spake, stake, sweepstake, take, tipsy-cake, undertake, wide-awake **AKE**

Awaken, betaken, mistaken, taken, wind-shaken **AKEN** *see* EN

Baker, breaker, caretaker, dress-maker, haymaker, jail-breaker, law-breaker, maker, matchmaker, peace-maker, Quaker, sailmaker, Shaker, shoemaker, spinnaker, tentmaker, un-dertaker **AKER** *see* ER

Abnormal, abysmal, admiral, adum-bral, antidotal, antipodal, apocryphal, arbital, astral, austral, autumnal, avowal, Bengal, betrayal, betrothal, cabal, carnal, cathedral, caudal, cen-tral, cerebral, cloistral, coastal, colos-sal, corral, crystal, demoniacal, de-posal, dihedral, disavowal, dismal, dis-missal, dorsal, ducal, enthral, epochal, feudal, Fingal, Funchal, gal, gyral, herbal, integral, interval, isothermal, jackal, Jubal, lachrymal, lethal, Luper-cal, madrigal, magistral, mammal, marshal, medal, missal, mistral, modal, narwhal, nasal, naval, offal, orchestral, pal, papal, Parsifal, paschal, pedal, panal, portrayal, postal, prodigal, pro-posal, Provençal, quintal, rascal, rear-admiral, rebuttal, rehearsal, renewal, reprisal, reversal, rock-crystal, sacer-dotal, sandal, scandal, seneschal, se-pulchral, signal, spectral, spiral, spousal, storm-signal, survival, synagogal, Taj

AL *see* AAL ANAL EAL EGAL ENAL ENTAL ERAL ERIAL ERNAL ESTAL ETAL EVAL IAL IBAL ICAL IDAL IMAL INAL ION-*al* IPAL ITAL

Mahal, teetotal, thermal, total, tri-
bunal, triumphal, universal, upheaval,
vandal, vassal, verbal, withdrawal,
withal

AL
IVAL
OCAL
ONAL
OPAL
ORAL
ORMAL
ORTAL
OVAL
OYAL
UAL
UGAL
URAL
URNAL
USAL
UTAL
ly-E**
s-ALS

Cabala, gala, Kalevala, Guatemala,
Jumala, La Scala, marsala, Sakuntala,
Shambhala

ALA
see
A**

Talc

ALC
see

Bald, emerald, herald, piebald, ri-
bald, scald, skald

ALD
see
ALL-*ed*
AUL-*ed*

Heraldry, ribaldry

ALDRY
see
E**

Airedale, ale, bale, chippendale,
dale, exhale, farthingale, female, gale,
gunwale, hale, impale, inhale, kale,

ALE
see
AIL

male, martingale, musicale, nightingale, pale, percale, regale, rummagesale, sale, scale, shale, stale, swale, tale, telltale, vale, whale, wholesale, Yale

ALE
EIL

Equivalent, prevalent

ALENT
see
ENT

Aleph

ALEPH
see
IPH

Behalf, calf, half, half and half, sea calf

ALF
see
APH

Ali, Bali, Bengali, Kali, Somali

ALI
see
I**

Australia, bacchanalia, paraphernalia, parentalia, penetralia, regalia, saturnalia, Thalia, Vestalia

ALIA
see
IA

Invalid, squalid, valid

ALID
see
ID

Aurora borealis, chrysalis, Count de Gabalis, cum grano salis, digitalis, oxalis

ALIS
see
IS*

Bilingualism, fatalism, formalism, idealism, imperialism, individualism, nationalism, rationalism, revivalism, royalism, socialism, vandalism

ALISM
see
ISM

Abnormality, actuality, banality, beastiality, carnality, conviviality, duality, equality, eternality, ethereality, fatality, finality, formality, frugality, generality, hospitality, inequality, intellectuality, liberality, locality, mentality, modality, mortality, municipality, neutrality, normality, originality, partiality, personality, plurality, potentiality, principality, prodigality, quality, rascality, reality, speciality, substantiality, technicality, tonality, totality, triviality, vitality

ALITY
see
E**
ITY

Equalize, idealize, immortalize, individualize, legalize, localize, materialize, moralize, mortalize, neutralize, penalize, rationalize, realize, scandalize, signalize, specialize, tantalize, visualize, vocalize

ALIZE
see
IZE

Balk, beanstalk, cakewalk, calk, chalk, cornstalk, intermittent talk, jaywalk, rope-walk, sheep-walk, sidewalk, small-talk, stalk, talk, walk

ALK
see
AWK

All, appall, ball, banquet-hall, baseball, basketball, befall, bird-call, blackball, bookstall, bugle-call, button-ball, call, carry-all, catcall, Chinese Wall, clarion-call, coffee-stall, Cornwall, croquet-ball, dancehall, downfall, enthrall, eyeball, fall, fish-ball, footfall, forestall, fruit-stall, gall, hall, highball, hold-all, install, mall, mudwall, music-hall, musketball, nightfall, overall, pall, pitfall, prison-wall, puffball,

ALL*
see
AUL
AWL
ed-ALD
y-E**
ALLY

rainfall, recall, roll call, sea-wall, small, **ALL***
spit ball, squall, stall, stonewall, tall,
tapestried-wall, tea-ball, thrall, wall,
waterfall, windfall

Shall **ALL****
see
AL

Callow, fallow, hallow, mallow, **ALLOW**
marsh mallow, sallow, shallow, tallow, *see*
wallow OW*

Ally, cynically, dally, diametrically, **ALLY**
dilly-dally, eternally, graphically, *see*
ideally, mathematically, morally, oc- E****
casionally, paradoxically, personally,
pragmatically, prosaically, rally, ras-
cally, reverentially, rurally, sally,
shilly-shally, stoically, tally, techni-
cally, totally, typically, tyrannically,
vitally

Balm, becalm, calm, doum palm, **ALM**
embalm, palm, psalm *see*
UALM

Buffalo, halo, water-buffalo **ALO**
see
O*

Anomalous, bicephalous, jealous, **ALOUS**
megacephalous, scandalous *see*
OUS

Alp, scalp **ALP**
see

Alpha **ALPHA**
see
A**

Cavalry, chivalry, rivalry **ALRY**
see
E**

Annals, cymbals **ALS**
see
AL-*s*

Alt, asphalt, basalt, cobalt, exalt, **ALT**
halt, malt, rock salt, salt, sea-salt, *see*
shalt, smalt, spring-halt AULT
s-ALTZ

Healthy, stealthy, wealthy **ALTHY**
see
E**

Alto, contralto, Rialto **ALTO**
see
O*

Casualty, fealty, loyalty, mayoralty, **ALTY**
penalty, realty, royalty, salty, vice- *see*
royalty E**

Waltz **ALTZ**
see
ALT-*s*

Bucephalus, Dædalus, Heliogabalus, **ALUS**
Sardanapalus, Tantalus *see*
US

Bivalve, calve, halve, needle valve, **ALVE**
salve, valve *see*

Abraham, Adam, Adullam, am, **AM**
amalgam, balsam, bantam, bedlam, *see*
beldam, buckram, cablegram, cam, AGM
clam, Coulee Dam, cram, dam, dram, AGRAM
Durham, epigram, flotsam, gam, ging- AMB
ham, gram, grand-slam, ham, Hiram, AMME
I am, imam, Islam, jam, jetsam, jim- AMN
jam, lam, macadam, madam, man- ASM
tram, marconigram, milldam, Omar OGRAM
Khayyam, pam, praam, pram, quan-
dam, ram, Rustam, salaam, scram,
sham, Siam, slam, Surinam, swam,
sweet-marjoram, telegram, Uncle Sam,
wham

Aceldama, Alabama, Bahama, cy- **AMA**
clorama, Dalai Lama, drama, Fuji- *see*
yama, Gautama, Kama, lama, llama, A**
mama, melodrama, pajama, Panama,
panorama, pranayama, Rama, Yama,
Yokohama

Dithyramb, iamb, jamb, lamb **AMB**
see
AM

Amble, bramble, preamble, scram- **AMBLE**
ble, shamble *see*
EL
LE

Aflame, blame, came, candle-flame, **AME***
dame, defame, fame, flame, frame, *see*
game, hallowed-flame, hame, inflame, AIM

lame, name, nickname, oriflame, over-
came, pen-name, same, selfsame,
shame, stepdame, surname, tame

AME*
AIME

Madame, Notre Dame

AME**
see
AM

Camel, caramel, enamel

AMEL
see
EL
LE

Amen, cyclamen, stamen, Tutank-
hamen

AMEN
see
EN

Armament, filament, firmament, la-
ment, ligament, lineament, medica-
ment, ornament, parliament, predica-
ment, sacrament, temperament, testa-
ment, tournament

AMENT
see
ENT

Gossamer, steamer, streamer, tamer

AMER
see
ER

Adamic, balsamic, ceramic, dynam-
ic, hydrodynamic, panoramic

AMIC
see
IC

Benjamin, gamin

AMIN
see
IN

Gramme, oriflamme, programme

AMME
see
AM

Damn   **AMN**
                                                  see
                                                  AM

Amor, clamor, enamor   **AMOR**
                                                  see
                                                  OR

Aid-de-camp, champ, clamp, cramp,   **AMP***
damp, decamp, encamp, firedamp,   *see*
glow-worm's lamp, lamp, postage-
stamp, ramp, safety-lamp, scamp,
spirit-lamp, stamp, tamp, tramp, vamp

Dismal Swamp, swamp   **AMP****
                                                  see
                                                  OMP

Pampa, Tampa   **AMPA**
                                                  see
                                                  A**

Damper, hamper, pamper, scamper,   **AMPER**
tamper   *see*
                                                  ER

Ample, example, sample, trample   **AMPLE**
                                                  see
                                                  EL
                                                  LE

Campus, grampus, hippocampus   **AMPUS**
                                                  see
                                                  US

Calamus, hippopotamus, ignoramus,   **AMUS**
mandamus, Morituri Salutamus, No-   *see*
stradamus   US

Bigamy, foamy, infamy, monogamy, poetogamy, polygamy, thingamy

AMY
see
E**

Afghan, Ahriman, Alaskan, Alderbaran, alderman, astrakhan, azan, backwoodsman, Balkan, ban, banyan, barrel-organ, began, birdman, bogeyman, Brahman, bran, brogan, bushman, Caliban, can, cancan, capstan, caravan, catamaran, cattleman, caveman, Chinaman, clan, clansman, clergyman, corban, courlan, Cretan, divan, dolman, draftsman, dustpan, Elizabethan, Etruscan, everyman, fan, fantan, fellowman, fireman, fisherman, foreman, Franciscan, freshman, fryingpan, Genghis Khan, gentleman, G-man, Gulistan, hackman, hardpan, harmattan, harridan, helmsman, heman, henchman, Heshvan, highwayman, Hindustan, horseman, hot-watercan, human, husbandman, inhuman, interurban, Iran, Ispahan, Jordan, kaftan, Kashan, khan, Khorassan, Ku-Klux-Klan, Kurdistan, layman, leman, leviathan, Libyan, longshoreman, madman, Magellan, man, marksman, marzipan, medicine-man, merchantman, middleman, midshipman, minute-man, molluscan, Musselman, Naaman, news organ, Nisan, Norman, Norseman, organ, orphan, Oscan, oysterman, pagan, pan, pavan, pecan, Peter Pan, plan, policeman, postman, Pullman, quartan, raglan, ragman, Ramadan, ran, randan, rataplan, rat-

AN*
see
ARIAN
ATAN
EAN**
EDIAN
ERAN
ESAN
IAN
ICAN
ICIAN
IGAN
ISAN
ITAN
OMAN
UAN

tan, redan, Redman, reman, rifleman, **AN***
Roman, rowan, sacristan, sampan,
sandman, sauce-pan, scan, Scotsman,
seaman, sedan, shaman, showman,
silvan, slogan, snowman, Solyman,
Soudan, span, Spartan, spick and span,
spokesman, St. Dunstan, steersman,
stewpan, suburban, suffragan, sultan,
suntan, superhuman, superman,
switchman, sylvan, talisman, tattan,
than, Theban, Tibetan, tincan, Titan,
toboggan, toucan, Trajan, Uhlan,
watchman, Welshman, yeggman, yeoman, Zoan

Swan, wan   **AN****
        see
        ON
        UAN

Ana, Apollonius of Tyanna, arcana,   **ANA**
banana, bandana, Cana, Diana, dulci-   *see*
ana, Ecbatana, fata morgana, Guiana,   A**
gymkhana, Havana, iguana, lantana,
liana, Louisiana, mañana, Narayana,
Nirvana, quotidiana, Ramayana, sul-
tana, vox humana

Bacchanal, banal, canal   **ANAL**
        see
        AL

Charabanc, franc   **ANC**
        see
        ANK

Abeyance, abidance, abundance, acquaintance, admittance, advance, aidance, allowance, ambulance, annoyance, appearance, appurtenance, arrogance, askance, assistance, assurance, attendance, avoidance, balance, barn dance, bechance, buoyance, chance, circumstance, clairvoyance, clearance, concomitance, concordance, connivance, contra-dance, contrivance, conveyance, countenance, country dance, dance, discordance, dissonance, distance, disturbance, durance, elegance, encumbrance, endurance, enhance, entrance, extravagance, finance, for instance, fragrance, France, freelance, furtherance, glance, governance, grievance, guidance, hindrance, ignorance, importance, inelegance, inheritance, instance, insurance, jubilance, lance, maintenance, mischance, misfeasance, monstrance, morrice-dance, nonchalance, nuisance, obeisance, observance, ordinance, ordnance, outdistance, overbalance, parlance, penance, perchance, performance, perseverance, petulance, pittance, prance, predominance, protuberance, quittance, reappearance, reconnaisance, redundance, relevance, reluctance, remembrance, remittance, remonstrance, renaissance, repugnance, resemblance, resonance, riddance, romance, semblance, severance, shawl-dance, sibilance, significance, stance, substance, sun-dance, superabundance, surveillance, temperance, tolerance, trance, unbalance, ut-

ANCE

see

ANSE
ANT*-*s*
ENCE
ENSE
ENT-*s*
IANCE
IENCE
UANCE

terance, valance, vengeance, vigilance, **ANCE**
war-dance

Blanch, branch, olive-branch, ranch **ANCH***
see
ANCHE

Stanch **ANCH****
see
AUNCH

Avalanche, carte blanche, Comanche **ANCHE**
see
ANCH*

Blatancy, buoyancy, chiromancy, **ANCY**
dactylomancy, discrepancy, expect- *see*
ancy, fancy, flagrancy, flippancy, hesi- E**
tancy, inconstancy, infancy, necro- EE
mancy, nonchalancy, occupancy, onei-
romancy, pyromancy, radiancy, re-
dundancy, relevancy, sycophancy, ten-
acy, truancy, vacancy, vagrancy, vi-
brancy

Aforehand, and, band, beforehand, **AND***
behindhand, Black Hand, bland, bor- *see*
derland, brand, brigand, cab-stand, IAND
command, contraband, countermand,
demand, disband, eland, elfland, Eng-
land, expand, fairyland, Ferdinand,
firebrand, flower-land, flowerstand,
free-hand, garland, gland, grand,
grandstand, grassland, Greenland,
hand, headland, highland, Holy Land,
husband, Iceland, inkstand, inland,
island, land, Lapland, Long Island,

lowland, mainland, misunderstand, moorland, my-land, mythland, New England, Newfoundland, New Zealand, off-hand, Promised Land, quicksand, remand, reprimand, salt-land, Samarkand, sand, saraband, secondhand, Shetland, shorthand, singingsand, sleight-of-hand, stand, strand, street-band, Switzerland, tableland, Tallyrand, thousand, underhand, understand, unhand, upland, vandalhand, warlike-band, washstand, wasteland, withstand, witness-stand, woodland, Zululand	**AND***
Gourmand, Roland, wand	**AND**** *see* OND
Ananda, propaganda, Uganda, veranda	**ANDA** *see* A**
Alexander, bystander, commander, corriander, gander, grander, Highlander, islander, meander, oleander, pander, philander, pomander, salamander, slander	**ANDER*** *see* ER
Squander, wander	**ANDER**** *see* ONDER
Candle, chandle, handle, manhandle, panhandle, rush candle, tallow candle	**ANDLE** *see* EL LE

Rembrandt

ANDT
see
ANT*

Thousandth

ANDTH
see

Apple brandy, bandy, brandy, candy, cherry brandy, handy, Normandy, rock candy, sandy

ANDY
see
E**

Aeroplane, bamboo-cane, bane, biplane, cane, cellophane, chicane, counterpane, crane, Dane, dogbane, elecampane, fleabane, henbane, humane, hurricane, hydroplane, inane, insane, lane, mane, marchpane, membrane, monoplane, mundane, pane, plane, profane, purslane, sane, soutane, sugarcane, supermundane, Tamerlane, thane, tisane, triplane, urbane, vane, volplane, wane, wolf's bane, weathervane, windowpane

ANE
see
AGNE
AIGN
AIN
EIGN
EIN

Castanet, planet

ANET
see
ET

Bang, boomerang, chain-gang, clang, fang, gang, hang, hoof-clang, mustang, orang-outang, out-sang, overhang, pang, parasang, Penang, rang, sang, shebang, slang, sprang, tang, twang, whang, whiz-bang, ylang ylang

ANG
see
ANGUE
INGUE

Arrange, change, derange, estrange, exchange, grange, interchange, mange, range, strange

ANGE*
see

Flange, mélange, orange   **ANGE****
                                        see

Anger, danger, endanger, manger,   **ANGER**
moneychanger, ranger   *see*
                                        ER

Angle, bangle, bespangle, dangle,   **ANGLE**
disentangle, entangle, mangle, new-   *see*
fangle, quadrangle, spangle, strangle, EL
tangle, triangle, wangle, wrangle   LE

Fandango, mango, tango   **ANGO**
                                        see
                                        O*

Cangue, gangue, harangue   **ANGUE**
                                        see
                                        ANG

Anglo-mania, decalcomania, dipso-   **ANIA**
mania, kleptomania, mania, miscella-   *see*
nia, Tasmania, Titania, Transjordania, IA
Transylvania, Urania

Botanic, galvanic, inorganic, inter-   **ANIC**
oceanic, mechanic, Messianic, mor-   *see*
ganic, oceanic, organic, panic, satanic, IC
titanic, transoceanic, volcanic

Christianity, humanity, inanity, in-   **ANITY**
sanity, sanity, urbanity, vanity   *see*
                                        E**
                                        ITY

Bank, blank, clank, crank, Cruik-   **ANK**
shank, dank, drank, embank, flank,   *see*
frank, gangplank, hank, lank, mounte-   ANC

bank, plank, point-blank, prank, rank, sank, savings-bank, shank, shrank, spank, stank, swank, tank, thank, yank **ANK**
S-ANX

Ankh **ANKH**
see
ANK

Longshanks, shanks, spindleshanks **ANKS**
see
ANK-*S*

Anna, canna, hosanna, manna, Polyanna, savanna, Susquehanna **ANNA**
see
A**

Banns **ANNS**
see
AN-*S*

Canny, cranny, Fanny, granny, nanny, tyranny, uncanny **ANNY**
see
E**

Cinzano, guano, llano, Milano, piano, soprano, volcano **ANO**
see
O*

Sans **ANS**
see
AN-*S*

Expanse, manse **ANSE**
see
ANCE

Aberrant, abundant, adamant, air-plant, ant, arrant, arrogant, ascendant, aslant, aspirant, benignant, blatant, bon vivant, buoyant, cant, celebrant, chant, claimant, clairvoyant, cognizant, confidant, consonant, constant, contestant, cormorant, Corybant, courant, covenant, currant, decant, descant, descendant, discordant, dormant, egg-plant, elegant, elephant, emigrant, enchant, equidistant, errant, expectant, extravagant, flagellant, flagrant, flamboyant, flippant, fondant, fragrant, gallant, gallivant, grant, hierophant, hydrant, ignorant, immigrant, implant, important, incessant, inconstant, inelegant, infant, informant, instant, irrelevant, jurant, Levant, lieutenant, malignant, merchant, ministrant, natant, nonchalant, observant, occupant, octant, pant, participant, passant, peasant, pedant, pendant, pennant, petulant, pheasant, pie-plant, plant, pleasant, poignant, postulant, powerplant, predominant, pregnant, protestant, puissant, pursuivant, quadrant, rant, redundant, regnant, relevant, reluctant, remnant, repugnant, resonant, restaurant, resultant, rubberplant, ruminant, search warrant, sextant, slant, stagnant, supplant, supplicant, sycophant, tenant, termagant, tolerant, transplant, trenchant, triumphant, tyrant, ululant, ungallant, unimportant, unpleasant, vacant, vagrant, verdant, vibrant, visitant, warrant

ANT*
see
ANDT
AUNT
EANT
ERANT
IANT
ICANT
ILANT
ITANT
UANT
ed-ED
ly - E**
S-ANCE
ANSE

Au courant, ci-divant, débutant, en passant, nonchalant, piquant, restaurant, soi-disant, want

ANT**
see
AUNT
ONT**

Andante, ante, bacchante, commandante, corybante, Dante, dilettante

ANTE
see
E*

Amaranth

ANTH
see

Antic, Atlantic, frantic, gigantic, pedantic, romantic, transatlantic, unromantic

ANTIC
see
IC

Canto, Campo Santo, coranto, esperanto

ANTO
see
O*

Errantry, gallantry, infantry, pageantry, pantry, peasantry, pedantry, pleasantry

ANTRY
see
E**

Scanty, shanty, warranty

ANTY
see
E**

Laudanum, tympanum

ANUM
see
UM

Manx, phalanx

ANX
see
ANK-*S*

Any, Bethany, botany, Brittany, company, dittany, epiphany, litany, mahogany, many, miscellany, Ro-

ANY
see
E**

many, Tammany, theophany, Tuscany, zany **ANY**

Bonanza, esperanza, extravaganza, stanza **ANZA**
see
A**

Cacao, cocao, curacao, Mindanao **AO**
see
O*

After-clap, burlap, cap, cat-nap, chap, clap, claptrap, crap, earlap, entrap, enwrap, fill-gap, flap, flytrap, fool's cap, gap, hanap, handicap, hap, Jap, kidnap, knap, kneecap, lap, madcap, mayhap, mishap, mobcap, mousetrap, nap, nightcap, on-tap, overlap, pap, Phrygian cap, pointed-cap, rap, rattle-trap, red cap, sap, satrap, scrap, shoulder-strap, skull-cap, slap, snap, stop-gap, strap, tap, thunder-clap, trap, Turk's cap, unwrap, Venus's-flytrap, wrap **AP***
see
APPE
ed-APT

Swap **AP****
see
OP

Ape, cape, drape, escape, fire-escape, gape, grape, landscape, misshape, nape, rape, red tape, scrape, shape, shipshape, tape **APE**
see
EPE

Brown paper, diaper, draper, newspaper, paper, rice-paper, sandpaper, skyscraper, wallpaper **APER**
see
ER

Jackanapes **APES**
see
APE-*s*

Anemograph, anopisthograph, bio- **APH**
graph, bolograph, chronograph, cine- see
matograph, epigraph, epitaph, graph, AFE**
gyrograph, hectograph, heliograph, ALF
hierograph, holograph, lithograph, AUGH
mimeograph, opistograph, pantograph, UAFF
paragraph, phonograph, photograph, *ed*-AFT
seraph, stenograph, stylograph, tele- *y*-APHY
graph

Autobiography, bibliography, biog- **APHY**
raphy, cacography, geography, heliog- see
raphy, lexicography, museography, E**
oceanography, orography, orthogra-
phy, phonography, photography, py-
rography, telephotography, topogra-
phy

Nappe **APPE**
see
AP*

Clapper, dapper, flapper, scrapper, **APPER**
snapper, wrapper see
ER

Apple, crab apple, dapple, grapple, **APPLE**
pineapple, scrapple see
EL
LE

Happy, sappy, scrappy, snappy **APPY**
see
E**

Craps, drumtaps, perhaps, snaps, taps

APS
see
AP*-*s*

Apse, collapse, elapse, lapse, relapse, trapse

APSE
see
AP*-*s*

Adapt, apt, deep-wrapt, inapt, rapt, slapt, wrapt

APT
see
AP*-*ed*
s-AP*-*s*

Plaque

AQUE*
see
AC

Opaque

AQUE**
see
AKE

Above par, Adar, afar, Akbar, Alcazar, almemar, altar, antimacassar, astylar, auto-car, avatar, bar, bazaar, beggar, below par, Belshazzar, bipolar, blazing-star, Bolivar, brownsugar, burglar, bursar, Caesar, calabar, calendar, car, caterpillar, cellar, char, cheddar, cigar, cinnabar, coal-tar, cooky-jar, cougar, crockery-jar, crossbar, crowbar, czar, D.A.R., day-star, debar, dog-star, evening-star, Excalibar, exemplar, far, feldspar, gar, Gaspar, Gibraltar, grammar, guitar, Hagar, handle-bar, hangar, horsecar, hussar, interstellar, isobar, Issachar, izar, jack-tar, jaguar, jar, jaunting-car,

AR*
see
ARE**
ARRE
EDAR
IAR
ILAR
OIR**
OLLAR
ULAR
ULGAR
YR
ed-ARD
s-ARS

Julian Calendar, lascar, lazar, Lochin- **AR***
var, lode star, lunar, Macassar, Mada-
gascar, Magyar, Malabar, maple sugar,
mar, medlar, molar, morning-star,
mortar, motor car, nectar, nenuphar,
Ninnar, Omar, par, pedlar, pillar,
Pindar, platform car, polar, Pompey's
Pillar, poplar, Potiphar, realgar, regis-
trar, salt cellar, samovar, sandbar,
scar, scholar, scimitar, Shinar, shoot-
ing-star, side-car, sitar, sleeping-car,
solar, spar, star, stellar, sugar, tar,
tartar, Templar, thus far, Trafalgar,
trolley-car, Vassar, vicar, vinegar,
Zanzibar, Zohar

Civil War, man-of-war, pre-war, war **AR****
see
ATOR
OR

Cithara, dulcamara, Ishvara, mas- **ARA**
cara, Para, Sahara, Sara, solfatara, *see*
Tara, taratantara, tiara A****

Arab, scarab, street-arab **ARAB**
see
AB*

Barb, garb, rhubarb **ARB**
see

Garble, marble, warble **ARBLE**
see
EL
LE

Arc, Joan of Arc, marc **ARC**
see
ARK

Arch, countermarch, larch, march, **ARCH***
outmarch, overarch, parch, starch *see*

Anarch, hierarch, monarch, oligarch, **ARCH****
patriarch, Petrarch, Plutarch, tetrarch *see*
ARK
S-OX

Anarchy, heptarchy, hierarchy, **ARCHY**
monarchy, oligarchy, tetrarchy *see*
E**

Abelard, afterward, Asgard, award, **ARD**
awkward, backward, backyard, bard, *see*
bastard, blizzard, bombard, boulevard, AR*-*ed*
brickyard, buzzard, calling-card, camel- IARD
opard, Camisard, canard, card, chard, UARD
church-yard, costard, coward, custard, *ly*-E**
dastard, discard, disregard, dockyard,
dullard, eastward, forward, foulard,
froward, gizzard, gold standard, green-
sward, haggard, halyard, hap-hazard,
hard, Harvard, hazard, hog's lard,
homeward, inward, izzard, laggard,
lard, leeward, leopard, lizard, mallard,
mansard, Midgard, mustard, nard,
niggard, northward, onward, orchard,
outward, pard, petard, placard, play-
ing-card, pochard, postcard, poultry-
yard, regard, retard, reward, reynard,
Richard, sard, Savoyard, scabbard,

Scotland Yard, seaward, shard, ship-yard, shoreward, skyward, sluggard, southward, standard, steelyard, stew-ard, stock-yard, straightforward, sward, tankard, thee-ward, thither-ward, toward, trump-card, turkey-buzzard, upward, us-ward, Utgard, vineyard, ward, wayward, westward, windward, wizard, yard

ARD

Cowardly, hardly, inwardly, nig-gardly, outwardly

ARDLY
see
E**

Aware, bare, beware, blare, care, compare, dare, declare, delftware, earthenware, ensnare, fanfare, fare, flare, flatware, glare, hardware, hare, insnare, mare, nightmare, pare, pebble-ware, plowshare, prepare, rare, scare, share, snare, spare, square, stoneware, tableware, tare, threadbare, thorough-fare, unaware, ware, warfare, wellfare

ARE*
see
AIR
EIR*
ERE**
IARE

Are, caviare

ARE**
see
AR*

Bearer, cupbearer, shearer, tale-bearer, wayfarer, wearer

ARER
see
ER

Dwarf, scarf, wharf

ARF
see

Barge, charge, countercharge, dis-charge, enlarge, large, marge, over-charge, recharge, surcharge, ultra-large

ARGE
see

Cargo, embargo, largo, supercargo   **ARGO**
see
O*

Aria, Ava Maria, cineraria, malaria,   **ARIA**
Samaria, wistaria   *see*
IA

Abcedarian, agrarian, antiquarian,   **ARIAN**
barbarian, humanitarian, librarian,   *see*
nonagenarian, proletarian, sectarian,   AN*
sexagenarian, utilitarian, vegetarian

Ballbearing, clearing, daring, faring,   **ARING**
glaring, hearing, paring, sea-faring   *see*
ING

Impresario, Lothario, scenario   **ARIO**
see
IO

Apollinaris, Paris, Polaris, Sybaris   **ARIS**
see
IS*

Charity, clarity, disparity, hilarity,   **ARITY**
irregularity, jocularity, parity, par-   *see*
ticularity, peculiarity, polarity, popu-   E**
larity, rarity, regularity, similarity,
singularity, solidarity, vulgarity

Ark, bark, birth-mark, book-mark,   **ARK**
bulwark, dark, Denmark, disembark,   *see*
ear-mark, embark, hark, highwater-   ARCH**
mark, landmark, lark, mark, mudlark,
Noah's ark, Ozark, park, Peruvian
bark, pitch dark, pock-mark, post-

mark, quotation-mark, remark, sark, shagbark, shark, shell-bark, skylark, snark, spark, stark, thumb-mark, tit-lark, watermark, wood-lark

ARK

Carl, gnarl, marl, snarl

ARL
see

Early, pearly, popularly, scholarly, similarly, singularly

ARLY
see
E**

Abandoned farm, alarm, arm, baby farm, charm, disarm, false-alarm, farm, forearm, harm, unharm

ARM*
see
ARME
S-ARMS

Lukewarm, swarm, warm

ARM**
see
ORM*

Gendarme

ARME
see
ARM*

Arms, coat-of-arms, fire-arms, men-at-arms

ARMS
see
ARM*-s

Warmth

ARMTH
see

Barn, darn, spun-yarn, tarn, yarn

ARN*
see

Forewarn, warn

ARN**
see
AWN

Carp, harp, jew's harp, scarp, sharp **ARP***
see

Warp **ARP****
see
ORP

Bizarre, Navarre **ARRE**
see
AR*

Arrow, barrow, drill-barrow, harrow, **ARROW**
marrow, narrow, sparrow, wheel-bar- *see*
row, yarrow OW*

Carry, charry, Du Barry, glengarry, **ARRY**
harry, marry, parry, quarry, remarry, *see*
starry, tarry E**

Champs de Mars, Mars **ARS**
see
AR*-*s*

Marse, parse, sparse **ARSE**
see

Harsh, marsh, salt-marsh **ARSH**
see

Apart, art, black art, braggart, cart, **ART***
chart, counterpart, dart, depart, dog- *see*
cart, Froissart, go-cart, hand-cart, EART
hart, impart, mart, Mozart, ox-cart,
part, pushcart, rampart, smart, start,
tart, upstart, weatherchart

Athwart, stalwart, thwart, wart **ART****
see
ORT

Barter, carter, charter, garter, self-starter, starter

ARTER
see
ER

Swarth

ARTH
see
ORTH*

Carve, starve, wharve

ARVE
see

Adversary, anniversary, apothecary, arbitrary, Barbary, binary, boundary, Calvary, canary, caravansary, cassowary, chary, cinerary, commentary, commissary, constabulary, contemporary, contrary, corollary, customary, dietary, dignitary, disciplinary, dispensary, documentary, dreary, dromedary, Dundreary, eleemosynary, elementary, emissary, fragmentary, functionary, glossary, granary, hoary, honorary, intercalary, involuntary, itinerary, Janizary, lapidary, legendary, library, literary, Mary, mercenary, military, momentary, monetary, notary, ovary, parliamentary, pituitary, planetary, plenary, primary, quandary, quaternary, rosary, rosemary, rotary, rudimentary, salary, sanitary, secondary, secretary, sedentary, solitary, summary, supernumerary, Tartary, temporary, tercentenary, Thackeray, Tipperary, tributary, tutelary, unitary, unwary, vagary, vary, vocabulary, voluntary, votary, wary, Zachary

ARY
see
AIRY
E**
IARY
INARY
ONARY
UARY

Abraxas, alas, Algeciras, arras, Atlas, balsas, Barabbas, Caiaphas, Candlemas, canvas, Carabas, Caracas, Christmas, coal-gas, Cordilleras, Dorcas, embarras, Esdras, fracas, gas, Hatteras, hippocras, Honduras, in vino veritas, Judas, Juventas, Kansas, laughing-gas, Lycidas, madras, Marsyas, Martinmas, Michaelmas, Midas, Mithras, nuda veritas, Pallas, pampas, per fas et nefas, Pocahontas, poison-gas, Puranas, sassafras, St. Nicholas, upas, Ushas, Vedas, Xmas

AS*
see
ASS
EAS
ORAS

As, has, whereas

AS**
see
AZ

Was

AS***
' see
AUSE

Airbase, base, bookcase, case, chase, crankcase, debase, crase, lower-case, paper-chase, pillowcase, purchase, show-case, staircase, steeple-chase, suitcase, vanity-case

ASE*
see
ACE
ed-AIST
ASTE

Chrysophrase, metaphrase, paraphrase, phase, phrase

ASE**
see
AISE
AZE

Abash, ash, balderdash, bash, brash, calabash, calash, cash, clash, crash, dash, flash, gash, gnash, goulash, hash, lash, mash, mountain ash, nettle rash,

ASH*
see
ACHE*

potash, plash, rash, sash, Shamash, slapdash, slash, smash, soda-ash, spatterdash, splash, succotash, thrash, trash, Wabash **ASH***

Backwash, swash, wash, whitewash **ASH*** *see* UASH

Dasher, dishwasher, gate-crasher, haberdasher, potato-masher, rasher **ASHER** *see* ER

Aphasia, Asia, Aspasia, athanasia, Australasia, Eurasia, fantasia, paronomasia **ASIA** *see* IA

Abrasion, evasion, invasion, occasion, persuasion, pervasion **ASION** *see* ION

Amasis, Anabasis, basis, elephantiasis, emphasis, hypostasis, oasis, protasis **ASIS** *see* IS*

Ask, bask, cask, damask, flask, gasmask, Iron Mask, mask, task, unmask **ASK** *see* ASQUE

Basket, casket, gasket, wastebasket **ASKET** *see* ET

Cataplasm, chasm, ectoplasm, enthusiasm, iconoclasm, phantasm, pleonasm, protoplasm, sarcasm, spasm **ASM** *see* AM EM

Diapason, freemason, Jason, mason **ASON**
see
ON

Asp, clasp, gasp, grasp, handclasp, **ASP**
hasp, rasp, unclasp, vulture-grasp, *see*
wasp *ed*-ED

Basque, casque, masque **ASQUE**
see
ASK

Applesass, ass, Balaam's ass, bass, **ASS**
brass, carcass, class, come-to-pass, *see*
compass, crass, crevass, cuirass, cut- AS*
lass, eelgrass, embarrass, encompass, EAS
eye-glass, fieldglass, glass, grass, harass, IAS
hourglass, isinglass, jackass, looking-
glass, marine glass, marsh-grass, mass,
middle-class, morass, opera-glass, out-
class, overpass, pass, pierglass, plate-
glass, repass, sandglass, sea bass,
sherryglass, spun glass, spy-glass,
stained-glass, sunglass, surpass, trass,
trespass, underpass, upperclass, wind-
lass, wineglass

Demi-tasse, en masse, Montparnasse **ASSE**
see
AS*
ASS

Brassy, embassy, glassy, massy, **ASSY**
sassy *see*
E**

Aghast, avast, ballast, blast, bombast, breakfast, broadcast, cast, contrast, downcast, enthusiast, fast, flabbergast, forecast, foremast, gymnast, half-mast, hast, iconoclast, inballast, jiggermast, jury-mast, last, long last, mast, metaphrast, outcast, outlast, overcast, paraphrast, past, peltast, plastercast, repast, sand-blast, seablast, shoemaker's last, steadfast, topmast, vast

AST*
see
ASK-*ed*
ASS-*ed*
ed-ED

Wast

AST**
see
AUST

Baste, chaste, cotton waste, distaste, foretaste, haste, lambaste, paste, post haste, taste, unchaste, waste

ASTE*
see
ACE-*d*
AIST
ASE*-*d*
ed-ED

Caste, half-caste

ASTE**
see
AST

Alabaster, aster, burgomaster, caster, courtplaster, disaster, faster, headmaster, master, piaster, pilaster, plaster, quarter-master, schoolmaster taskmaster, Zoroaster

ASTER
see
ER

Bombastic, drastic, ecclesiastic, elastic, fantastic, mastic, monastic, plastic, sarcastic, scholastic, spastic

ASTIC
see
IC

Ghastly, lastly, vastly **ASTLY**
see
E**

Dynasty, hasty, nasty, pasty, tasty **ASTY**
see
E**

Embrasure, measure, pleasure, tape **ASURE**
measure, treasure *see*
URE

Apostasy, easy, ecstasy, fantasy, **ASY**
free-and-easy, idiosyncrasy, phantasy *see*
E**

Acrobat, aerostat, Allat, Al Sirat, **AT***
Ararat, arhat, aristocrat, assignat, at, *see*
autocrat, automat, baccarat, bat, blat, IAT
bobcat, bodhisat, brat, brick-bat, carat,
cat, caveat, chat, chit-chat, civet cat,
combat, concordat, cravat, cricket-bat,
crush-hat, democrat, diplomat, ducat,
fat, format, ghat, gnat, habitat, hat,
heliostat, hell-cat, Herat, high-hat,
hors de combat, Jack Sprat, Jehosha-
phat, jurat, Kit-cat, Maat, Magnificat,
Monteserrat, mudflat, muscat, musk-
rat, pat, pit-a-pat, plutocrat, pole-cat,
rat, rat-a-tat, Rubaiyat, sat, Shebat,
slat, spat, tat, that, that's that, theo-
crat, thereat, Tiamat, tit-for-tat, tom-
cat, top-hat, vat, wax fat, wharf-rat,
whereat, wildcat, ziggurat

Somewhat, squat, swat, what **AT****
see
IOT

Nougat

AT***
see
A**

Automata, cantata, crux-ansata, data, errata, inamorata, Mahabharata, natura naturata, persona grata, pro rata, sonata, strata, ultimata

ATA
see
A**

Fatal, natal, prenatal

ATAL
see
AL

Charlatan, Satan, tarlatan, Yucatan

ATAN
see
AN*

Batch, boxing-match, catch, cross-patch, dispatch, hatch, latch, lifted-latch, match, melon-patch, nuthatch, overmatch, patch, potlatch, safety-match, scratch, snatch, sulphur match, thatch, unlatch

ATCH*
see
ACH**

Dog-watch, night-watch, stop-watch, watch, wrist-watch

ATCH**
see
OTCH

Abate, accommodate, adumbrate, agate, annotate, antedate, ate, bifurcate, billingsgate, bookplate, breastplate, caliphate, carbohydrate, carnate, celebrate, celibate, checkmate, chief mate, cognate, compensate, concentrate, confiscate, conflagrate, conflate,

ATE
see
AIT
AVATE
EAT**
EATE
EBATE

conjugate, co-ordinate, copperplate, correlate, corrugate, coruscate, crate, cremate, date, deflagrate, deflate, demonstrate, desecrate, designate, dictate, dinnerplate, discarnate, distillate, divagate, door-plate, edentate, electroplate, elevate, elongate, elucidate, emigrate, equilibrate, estate, exculpate, exhilarate, expurgate, extirpate, fashionplate, fate, filtrate, first-rate, floodgate, frustrate, gate, Golden Gate, grate, gyrate, hate, helpmate, hibernate, hydrate, illustrate, importunate, impregnate, incarnate, incubate, inculcate, inflate, ingrate, inmate, innate, insenate, instate, insulate, interpenetrate, interrogate, interstate, inundate, late, lucubrate, lustrate, magistrate, magnate, mandate, mate, messmate, methylate, migrate, narrate, negate, Newgate, nictate, nitrate, obfuscate, objurate, orchestrate, ornate, oscillate, ovate, overrate, overstate, palate, pate, penetrate, perpetrate, phosphate, placate, plate, playmate, pomegranate, potentate, promulgate, propagate, prostrate, pulsate, rate, recapitulate, reinstate, remonstrate, roller-skate, rotate, sate, schoolmate, scintillate, second-mate, second-rate, sedate, separate, serrate, skate, slate, sluice-gate, stagnate, stalemate, state, syncopate, tergiversate, tessellate, tinplate, titillate, tollgate, translate, truncate, upto-date, vacate, vacillate, variegate, vegetate, vertebrate, vibrate, Vulgate, wooly-pate

ATE

ECATE
EGATE
EIGHT*
ELATE
ENATE
ERATE
ETE**
IATE
ICATE
IDATE
IGATE
ILATE
IMATE
INATE
IPATE
IRATE
ITATE
IVATE
OATE
OBATE
OCATE
OGATE
OLATE
ONATE
ORATE
OVATE
UATE
ULATE
URATE
S-ATES

Accurately, alternately, desolately, lately, innately, intimately, irately, ornately, passionately, philately, precipitately, sedately, separately, stately

ATELY
see
E**
ELY

Alma-Mater, crater, Dis pater, fire-eater, greater, idolater, later, man-eater, pater, Stabat Mater, sweater, theater

ATER
see
ER

United States

ATES*
see
ATE-*S*

Fides Achates, Harpocrates, Hippocrates, Mithridates, Socrates

ATES**
see
ES

Aftermath, Ardath, bath, bridle-path, by-path, footbath, footpath, Goliath, hath, lath, math, mudbath, path, Sabbath, sandbath, showerbath, sitz-bath, towpath, Turkish-bath, war-path, wrath

ATH
see
OPATH

Bathe, enswathe, lathe, rathe, scathe, spathe, swathe

ATHE
see

Allopathy, antipathy, apathy, homeopathy, neuropathy, sympathy, telepathy

ATHY
see
E**

Amati, Frascati, Haimavati, Illuminati, literati, Parvati, Sarasvati

ATI
see
I**

Acrobatic, anastigmatic, aquatic, aristocratic, aromatic, Asiatic, autocratic, automatic, axiomatic, chromatic, climatic, diplomatic, dogmatic, dramatic, ecstatic, Eleatic, emblematic, emphatic, epigrammatic, erratic, fanatic, fluviatic, hieratic, hypostatic, idiomatic, lunatic, lymphatic, mathematic, melodramatic, miasmatic, morganatic, operatic, phlegmatic, piratic, plutocratic, pneumatic, polychromatic, pragmatic, prismatic, problematic, rheumatic, sabbatic, semi-aquatic, static, systematic, thematic, theocratic, trichromatic

ATIC
see
IC

Literatim, verbatim

ATIM
see
IM

Gelatin, Latin, matin, satin

ATIN
see
IN

Fascinating, grating, hibernating, lubricating, pulsating, rating

ATING
see
ING

Abdication, acclamation, accusation, administration, admiration, adulation, adumbration, affectation, affirmation, agitation, alteration, amplification, animation, appellation, arborization, attenuation, auto-intoxication, avocation, calculation, cantillation, carnation, causation, cessation, circulation, citation, civilization, collation,

ATION
see
IATION
ION

combination, communication, compensation, concatenation, concentration, condemnation, condensation, configuration, confirmation, conformation, conglomeration, congregation, consolation, constellation, consternation, consultation, consummation, contamination, contemplation, coöperation, co-ordination, coronation, corporation, counter-irritation, culmination, dedication, degustation, delegation, deportation, destination, dilapidation, dilation, discrimination, disintegration, dispensation, dissertation, dissipation, distillation, donation, duration, elevation, elimination, elucidation, emanation, embrocation, emigration, emulation, encrustation, enumeration, equation, eradication, estimation, evocation, exaggeration, exaltation, exhiliration, expectation, expiration, exploitation, expostulation, extenuation, exudation, exultation, fixation, flirtation, fluctuation, fornication, fortification, fulmination, fumigation, generalization, gestation, glorification, gradation, graduation, gravitation, gurgitation, gustation, hallucination, hesitation, identification, illation, illumination, illustration, imitation, impersonation, incantation, incarnation, incineration, incrustation, individualization, individuation, inflammation, inflation, information, innovation, insolation, inspiration, installation, insubordination, insulation, interpenetration, interpolation, interpretation, interrogation, in-

ATION

toxication, inundation, investigation, irritation, isolation, iteration, jubilation, laceration, legation, levitation, libation, liberation, libration, limitation, location, lubrication, lucubration, lustration, manifestation, manipulation, materialization, mediation, meditation, mensuration, migration, miscalculation, miscreation, mitigation, moderation, modulation, mutation, mutilation, natation, nation, negation, notation, nullification, obfuscation, oblation, obligation, observation, occupation, oration, organization, orientation, oscillation, osculation, ossification, ostentation, ovation, pagination, participation, particularization, peculation, peregrination, perspiration, plantation, population, potation, precipitation, predestination, presentation, preservation, privation, probation, proclamation, prolongation, propagation, provocation, publication, pulsation, punctuation, purification, quotation, radiation, ramification, ration, recantation, recapitulation, reclamation, recreation, recrimination, recuperation, reformation, reforestration, refrigeration, regeneration, regimentation, regulation, reincarnation, reiteration, relation, reparation, repastination, representation, reputation, reservation, respiration, resuscitation, revelation, reverberation, revocation, rotation, ruination, salutation, salvation, sanitation, simulation, speculation, stabilization, stagnation, station, stimulation, sub-

ATION

ordination, supererogation, supplica- **ATION**
tion, tabulation, temptation, tergiver-
sation, tintinnabulation, transfigura-
tion, translation, transmigration, trans-
mogrification, transmutation, trans-
portation, trepidation, tribulation, un-
dulation, unification, vacation, vac-
cination, valuation, vaticination, vege-
tation, veneration, ventilation, verifi-
cation, vexation, vibration, violation,
visitation, visualization, vituperation,
vocalization, vocation

Clematis, gratis **ATIS**
see
IS*

Affirmative, alternative, causative, **ATIVE**
communicative, comparative, corrobo- *see*
rative, curative, decorative, derivative, IVE**
evocative, excitative, figurative, form-
ative, germinative, illative, illustrative,
imaginative, imperative, initiative, in-
sinuative, laxative, legislative, lucra-
tive, mediative, meditative, modifica-
tive, narrative, native, negative, nomi-
native, operative, optative, palliative,
predicative, prerogative, preservative,
provocative, purgative, putative, rela-
tive, remunerative, representative, res-
torative, sanative, sedative, superla-
tive, talkative, tentative, terminative,
vocative

Agitato, animato, appogiato, ben **ATO**
trovato, Cato, inamorato, obligato, *see*
pizzicato, Plato, potato, rabato, stac- O*
cato, tomato, vibrato

Accelerator, administrator, agitator, alligator, arbitrator, aviator, curator, dictator, educator, elevator, emigrator, equator, escalator, fornicator, generator, gladiator, imperator, impersonator, incinerator, incorporator, incubator, indicator, instigator, insulator, investigator, liberator, lubricator, mediator, moderator, narrator, navigator, nominator, orator, perambulator, percolator, perpetrator, prestidigitator, prevaricator, procrastinator, procurator, prognosticator, promulgator, radiator, refrigerator, senator, spectator, speculator, testator, translator, ventilator, vibrator

ATOR
see
AR**
OAR
OR

Amatory, anticipatory, conservatory, consignatory, dedicatory, depreciatory, derogatory, dilatory, evocatory, feudatory, fumatory, gyratory, indicatory, inflammatory, laboratory, laudatory, lavatory, mandatory, migratory, objurgatory, obligatory, observatory, oratory, predatory, prefatory, preparatory, propitiatory, purgatory, reformatory, respiratory, sudatory, vibratory

ATORY
see
E**
ORY

Amphitheatre, theatre

ATRE
see
ER

Idolatry, ophiolatry, psychiatry

ATRY
see
E**

Captain Marryatt, kilowatt, watt **ATT**
see
OT

Batter, chatter, clatter, flatter, hat- **ATTER**
ter, matter, patter, platter, scatter, *see*
shatter, smatter, spatter, splatter, ER
subject-matter

Battle, cattle, prattle, rattle, Seattle, **ATTLE**
sham-battle, tattle, tittle-tattle, wattle *see*
EL
LE

Ageratum, Atum, erratum, poma- **ATUM**
tum, stratum, substratum, superstrat- *see*
um, ultimatum UM

Armature, caricature, creature, cur- **ATURE**
vature, denature, entablature, feature, *see*
illnature, immature, judicature, legis- EUR
lature, ligature, literature, mature,
miniature, nature, nomenclature, premature, signature, temperature

Afflatus, apparatus, hiatus, salera- **ATUS**
tus, Pisistratus *see*
US

Esau, Nassau **AU***
see
AW

Esquimau, landau, Pau **AU****
see
O*

Jungfrau, tau	**AU*****
	see
	OW**
Bedaub, daub	**AUB**
	see
	AB**
	OB*
Sauce	**AUCE**
	see
	OS*
	OSS
Debauch	**AUCH**
	see
Applaud, defraud, fraud, gaud, laud, maraud, Maud	**AUD**
	see
	AW-*ed*
	ed-ED
Quohaug	**AUG**
	see
	OG
Gauge	**AUGE**
	see
	AGE
Laugh	**AUGH***
	see
	AFE
Faugh	**AUGH****
	see
	AW

Aught, caught, distraught, dread-naught, fearnaught, fraught, naught, onslaught, self-taught, taught, un-taught, well-taught

AUGHT*
see
AUT*
OUGHT

Draught

AUGHT**
see
AFT

Haughty, naughty

AUGHTY
see
E**

Caterwaul, caul, Gaul, haul, maul, overhaul, Paul, Saul

AUL
see
AWL
ed-ALD

Assault, catapault, default, fault, somersault, treasure-vault, vault

AULT
see
ALT
S-ALTZ

Capernaum, meerschaum

AUM
see
UM

Faun, Marble Faun

AUN
see
AWN

Craunch, haunch, launch, paunch, staunch

AUNCH
see
ANCH**

Aunt, daunt, flaunt, gaunt, haunt, jaunt, taunt, vaunt

AUNT
see
ANT**
ed-ED
S-ONSE

Bucentaur, centaur, dinosaur, mino-
taur, plesiosaur

AUR
see
OR

Epidaurus, ichthyosaurus, plesio-
saurus, Taurus, thesaurus

AURUS
see
URUS
US

Santa Claus

AUS
see
AUSE

Applause, because, cause, clause,
pause

AUSE
see
AUS
AW-*s*

Exhaust, Faust, holocaust

AUST
see
OST*

Gauze

AUZE
see
AUSE

Aeronaut, Argonaut, juggernaut,
taut

AUT*
see
AUGHT*

Sauerkraut

AUT*
see
OUT

Nautch

AUTCH
see

Mauve **AUVE**
see
OVE*

Slav **AV**
see
AVE**

Ava, Balaklava, Bhairava, cassava, **AVA**
guava, Java, lava *see*
A**

Aggravate, excavate **AVATE**
see
ATE

Architrave, behave, brainwave, **AVE***
brave, cave, close shave, concave, *see*
conclave, crave, deprave, engrave, AIVE
enslave, forgave, galley-slave, grave,
hairwave, heatwave, Hertzian wave,
knave, lave, marcel wave, margrave,
misbehave, nave, octave, pilgrim-stave,
quarry-slave, rave, save, sea-wave,
shave, shortwave, slave, stave, tidal
wave

Have **AVE****
see
AV

Caravel, gavel, gravel, navel, ravel, **AVEL**
travel, unravel *see*
EL
LE

Craven, engraven, haven, heaven, **AVEN**
leaven, raven, smooth-shaven *see*
EN

Cadaver, claver, engraver, graver, palaver, quaver, shaver, waver

AVER
see
ER

Gravy, navy, wavy

AVY
see
E**

Blue law, bucksaw, cat's-paw, caw, Choctaw, claw, coleslaw, draw, flaw, forepaw, foresaw, gew-gaw, guffaw, handsaw, haw, hee-haw, in-law, jackdaw, jackstraw, jaw, jig-saw, kickshaw, law, lockjaw, macaw, mackinaw, maw, outlaw, paw, pawpaw, pshaw, raw, rickshaw, Saginaw, Salic Law, scrollsaw, see-saw, straw, taw, thaw, underjaw, Warsaw, withdraw

AW
see
AWE
UAW
ed-AUD
s-AUSE
OR-*s*

Away, caraway, castaway, fadeaway, far-away, fly-away, rockaway, runaway, stayaway, stowaway, straightaway, while away

AWAY
see
A**

Bawdry, tawdry

AWDRY
see
E**

Awe, overawe

AWE
see
AW

Awk, fish-hawk, gawk, henhawk, Mohawk, moulting-hawk, news hawk, sparrowhawk, squawk, tomahawk

AWK
see
ALK
y-E**

Awl, bawl, brawl, cawl, crawl, drawl, goat-shawl, scrawl, shawl, sprawl, trawl, yawl

AWL
see
UALL
ed-ALD

Brawn, dawn, day-dawn, deep-drawn, drawn, false-dawn, fawn, lawn, long-drawn, overdrawn, pawn, prawn, rosy-fingered dawn, sawn, spawn, with-drawn, yawn

AWN
see
ARN**
ONE**
ORN

Ajax, anthrax, anti-climax, battle-ax, bees-wax, borax, climax, flax, Hali-fax, head-tax, income tax, lax, opopa-nax, overtax, Pax, pickax, poll-tax, relax, sealing-wax, smilax, surtax, syn-tax, tax, thorax, toad-flax, wax, zax

AX*
see
AC-*s*
ACHS
ACK-*s*
ACT-*s*

Coax, hoax

AX**
see
OKE-*s*

Affray, airway, allay, All Fool's Day, All Soul's Day, alpha-ray, alway, any-way, Appian Way, arbor day, archway, array, assay, astray, ay, bay, Bay of Biscay, belay, beta-ray, betray, blue-jay, Bombay, Botany, Bay, bray, breakfast tray, by-play, byway, Ca-thay, causeway, Charlotte Corday, clay, cutaway, dapple-gray, daresay, day, decay, defray, delay, disarray, dismay, display, doomsday, doorway, dray, everyday, essay, fast day, fay, field day, flay, foray, fray, Friday, gainsay, gamma-ray, gangway, gay, gray, half-pay, halfway, hatchway,

AY
see
A*
AWAY
EIGH
EY
UAY
UET**
ed-ADE*
    AID*
s-A*-*s*
AISE
AIZE
ASE**
AYS

hay, headway, heyday, highway, holi-
day, horseplay, hurray, inlay, jay,
Judgment-day, lamp-ray, Labor-day,
lay, leeway, mainstay, Malay, Manda-
lay, man Friday, market-day, mascu-
line-array, may, midday, midway,
Milky-Way, miracle-play, mislay,
Monday, Mother's day, natal-day,
nay, noonday, Norway, nosegay, now-
aday, N-ray, Ojibway, outlay, out-of-
the-way, outstay, passageway, Passion
Play, pathway, pay, photo-play, play,
popinjay, portray, pray, prepay, pri-
vate-way, railway, ray, redletter day,
relay, repay, roundelay, runaway, run-
way, Saint's-Day, Saturday, say, shay,
silver-gray, slay, sluice-way, soothsay,
speedway, spillway, splay, spray, stay,
sting ray, stray, subway, Sunday,
sway, tag-day, Thursday, today, To-
kay, Tuesday, ultra violet ray, under-
pay, underway, war-array, water-way,
waylay, Wednesday, welladay, Whit-
sunday, workaday, X-ray, yesterday

AY

Himalaya, Maya

AYA
see
A**

Assayer, layer, payer, piano-player,
prayer, slayer, soothsayer, sprayer,
taxpayer

AYER
see
ER

Bygone-days, fable-days, now-a-
days, salad days, side-ways

AYS
see
AY-S

Alcatraz, Boaz, Shiraz, topaz	**AZ** *see* AS** AZZ
Ormazd	**AZD** *see*
Ablaze, amaze, blaze, craze, daze, emblaze, faze, gaze, glaze, haze, maze, raze, stargaze	**AZE** *see* AISE AY-*s* *y*-AZY
Bombazine, magazine	**AZINE** *see* INE**
Amazon, blazon, emblazon	**AZON** *see* ON
Jazz	**AZZ** *see* AZ
Crazy, glazy, hazy, lazy	**AZY** *see* E**

E SOUNDS

Acme, adobe, agape, Ananke, ane-   **E***
mone, Aphrodite, Ariadne, Astarte,   *see*
Ate, be, bene, campanile, Chile, Chloe,   **A***
Circe, Comanche, Cybele, Danae,
Daphne, dele, Don Quixote, epitome,
Euterpe, evoe, festina lente, finale,
fricasse, Ganymede, Ge, Gethsemane,
Goethe, he, Hebe, Il Trovatore, King
Rene, Lao-Tse, Lethe, macrame, may-
be, me, m.d., Melpomene, Miserere,
Mitylene, Nepenthc, netsuke, Nike,
Niobe, nota bene, padre, phoebe,
Phryne, Proserpine, Psyche, recipe,
sake, salame, Selene, Semele, sesame,
she, sotto voce, stele, tele, the, tse-tse,
ukulele, Ultima Thule, viva-voce, we,
would-be, Yangtse, ye, Zantippe

Abruptly, accordingly, adroitly,   **E****
Allegheny, amply, anchovy, angry,   *see*
anomaly, army, aunty, avowedly,   ABBY
baby, badly, bankruptcy, bel-esprit,   ABLY
belfry, belly, biddy, bigotry, blackly,   ACITY
blameworthy, Blavatsky, blindly,   ACY
bloodthirsty, booby, bossy, brawny,   ADY
briskly, buddy, buggy, bunchy, Bur-   AE
gundy, bushy, busy, caddy, calumny,   AIN-*ly*
canopy, certainly, certainty, cheeky,   AINT-*ly*
chiefly, choosy, chunky, clingingly,   AIRY

clumsy, cocky, colonelcy, conspiracy, controversy, copy, corruptly, country, county, coyly, cozy, crafty, cuppy, curtly, daily, daisy, darkly, deftly, deucedly, dicky, dingy, dirty, doughty, downy, dowry, dreary, drowsy, dumpy, early, easy, eighty, elegy, empty, entreaty, envy, epilepsy, eurythmy, faulty, fifty-fifty, filthy, finicky, fishy, flaky, flatly, fleshy, flimsy, flinty, flossy, flunky, fool-hardy, forestry, forty, frailty, frenzy, freshly, friendly, frisky, frosty, frowsy, fusty, fuzzy, galaxy, garden-party, gaudy, gawky, gayly, ghostly, glossy, godly, goodly, goofy, gossipy, gramercy, greatly, grimy, grisly, grouchy, grumpy, guilty, half-empty, haply, happy-go-lucky, harpy, hazy, heady, healthy, heathenishly, heavy, hoity-toity, honestly, hooky, horny, huffy, husbandry, hypocrisy, idiocy, imperiously, industry, inly, Italy, ivy, jaunty, jelly, jeopardy, Jewry, jiffy, jointly, jolly, jumpy, kilty, kindly, kingly, lanky, larceny, leafy, lethargy, liberty, Lombardy, lousy, lucky, lumpy, lycanthropy, mammy, meaty, mercy, mimicry, minstrelsy, miry, missy, misty, monopoly, mostly, mouldy, muchly, muddy, mumsy, Muscovy, namby-pamby, narrowly, natty, nearly, neatly, neighborly, nervy, newly, newsy, nifty, nightly, nimbly, nippy, noisy, noteworthy, novelty, oily, oozy, orgy, outlawry, overstudy, paddy, palfry, palsy, paltry, panicky, panoply, pansy, partly,

E**

AL-*y*
ALDRY
ALITY
ALLY
ALRY
ALTHY
ALTY
AMY
ANCY
ANDY
ANITY
ANNY
ANT*-*ly*
ANTE
ANTRY
ANTY
ANY
APHY
APPY
ARCHY
ARDLY
ARITY
ARLY
ARRY
ARY
ASSY
ASTLY
ASTY
ASY
ATELY
ATHY
ATORY
ATRY
AUGHTY
AVY
AZY

party, pastry, patty, pebbly, perfidy, perilously, perky, pesky, philanthropy, pigmy, pithy, pixy, plucky, podgy, poky, polyandry, poppy, porphyry, pot-belly, poultry, praiseworthy, priestly, priory, privy, progeny, pudgy, Punch and Judy, puppy, pussy, rainy, raspy, ready, regularly, remedy, revelry, risky, rocky, roughly, ruby, ruddy, Rugby, rusty, rutty, sacristy, saintly, saucy, scaly, scraggy, scratchy, scrawny, scurvy, seaworthy, secretly, sentry, shabby, sharply, sharpy, shifty, shindy, shoddy, sightly, sissy, sketchy, slangy, slightingly, slimy, smithy, smugly, snoozy, snugly, softly, softy, solemnly, sooty, sovereignty, sparingly, speak-easy, spiffy, spongy, sporty, sprightly, spunky, squally, steady, stealthy, stingy, stocky, strategy, study, subsidy, sultry, superbly, surly, suzerainty, swanky, swarthy, tansy, tantivy, tapestry, tawdry, tawny, taxidermy, tetchy, theory, therapy, Thessaly, thinly, third-party, thirty, thorny, thoroughly, thrifty, throaty, tidy, timothy, toady, toby, toddy, tootsy-wootsy, topsy-turvy, trebly, tricky, twenty, ugly, understudy, unearthly, uneasy, unerringly, unfriendly, ungainly, unknowingly, unlucky, unsteady, unwieldy, veery, vestry, villainy, wanly, waxy, wealthy, weary, weekly, wheezy, whimsy, willingly, windy, wintry, wishy-washy, wooly, wordy, wormy, worry, worthy, wrongly, yearly

E**

EA*

EALTH-y

ECTLY

ECY

EDY

EE

EEDY

ELRY

ELY

EMY

ENARY

ENCY

ENLY

ENNY

ENTLY

ENTRY

ENTY

ERGY

ERITY

ERLY

ERRY

ERY

ESTY

ESY

ETRY

ETTY

ETY

EVY

EWY

EY**

I**

IARY

IBLY

ICACY

ICITY

ICKLE

E**
ICY
IDITY
IDLY
IE*
IETY
IGHTY
IGY
ILITY
ILLY
ILY
INARY
ING-*ly*
INKY
INNY
INTLY
INY
IPSY
IRACY
IRY
ISH-*ly*
ISKY
ISTRY
ITTY
ITY
IVERY
IVITY
OBBY
OCHE
ODY
OGGY
OGY
OLLY
OLY
OMY
ONLY
ONRY

E**

ONY
OODY
OPHY
OPPY
OQUY
ORITY
ORRY
ORY
OSITY
OSY
OSYNE
OTRY
OUSLY
OWDY
OWLY
OWY
UAL-*y*
UALLY
UARY
UBBY
UGGY
UITY
ULKY
ULLY
ULTY
ULY*
UMMY
UNDRY
UNDY
UNNY
UNY
UPTCY
URDY
URGY
URITY
URLY

E**
    URRY
    URTLY
    URY
    USTY
    USY
    UTTY
    UTY
    YE**
    S-EASE*
    IE*-S

Beeftea, blue-sea, cambric tea, chartless sea, choppy sea, Dead Sea, flea, guinea, high-sea, lea, over sea, pea, plea, Red Sea, sea, sweet-pea, tea, undersea, unsailed-sea

EA*
    see
    E**
    S-ADES*
    EASE*

Adrastea, area, azalea, Boadicea, Bona Dea, cetacea, Chaldea, Crimea, Ea, Gaea, Galatea, hydrangea, Idumea, kea, Korea, Laodicea, Leucothea, Medea, nausea, panacea, Penthesilea, Rhea, spiræa, trachea

EA**
    see
    A**

Yea

EA***
    see
    A*

Changeable, impermeable, ineffaceable, malleable, peaceable, permeable, serviceable, sizeable, traceable, unchangeable

EABLE
    see
    EL
    LE

Peace

EACE
    see
    EASE**

Beach, bleach, cleach, each, im-
peach, over-reach, peach, preach,
reach, teach

EACH
see
EECH
es-EZ

Beacon, deacon

EACON
see
ON

Arrow-head, balm of Gilead, bed-
spread, bedstead, behead, big-head,
block-head, Book of the Dead, bread,
brownbread, bulkhead, bullhead, cab-
bage-head, copperhead, dead, dead-
head, dread, drowsi-head, dunderhead,
figurehead, forehead, gingerbread, gor-
gon-head, hammer-head, head, hogs-
head, homestead, instead, lead, logger-
head, masthead, Oread, overhead,
overspread, pilot-bread, pinhead, read,
roadstead, Roundhead, saphead, shew-
bread, shortbread, sleepy-head, sore-
head, spearhead, spread, squarehead,
stead, sweetbread, thread, towhead,
tread, turtlehead, unread

EAD*
see
ACT-*ed*

Bead, knead, lead, mead, plead,
read, reread

EAD**
see
EDE

Breadth

EADTH
see
EDTH

Bay-leaf, clover-leaf, fallen-leaf, fig-
leaf, flyleaf, goldleaf, leaf, palm-leaf,
rose-leaf, sheaf

EAF*
see
EEF
IEF
S-EAVE-*S*

Deaf

EAF**
see
EF

Acreage, lineage, mileage

EAGE
see
AGE*

Beagle, eagle, gold-eagle, spread-eagle

EAGLE
see
EL
LE

Beak, bespeak, bleak, creak, freak, grosbeak, leak, outspeak, peak, sneak, speak, spring-aleak, squeak, streak, teak, tweak, weak, wreak

EAK*
see
EAKE
EEK
IQUE

Beefsteak, break, daybreak, heart-break, outbreak, steak

EAK**
see
AKE

Anneal, appeal, armorial seal, cochi-neal, commonweal, conceal, congeal, deal, heal, leal, meal, misdeal, New Deal, oatmeal, peal, piecemeal, repeal, reveal, seal, self-heal, solomon's seal, squeal, steal, teal, veal, weal, zeal

EAL*
see
EEL
ILE**
ed-IELD

Realm

EALM
see
ELM

Dealt

EALT
see
ELT

Commonwealth, health, stealth, wealth

EALTH
see
ly-E**

Beam, bream, coldcream, Cold-stream, cream, crossbeam, day-dream, Devonshire cream, dream, gleam, gulf-stream, hornbeam, ice-cream, mid-stream, moonbeam, ream, scream, seam, steam, stream, sunbeam, team

EAM
see
EEM
IME**

Bean, bemean, clean, dean, demean, dry-clean, glean, jean, lean, mean, string-bean, unclean, wean, yean

EAN*
see
EEN
INE**

Atlantean, Caribbean, cerulean, ce-tacean, crustacean, Epicurean, Hercu-lean, hyperborean, Korean, Mediter-ranean, mid-ocean, nectarean, ocean, pæan, Promethean, protean, pygmean, subterranean, superterranean, terpsi-chorean, terranean, unknown-ocean

EAN**
see
AN*
EN
IEN*

Miscreant, pageant, recreant, ser-geant

EANT
see
ANT*

Ash-heap, cheap, heap, leap, neap, reap, sand-heap

EAP
see
EEP

Appear, blear, clear, crystal-clear, dear, disappear, dog-ear, drear, ear, endear, fear, gear, hear, King Lear, lean-year, leap-year, linear, lunar year, my dear, near, overhear, reappear, rear, sear, smear, solar year, spear, steering-gear, tear, year, yesteryear

EAR*
see
EER
ERE
IER
ed-EARD**

Bear, bugbear, forebear, Great Bear, koala bear, northern-bear, pear, polar-bear, prickly pear, swear, tear, teddy-bear, underwear, wear

EAR**
see
AIR
ARE*

Research, search

EARCH
see
ERCH
IRCH
URCH

Heard, overheard, unheard

EARD*
see
ERD
URD

Beard, Bluebeard, Old Man's beard, shaggy-beard

EARD**
see
EAR*-*ed*

Shakespeare

EARE
see
EER

Earl, mother-of-pearl, pearl, seed-pearl

EARL
see
IRL
URL

Earn, learn, unlearn, yearn

EARN
see
ERN
URN

Hearse, rehearse

EARSE
see
ERCE
ERSE
URSE

Bleeding-heart, broken-heart, faint-heart, heart, inmost-heart, sweetheart **EART** *see* ART*

Dearth, earth, fuller's earth, hearth, unearth **EARTH** *see* ERTH

Æneas, Boreas, pancreas **EAS*** *see* AS*

Seven Seas **EAS**** *see* ESE

Appease, disease, displease, ease, heartease, please **EASE*** *see* ADES* E*-*s* EESE*

Axle-grease, cease, crease, decease, decrease, elbow-grease, increase, lease, release, surcease **EASE**** *see* EECE *ed*-IEST**

Leash **EASH** *see* EESH

High treason, rainy season, reason, season, treason **EASON** *see* ASON ON

Beast, east, Far East, feast, least, love-feast, Near East, northeast, southeast, yeast	**EAST*** *see* IEST** ISTE YST**
Abreast, breast, redbreast	**EAST**** *see* EST
Aisle-seat, backseat, bearded-wheat, beat, bleat, box-seat, browbeat, buckwheat, cheat, cleat, countryseat, crabmeat, deadbeat, defeat, drumbeat, eat, entreat, feat, forcemeat, heartbeat, heat, maltreat, meat, mince-meat, mistreat, neat, overeat, peat, repeat, reseat, rustic-seat, seat, sweetmeat, treat, unseat, wheat	**EAT*** *see* EET EIT* *ed*-ED
Great	**EAT**** *see* EATE
Sweat, threat	**EAT***** *see* ET
Aureate, baccalaureate, create, laureate, miscreate, nauseate, permeate, procreate, recreate, roseate	**EATE** *see* ATE EAT**
Beneath, bequeath, heath, 'neath, sheath, smoke-wreath, underneath, wreath	**EATH*** *see* EATHE EETH

Breath, death **EATH****
see
AITH**
ETH

Breathe, sheathe, unsheathe, wreathe **EATHE**
see
EATH*

Cordovan leather, feather, heather, **EATHER**
leather, pinfeather, sole leather, weath- *see*
er, white feather ER

Bandeau, beau, bureau, chateau, **EAU**
manteau, plateau, portmanteau, ron- *see*
deau, Rousseau, tableau, tonneau, O*
trousseau, weather bureau

Bereave, cleave, eave, heave, inter- **EAVE**
weave, leave, sheave, sick-leave, weave *see*
EEVE
EVE
S-EAF*-S

Beaver, weaver **EAVER**
see
ER

Bab el Mandeb, cobweb, cubeb, deb, **EB**
Horeb, neb, pleb, Seb, spider-web, web *see*
EBB

Debate, rebate **EBATE**
see
ATE

Ebb **EBB**
see
EB

Glebe, grebe, plebe

EBE
see

Algebra, zebra

EBRA
see
A**

Debt

EBT
see
ET

Aztec, Quebec, sec, spec, Toltec, xebec

EC
see
ECK

Deprecate, Hecate, hypothecate, imprecate

ECATE
see
ATE

Decent, indecent, recent

ECENT
see
ENT

Beck, bedeck, breakneck, by heck, check, crookneck, deck, fleck, flyspeck, gooseneck, henpeck, kopeck, leatherneck, longneck, low-neck, mizzen-deck, neck, peck, pinchbeck, quarter-deck, rebeck, recheck, reck, roughneck, rubberneck, shipwreck, smart-aleck, speck, stiff-neck, swan-neck, upperdeck, wreck

ECK
see
EK
EQUE
ed-ECT
s-EX

Freckle, heckle, speckle

ECKLE
see
EL
LE

Abject, affect, architect, bisect, circumspect, collect, confect, connect, correct, defect, deflect, deject, detect, dialect, direct, disinfect, disrespect, dissect, effect, eject, elect, erect, expect, genuflect, imperfect, incorrect, indirect, infect, inflect, inject, insect, inspect, intellect, intersect, introspect, neglect, object, perfect, pluperfect, prefect, prelect, project, prospect, protect, recollect, reflect, reject, respect, resurrect, retrospect, sect, select, self-respect, stage-effect, stick insect, subject, suspect

ECT
see
ECK-*ed*
S-ECK-*s*
EX

Correctly, directly, objectly, perfectly ¡

ECTLY
see
E**

Collector, deflector, detector, director, elector, erector, Hector, inspector, projector, prospector, protector, rector, reflector, sector, stamp-collector, tax-collector

ECTOR
see
OR

Fleecy, prophecy, secrecy

ECY
see
E**

Accented, accosted, accredited, addle-pated, affrighted, aged, agitated, anointed, antiquated, barricaded, bed, beloved, benighted, bigoted, biped, bird-witted, bled, blended, blessed, bloodshed, bobsled, booted, bow-legged, branded, bred, brooded,

ED*
see
AID**
EAD
ID
IED**
UID

bruited, buffeted, carted, catfooted, close-fisted, coasted, cold-blooded, comforted, conceited, confounded, corroded, crabbed, crowned, cursed, dark-red, defeated, deflected, disquieted, double-bed, dumbfounded, elated, elected, ended, evil-minded, fair-minded, false-hearted, feather-bed, fed, fled, fretted, garden-bed, half-hearted, high-minded, hoisted, home-bred, hon-eyed, hot-bed, hot-headed, hundred, ill-bred, imbed, inbred, indebted, infra-red, invented, jagged, jewel-studded, kilted, kindred, knotted, lamented, learned, led, left-handed, light-footed, long-winded, lowbred, Manfred, milk-fed, misled, Mohammed, naked, nar-row-minded, newly-wed, nodded, one-sided, over-fed, oyster-bed, pixilated, precipated, prompted, quadruped, rail-roaded, recommended, red, red-handed, reported, resounded, restricted, resusci-tated, sacred, Samoyed, shed, shredded, single-bed, single-handed, slab-sided, sled, snowshed, sober-minded, sped, spirited, spoon-fed, spotted, stark-naked, stilted, stout-hearted, sure-footed, talented, Tancred, thorough-bred, translated, trundle-bed, un-abated, unaccented, uncomforted, un-derbred, underfed, unpolluted, un-spotted, unsuited, untested, untrans-lated, unwarranted, unwed, unwonted, variegated, vested, wafted, watershed, well-fed, whole-hearted, wicked, wooded, woodshed, worsted, wretched, zed

ED*

ACT-*ed*
ANT*-*ed*
ASP-*ed*
AST-*ed*
ASTE-*d*
AUD-*ed*
AUNT-*ed*
EAD*-*ed*
EAT*-*ed*
EDE-*d*
END-*ed*
ET-*ed*
ICT-*ed*
IDE-*d*
IED**
IELD-*ed*
IFT-*ed*
IGHT-*ed*
ILT-*ed*
IT-*ed*
OAST-*ed*
OINT-*ed*
ORD*-*ed*
OST*-*ed*
ULT-*ed*
UTE-*d*

Accursed, airconditioned, Argus-
eyed, backed, barelegged, beloved,
bereaved, bleached, brazen-faced,
breathed, caracoled, cloyed, cowled,
cured, curtained, dark-eyed, dead-eyed,
delved, deranged, drenched, drowsed,
electrotyped, endorsed, enveloped,
etched, far-fetched, fettered, flagged,
fringed, frog-eyed, full-fledged, gnarled,
gypped, hallowed, hardboiled, hen-
pecked, horned, Janus-faced, keyed,
landlocked, low-necked, mottled, mul-
lioned, newly-wed, pampered, par-
celled, peopled, petered, pillowed,
refurbished, reserved, riprapped, rock-
ribbed, scowled, sequestered, shame-
faced, skewered, slant-eyed, smacked,
snarled, so-called, star-spangled,
stitched, strait-laced, stuccoed, sway-
backed, tattered, tempered, three-
cornered, two-faced, unlettered, un-
peopled, unreined, unremembered, un-
scathed, untrammeled, wed, well-
groomed, winced, winged, withered

ED**
see

Edda

EDDA
see
A**

Accede, antecede, cede, centipede,
concede, expede, impede, intercede,
precede, recede, rede, retrocede, se-
cede, stampede, supersede, Swede,
velocipede, Venerable Bede

EDE*
see
EED
ed-ED

Suede

EDE**
see
ADE

Dredge, edge, fledge, foreknowledge, kedge, keen-edge, knowledge, ledge, mountain-edge, on edge, pledge, sedge, selvedge, sledge, waters-edge, wedge

EDGE
see
AGE*
EAGE
EGE
IDGE

Comedian, median, tragedian

EDIAN
see
AN*
IAN

Accredit, credit, edit, discredit

EDIT
see
IT

Credo, teredo, Toledo, torpedo, tuxedo

EDO
see
O*

Hundredth

EDTH
see
EADTH

Aqueduct, deduct

EDUCT
see
UCT

Comedy, higgledy-piggledy, remedy, tragedy

EDY
see
E**

Absentee, agree, alee, apogee, ash-tree, banshee, bee, bootee, Bo-tree, bumblebee, calipee, carefree, Chaldee, Cherokee, chick-a-dee, chimpanzee, coatee, coffee, committee, conferee, Cree, debauchee, devotee, disagree,

EE
see
E**
IGREE
S-IES**
IEZE

divorcee, dungaree, elderberry-tree, **EE**
employee, fancy-free, fee, fiddle-dee-
dee, fig-tree, flee, foresee, free, fricassee,
fringe-tree, Galilee, garnishee, gee,
ghoulish-glee, glee, goatee, grandee,
guarantee, hard-alee, hat-tree, honey-
bee, indorsee, jamboree, jubilee, Judas-
tree, knee, lee, legatee, lessee, levee,
marquee, mulberry-tree, nominee, ogee,
oversee, parent-tree, Parsee, patentee,
Pawnee, payee, Pharisee, pledgee,
pongee, presentee, prithee, puttee,
quilting-bee, rappee, referee, refugee,
repartee, rupee, Sadducee, scot-free,
scree, see, set-free, settee, Shawnee,
shoe-tree, snicker-snee, soiree, spelling-
bee, spondee, spree, squeegee, suttee,
talkee-talkee, tee, te-hee, tepee, thee,
third degree, three, toffee, tree, trustee,
vendee, warrantee, wee, whoopee,
Yankee, Zuyder Zee

Fleece, golden-fleece, Greece   **EECE**
                                   see
                                 EESE**

Beech, beseech, breech, leech,   **EECH**
screech, speech, village-leech   *see*
                                 EACH
                                 es-EZ

Agreed, aniseed, apostle's creed, **EED**
bindweed, birdseed, bleed, breed,   *see*
chickweed, cotton-seed, creed, cross- EAD**
breed, decreed, deed, exceed, feed, flax- EDE
seed, freed, full speed, gleed, Godspeed, YD
greed, half-breed, hayseed, heed, in- *ed*-ED
deed, Indian weed, ironweed, jewel- *y*-EEDY

weed, knock-kneed, knotweed, linseed, **EED**
meed, misdeed, need, overfeed, pig-
weed, pokeweed, poppy-seed, proceed,
reed, screed, seaweed, seed, sneeze-
weed, speed, steed, stinkweed, succeed,
title-deed, tobacco-weed, treed, tweed,
weak-kneed, weed, whispering-reed

Darning needle, pine needle, needle, **EEDLE**
wheedle   *see*
                                         EL
                                         LE

Greedy, needy, reedy, seedy, speedy, **EEDY**
weedy   *see*
                                         E**

Beef, coral-reef, reef, shereef   **EEF**
                                       see
                                        IEF

Cheek, cleek, creek, Greek, hide-   **EEK**
and-seek, leek, meek, next-week, peek, *see*
reek, seek, sleek, week   EAK*
                                       IEK
                                       IQUE

Balance-wheel, cartwheel, chain-   **EEL**
wheel, cogwheel, creel, despot's heel, *see*
eel, emery wheel, feel, Ferris-wheel, EAL*
flywheel, genteel, heel, high-heel, Jez- ILE**
reel, keel, kneel, millwheel, newsreel, *ed*-IELD
paddle-wheel, peel, potter's wheel,
prayer wheel, reel, shabby-genteel,
spinning-wheel, steel, Virginia reel,
water-wheel, wheel

Beseem, deem, esteem, redeem, seem, self-esteem, teem

EEM
see
EME

Aberdeen, a-tween, baleen, between, bowling green, canteen, careen, Colleen, e'en, eighteen, fellaheen, fifteen, fourteen, go-between, green, Hallowe'en, has-been, keen, lateen, Maureen, might-have-been, nankeen, nineteen, ocean-green, overween, Paris-green, peen, preen, putting green, queen, sateen, screen, sea-green, seen, seventeen, sheen, sixteen, smoke-screen, spleen, thirteen, tureen, 'tween, umpteen, unseen, velveteen, village-green, ween, wintergreen

EEN
see
EAN*
ENE
IEN**
IENE
S-EENS

Greens, smithereens, teens

EENS
see
EEN-*S*

Asleep, Bo-peep, cheep, chimneysweep, clean sweep, creep, deep, donjon-keep, keep, knee-deep, oversleep, peep, sheep, skin-deep, sleep, steep, sweep, upkeep, weep, well-sweep, Uriah Heep

EEP
see
EAP

Carpet-sweeper, creeper, deeper, gamekeeper, housekeeper, keeper, lighthouse-keeper, office seeker, peeper, seeker, sky-sleeper, steeper, sweeper

EEPER
see
ER

Auctioneer, beer, buccaneer, cameleer, carabineer, career, chanticleer, charioteer, cheer, compeer, decreer,

EER
see
EIR**

deer, domineer, engineer, fallow-deer, **EER**
freer, gazetteer, ginger-beer, jeer, leer,   ERE*
mountaineer, muleteer, musk-deer,   IER**
musketeer, mutineer, nearbeer, over-   *ed*-EARD**
seer, peer, pioneer, privateer, profiteer,
queer, racketeer, reindeer, rootbeer,
seer, sheer, sight-seer, sneer, spruce
beer, steer, veer, veneer, volunteer

Lees, Maccabees, Pyrenees   **EES**
  see
  E**-*s*
  EE-*s*
  ES*

Cheese, creese, Edam cheese, head- **EESE***
cheese, Swiss cheese   *see*
  EASE*
  EEZE

Geese   **EESE****
  see
  EASE**
  EECE
  ESE
  IS***

Baksheesh, hasheesh   **EESH**
  see
  EASH

Afreet, balance-sheet, beet, bitter- **EET**
sweet, Blackfeet, crow's-feet, discreet,   *see*
feet, fleet, greet, indiscreet, meadow-   EIPT
sweet, meet, parakeet, peet, proof-   EIT*
sheet, sheet, skeet, sleet, stern-sheet,   ETE*
stocking-feet, street, sweet, tweet,
Wall Street, winding-sheet

Dragon's teeth, false teeth, teeth   **EETH**
see
EATH*

Seethe, teethe   **EETHE**
see
EATHE

Beeve, peeve, reeve, sleeve   **EEVE**
see
EIVE

Breeze, faintest-breeze, freeze, land-breeze, sneeze, squeeze, sweetscented-breeze, wheeze   **EEZE**
see
EASE*
EIZE
IEZE
IE*-*s*

Chef, clcf   **EF**
see
EAF

Bereft, cleft, deft, heft, left, reft, theft, weft   **EFT**
see

Defy, liquefy, putrefy, stupefy   **EFY**
see
I*

Bandy-leg, beg, cribbage-peg, dreg, kcg, leg, mumbletypeg, nutmeg, peg   **EG**
see
AGUE*
EGG

Illegal, legal, regal, vice-regal   **EGAL**
see
AL

Aggravate, congregate, delegate, leg-ate, relegate, segregate   **EGATE**
see
ATE

Allege, college, cortège, privilege, sacrilege   **EGE**
see
EDGE
IDGE

China-egg, egg, nest-egg, ostrich-egg, yegg   **EGG**
see
EG

Legion, region   **EGION**
see
ION

Apothegm, phlegm   **EGM**
see
EM

Abednego, alter ego, ego, forego   **EGO**
see
O*

Daddylonglegs, dregs, sea-legs   **EGS**
see
EG-*s*

Eh, El Gezireh, Gizeh, Nineveh, Tecumseh   **EH**
see
A*

Lorelei   **EI***
see
I*

Lei, rei **EI****
see
AY

Cassiopeia, hygeia, pharmacopæia **EIA**
see
IA

Nereid, Perseid **EID**
see
ID

Beige **EIGE**
see
EGE

Inveigh, neigh, outweigh, Raleigh, **EIGH**
sleigh, weigh *see*
EY*
ed-AID*

Eight, feather weight, freight, heavy- **EIGHT***
weight, hundred-weight, paperweight, *see*
pennyweight, weight ATE

Height, mountain-height, sleight **EIGHT****
see
IGHT

Deign, feign, foreign, reign, sover- **EIGN**
eign *see*
AIN

Nonpareil, unveil, veil **EIL***
see
AIL
ALE

Ceil   **EIL****
                                               see
                                               EEL

Hussein, mullein, protein, Shin Fein, skein, vein   **EIN***
       see
       AIN

Frankenstein, Holstein, Rubenstein, stein   **EIN****
       see
       INE

Seine, vicereine   **EINE**
       see
       AIN–

Being, fleeing, freeing, seeing   **EING**
       see
       ING

Feint   **EINT**
       see
       AINT

Receipt   **EIPT**
       see
       EAT*

Heir, their   **EIR***
       see
       ERE**

Weir   **EIR****
       see
       EAR

Weird	**EIRD** *see* EARD** EAR-*ed*
Edelweiss, gneiss	**EISS** *see* ICE*
Conceit, deceit	**EIT*** *see* ETE
Albeit, counterfeit, forfeit	**EIT**** *see* IT
Deity, homogeneity, ipseity, seity, spontaneity	**EITY** *see* E** ITY
Apperceive, conceive, deceive, perceive, preconceive, receive	**EIVE** *see* IEVE*
Seize	**EIZE** *see* EEZE ES*
Baalbek, Melchizedek, Sebek, topek, trek, Vathek	**EK** *see* ECK
Eke	**EKE** *see* EEK

Angel, apparel, archangel, asphodel, **EL**
barrel, befel, Beth-el, brothel, calomel, *see*
cancel, cantonflannel, chancel, channel, ABEL
charnel, chattel, chisel, citadel, compel, AEL
corbel, counsel, cudgel, damozel, dam- AMEL
sel, dispel, easel, El, evangel, excel, AVEL
expel, fardel, flannel, flour-barrel, gam- ELL
brel, gimel, hazel, hostel, hydromel, ENNEL
impel, infidel, Israfel, jewel, Jezebel, EREL
kernel, kummel, lapel, laurel, libel, ERYL
lintel, marvel, minstrel, missel, model, EVEL
mongrel, morsel, Mount Carmel, mus- IEL
catel, mussel, nickel, Noel, panel, IVEL
parallel, parcel, pastel, personnel, pet- OVEL
rel, pimpernel, pommel, pretzel, propel, OWEL
quarrel, rebel, remodel, repel, rondel, UEL
satchel, scalpel, scoundrel, scrannel, UNNEL
sentinel, shekel, shrapnel, sorrel, span- USEL
drel, stormy petrel, tael, tassel, tim- YL
brel, tinsel, trammel, vessel, wastrel, *ed*-ELD
weasel, Whitechapel, witch-hazel, *y*-E**
woodsorrel, yodel, yokel ELY

Addle, air-castle, amble, ample, **LE**
ankle, Aristotle, astraddle, axle, baffle, *see*
bamboozle, battle, beagle, beetle, ABBLE
boodle, bridle, bubble, bugle, bundle, ABLE
bungle, burble, burgle, carbuncle, ACKLE
castle, cat's-cradle, cattle, chortle, ACLE
church-steeple, clientele, cockle, cod- ADDLE
dle, Constantinople, couple, cradle, AMBLE
crossword-puzzle, crumple, cuttle, AMPLE
dawdle, dazzle, decuple, dingle, dis- ANDLE
mantle, double, embezzle, empurple, ANGLE
entitle, fettle, foible, fondle, foozle, APPLE
forecastle, frazzle, gargle, gentle, gur- ARBLE
gle, haggle, idle, inveigle, jungle, ATTLE

kindle, kirtle, ladle, mantle, maple, meddle, mollycoddle, monocle, mottle, muffle, muscle, myrtle, new-fangle, noodle, nozzle, octuple, ogle, oodle, pebble, peddle, peduncle, people, piffle, pinochle, poodle, purple, quadruple, quintuple, raffle, rankle, razzle-dazzle, reshuffle, Roman candle, rubble, schnozzle, scuffle, septuple, shuffle, shuttle, snaffle, snuffle, socle, spangle, sparkle, stag-beetle, staple, startle, stubble, subtle, supple, temple, tickle, tinkle, tipple, title, toddle, tousle, treacle, treadle, treble, trouble, truffle, trundle, tussle, tweedle, uncle, un-ruffle, waffle, waggle

LE

EABLE
EAGLE
ECKLE
EEDLE
ELLE
EMBLE
ESTLE
ETTLE
IABLE
IBBLE
IBLE
ICKLE
ICLE
IDDLE
IDLE
IFLE
IGGLE
IMBLE
IMPLE
INDLE
INGLE
INKLE
IPLE
IPPLE
IRCLE
ISTLE
ITTLE
IZZLE
OBBLE
OBLE
OGGLE
OPLE
OSTLE
UBLE
UCKLE
UDDLE

LE
UGGLE
UMBLE
URDLE
URTLE
USTLE
UZZLE
YCLE

Belate, elate, prelate, relate **ELATE**
see
ATE

Belch, squelch **ELCH**
see

Beheld, eld, geld, held, meld, upheld, **ELD**
weld, withheld *see*
EL-*ed*

Veldt **ELDT**
see
ELT

Careless, defenceless, gestureless, **ELESS**
guileless, homeless, lifeless, measure- *see*
less, nevertheless, noiseless, priceless, ES**
purposeless, senseless, shameless, shoe- ESCE
less, spaceless, tasteless, timeless, use- ESS
less, vagueless, valueless, verdureless,
wireless

Bandelet, bracelet, corselet, ocelet, **ELET**
omelet, wavelet *see*
ET

Delf, elf, herself, himself, itself, my- **ELF**
self, oneself, pantry-shelf, pelf, self, *see*
shelf, thing-in-itself, thyself, yourself

Twelfth **ELFTH**
see

Elia, Cordelia, lobelia, Ophelia, **ELIA**
parahelia *see*
IA

Goblin, javelin, zeppelin **ELIN**
see
IN

Elk **ELK**
see

Alarum-bell, ankle-bell, artesian **ELL**
well, befell, bell, blue-bell, bombshell, *see*
buy-and-sell, cell, churchbell, cockle- EL
shell, convent bell, cowbell, curfewbell, ELLE
dell, diving-bell, doorbell, dumb-bell,
dwell, eggshell, ell, fare-thee-well, fare-
well, fell, foretell, ground swell, hare-
bell, heather-bell, hell, jell, knell, mis-
spell, nutshell, Oliver Cromwell, over-
sell, pell-mell, quell, resell, retell,
school-bell, seashell, sell, shell, sleigh-
bell, smell, spell, swell, tell, tortoise-
shell, vesper-bell, well, whitewashed-
cell, William Tell, yell

Capella, citronella, fenestrella, Isa- **ELLA**
bella, nigella, pimpinella, predella, *see*
prunella, stella, tarantella, umbrella, A**
villanella

Bagatelle, coutelle, damozelle, fon- **ELLE**
tanelle, Gabrielle, gazelle, immortelle, *see*
La Pucelle, mademoiselle, Moselle, ELL
nacelle, spirituelle, villanelle

Dardanelles

ELLES
see
ELL-*S*

Bookseller, screw propeller, speller, story-teller, teller

ELLER
see
ER

Cello, hello, martello, Othello, punchinello, violoncello

ELLO
see
O*

Bed-fellow, fellow, Longfellow, mellow, yellow

ELLOW
see
O*
OW*

Elm, helm, overwhelm, slippery-elm, St. Anselm, whelm

ELM
see
EALM

Felon, Fenelon, melon, watermelon

ELON
see
ON

Help, kelp, whelp, yelp

ELP
see

Hostelry, jewelry, revelry

ELRY
see
E**

Else

ELSE
see

Belt, delt, dwelt, felt, heartfelt, knelt, lifebelt, melt, pelt, smelt, spelt, welt

ELT
see
EALT

Svelte	**ELTE** *see* ELT
Helter-skelter, shelter, swelter, welter	**ELTER** *see* ER
Delve, helve, shelve, twelve	**ELVE** *see* S-ELVES
Elves, ourselves, selves, shelves, themselves, yourselves	**ELVES** *see* ELVE-S

Antiquely, blithely, chastely, coarsely, comely, completely, concretely, contumely, conversely, crudely, divinely, entirely, exquisitely, freely, homely, inanely, infinitely, intuitively, lately, leisurely, lithely, loosely, lovely, merely, naïvely, namely, obliquely, obtrusively, precisely, princely, profusely, purely, rarely, relatively, rely, safely, savagely, scarcely, shapely, sincerely, solely, sorely, strangely, sublimely, supremely, surely, tamely, tensely, timely, unlovely, untimely, vaguely, wifely

ELY
see
ATELY
E**
EL-*y*

Ad valorem, anadem, anthem, begem, cave canem, diadem, emblem, gem, harem, hem, ibidem, idem, item, Jerusalem, Moslem, poem, postmortem, problem, proem, pro tem, sachem, Shem, solar system, stem, stratagem, system, tandem, them, theorem, totem, Zemzem

EM
see
AM
ASM
EGM
EMN
IAM
IEM

Alma Tadema, anathema, cinema, eczema, ulema

EMA
see
A*

December, dismember, ember, member, November, remember, September

EMBER
see
ER

Assemble, dissemble, reassemble, resemble, tremble, tout ensemble

EMBLE
see
EL
LE

Bireme, blaspheme, Carême, extreme, La Bohème, quinquereme, scheme, supreme, theme, trireme

EME
see
EAM
IME**

Accoutrement, achievement, acquirement, amusement, assuagement, at-one-ment, attunement, bereavement, casement, cement, cerement, chastisement, clement, denouement, displacement, divulgement, element, embezzlement, encouragement, enlargement, escapement, excitement, impalement, implement, improvement, inclement, infringement, management, measurement, movement, pavement, postponement, pronouncement, refinement, reimbursement, reinforcement, requirement, retirement, settlement, sub-basement, supplement, tenement, vehement

EMENT
see
ENT

Bessemer, blasphemer, schemer

EMER
see
ER

Condemn, contemn, solemn	**EMN** *see* EM
Demon, lemon	**EMON** *see* ON
Hemp	**EMP** *see*
Attempt, contempt, exempt, pre-empt, tempt, unkempt	**EMPT** *see*
Academy, alchemy, blasphemy, Domremy, enemy, Ptolemy	**EMY** *see* E**

Aden, ashen, Aten, auf wiedersehen, barren, batten, begotten, beholden, bitten, boughten, brazen, brethren, brighten, burden, chicken, chosen, cozen, crestfallen, dampen, darken, delicatessen, den, dew-beladen, Dolly Varden, dolmen, down-trodden, dozen, Dryden, Eden, embolden, enliven, fatten, fen, flaxen, forbidden, forgotten, foughten, frighten, frozen, Galen, garden, gentlemen, glen, glisten, gluten, goose-pen, Goshen, gotten, guinea-hen, harden, hasten, heathen, heavy-laden, hen, herb-garden, hidden, hoyden, Hymen, hyphen, idle-pen, ill-gotten, ken, kindergarten, kinsmen, kitchen, kitten, laden, lengthen, lenten, lessen, lichen, lighten, liken, linden, linen, listen, madden, mad-men, Mag-

EN
see
AMEN
AKEN
ASTE-*n*
AVEN
EAN**
EMEN
ENNE
EVEN
IEN*
IMEN
IZEN
OGEN
OKE-*n*
OKEN
OMEN
OVEN
UMEN

EN

YGEN

ly-E**

s-ENS

dalen, maiden, marshy-fen, men, menhaden, mitten, mizzen, moisten, molten, mullen, Munchausen, newfallen, oaken, oaten, often, olden, open, Origen, overladen, paten, pen, pig-pen, pollen, poverty-stricken, quicken, quill-pen, redden, re-open, risen, roof-garden, rotten, sadden, Saracen, schoolmen, silken, siren, smarten, soften, storm-driven, strengthen, stricken, sudden, sullen, swollen, table-linen, ten, terror-stricken, then, thicken, tungsten, unforsaken, unloosen, untrodden, vestry-men, vixen, warden, warren, waxen, weather-beaten, wen, when, whiten, wooden, wormeaten, wren, written, Yemen, yen

ENA
see
A**

Arena, Athena, duena, hyena, novena, phenomena, philopena, Porsena, prolegomena, subpœna, verbena

ENADE
see
ADE*

Grenade, hand-grenade, promenade, serenade

ENAL
see
AL

Arsenal, Juvenal, phenomenal, venal

ENARY
see
ARY

Centenary, mercenary, septenary

ENATE
see
ATE

Hyphenate, oxygenate, rejuvenate, senate

Absence, abstinence, acquiescence, adolescence, appetence, back fence, belligerence, cadence, circumference, coincidence, commence, condolence, conference, confidence, continence, corpulence, correspondence, credence, decadence, defence, difference, diffidence, diligence, divergence, divulgence, effulgence, eminence, essence, evidence, excellence, excrescence, fence, Florence, florescence, fraudulence, hence, immanence, impertinence, impotence, impudence, inadvertence, incandescence, incidence, incompetence, inconsequence, independence, indigence, indolence, indulgence, inference, influence, innocence, insistence, intelligence, interference, intumescence, iridescence, irreverence, jurisprudence, lapidescence, magnificence, negligence, nonoccurrence, occurrence, offence, omnipotence, omnipresence, opulence, parexcellence, pence, penitence, persistence, Peter-pence, petrescence, phosphorescence, pre-eminence, preference, presence, prevalence, prominence, Provence, providence, prudence, quintessence, recurrence, redolence, reference, reminiscence, renascence, residence, resplendence, resurgence, reticence, reverence, self-defence, senescence, silence, sixpence, snake fence, subsistence, sufferance, thence, tower-of-silence, transference, turbulence, violence, virulence, whence

ENCE
see
ANCE
ANT*-*s*
ENSE
ENT-*s*
IENCE
UENCE

Bench, blench, clench, drench, French, intrench, monkey-wrench,

ENCH
see

oak-bench, quench, retrench, stench, **ENCH**
stone-bench, trench, unclench, wench,
workbench, wrench

Agency, appetency, clemency, co- **ENCY**
gency, cognency, competency, con- *see*
sistency, constituency, contingency, E**
currency, decency, deficiency, delin-
quency, despondency, efficiency,
emergency, exigency, fervency, fre-
quency, impotency, inadvertency, in-
cipiency, inclemency, inconsistency,
incumbency, independency, indigency,
infrequency, leniency, nascency, pat-
ency, permanency, persistency, perti-
nency, potency, pungency, regency,
tendency, transparency

Amend, append, ascend, attend, **END**
befriend, bend, blend, candle-end, *see*
commend, comprehend, condescend, UEND
contend, defend, depend, descend, dis- *ed*-ED
tend, dividend, emend, end, expend, *ly*-E**
extend, fend, forfend, friend, Godsend,
impend, intend, interblend, legend,
lend, mend, offend, pend, perpend,
portend, pretend, recommend, rend,
reprehend, reverend, send, spend,
superintend, suspend, tail-end, tend,
transcend, trend, unbend, vend, vili-
pend, wend, Zend

Addenda, agenda, hacienda **ENDA**
see
A**

Bartender, defender, double-ender, **ENDER**
engender, expender, fender, gender, *see*
lavender, legal-tender, mender, offend- ER

er, pretender, provender, sea-lavender, spender, surrender, suspender, tender **ENDER**

Crescendo, diminuendo, innuendo **ENDO**
see
o*

Calends, odds-and-ends **ENDS**
see
END-*s*

Acetylene, contravene, convene, damascene, epicene, ethylene, gangrene, hygiene, intervene, kerosene, Magdalene, Nazarene, Nicene, obscene, pliocene, pyrene, scene, serene, supervene **ENE**
see
EEN
IEN**
INE**

Eye-opener, gardener, listener, scrivener **ENER**
see
ER

Genet, Plantagenet, tenet **ENET**
see
ET

Ginseng **ENG**
see
ING

Avenge, challenge, lozenge, revenge, scavenge, Stonehenge **ENGE**
see

Length, strength, wave-length, whole-length **ENGTH**
see

Armenia, gardenia, Iphigenia, mil- **ENIA**
lenia, neomania   *see*
                                   IA

Arsenic, eugenic, hygienic, Sara- **ENIC**
cenic, scenic   *see*
                                   IC

Amenity, serenity   **ENITY**
                                   see
                                   ITY

Evenly, heavenly, keenly, openly, **ENLY**
queenly, slovenly, suddenly   *see*
                                   EN-*ly*

Antenna, Avicenna, gehenna, henna, **ENNA**
Porsenna, senna, Sienna, Vienna   *see*
                                   ENA

Cayenne, comedienne, Parisienne,   **ENNE**
tragedienne   *see*
                                   EN

Fennel, kennel   **ENNEL**
                                   see
                                   EL

Catch-penny, fenny, fippenny, ha'- **ENNY**
penny, penny, spinning-jenny   *see*
                                   E**

Amiens, Athens, Camoëns, Dickens, **ENS**
dozens, homo sapiens, lens, nolens *see*
volens, wooded glens   EN-*s*

Condense, dense, dispense, expense, frankincense, horse sense, immense, incense, intense, license, nonsense, offense, pretense, recompense, sense, suspense, tense

ENSE
see
ENCE
ENT-*s*

Censer, condenser, denser

ENSER
see
ER

Abhorrent, accent, acknowledgment, adjournment, adolescent, adornment, advent, albescent, alignment, amendment, annulment, antecedent, apartment, arborescent, ardent, argent, arpent, ascent, astonishment, astringent, bent, bewilderment, bombardment, brazen serpent, cent, cerement, circumfluent, circumvent, cogent, comment, competent, consent, consignment, consistent, content, convergent, co-respondent, correspondent, crescent, current, decadent, descent, deterrent, diligent, disalignment, discernment, discontent, dissent, divergent, embankment, emulgent, encampment, endearment, enjoyment, enrollment, enthralment, environment, equipment, escarpment, establishment, evanescent, event, excellent, existent, extent, ferment, fervent, foment, fragment, fulfilment, gent, Ghent, horrent, illcontent, impellent, impotent, inadvertent, incandescent, incoherent, incompetent, inconsistent, incumbent, indent, independent, indictment, indigent, innocent, insolvent, insurgent,

ENT
see
ACENT
AGENT
ALENT
AMENT
ECENT
EMENT
ERENT
ICENT
IDENT
IENT
IMENT
INENT
OLENT
ONENT
UENT
ULENT
ULGENT
UMENT
ly-ENTLY
s-ENCE

intelligent, intent, interlucent, intermittent, intumescent, invent, irides-
cent, judgment, lambent, latent, lat-
escent, lent, lucent, magnificent, mal-
adjustment, malcontent, nascent, non-
existent, non-payment, oddment, oint-
ment, omnipotent, omnipresent, opal-
escent, parchment, parent, patent,
payment, pendent, penitent, pent,
percent, permanent, persistent, phos-
phorescent, pigment, potent, prece-
dent, present, prevent, prudent,
pschent, pungent, punishment, putres-
cent, quiescent, ravishment, recent,
red cent, redolent, refreshment, re-
fringent, refulgent, regent, relent, re-
·lucent, reminiscent, rent, repellent,
repent, resent, resentment, resplend-
ent, respondent, resurgent, retrench-
ment, rodent, scent, segment, senes-
cent, sent, serpent, shipment, silent,
solvent, spent, stringent, student,
superincumbent, superintendent, tal-
ent, tangent, tent, torment, torrent,
transcendent, translucent, transparent,
treatment, tumescent, Turkish crescent, unbent, under-current, under-
went, unravelment, urgent, vent, vest-
ment, vice-regent, well-content, went

ENT

Accidental, continental, detrimental,
elemental, experimental, fundamental,
incidental, instrumental, mental, mon-
umental, occidental, Oriental, orna-
mental, parental, regimental, rental,
sacramental, temperamental, trans-
continental

ENTAL
see
AL

Carpenter, center, enter, re-enter, renter, self-center

ENTER
see
ER

Eleventh, n-th, seventh, tenth

ENTH
see

Amentia, dementia

ENTIA
see
IA

Eloquently, eminently, frequently, gently, innocently, intently, patiently, penitently, permanently, presently, prominently, prudently

ENTLY
see
E**
ENT-*ly*

Memento, pimento

ENTO
see
O*

Entry, gentry, sentry

ENTRY
see
E**

Plenty, twenty, seventy

ENTY
see
E**

Borneo, Camdeo, cameo, Galileo, Laus Deo, Leo, Montevideo, nil sine Deo, rodeo, Romeo, vireo

EO
see
O*

Sheol

EOL
see
OL

Anacreon, bludgeon, burgeon, cameleon, clay pigeon, curmudgeon, dudgeon, dungeon, eon, escutcheon, gal-

EON
see
ON

leon, Gideon, luncheon, melodeon, **EON**
Napoleon, neon, Odeon, pantheon,
peon, pigeon, stoolpigeon, sturgeon,
surgeon, truncheon, widgeon

Alliaceous, aqueous, argillaceous, **EOUS**
beauteous, cinereous, consanguineous, *see*
contemporaneous, courageous, courte- AMUS
ous, erroneous, fabaceous, ferreous, EUS*
gallinaceous, gaseous, gorgeous, hetero- IOUS
geneous, hideous, homogeneous, igne- OUS
ous, instantaneous, ligneous, malva- UOUS
ceous, miscellaneous, osseous, out- US
rageous, papaveraceous, piteous, right- *ly*-OUSLY
eous, saponaceous, simultaneous, spon-
taneous, subaqueous, subterraneous,
succedaneous, terraqueous, vitreous

Amenhotep, doorstep, footstep, **EP**
goose step, instep, lockstep, mint- *see*
julep, misstep, overstep, pep, prep,· S-EPS
quick step, rep, side-step, step, two-
step

Crêpe **EPE**
see
APE

Steppe **EPPE**
see
EP

Biceps, corbiesteps, forceps **EPS**
see
EP-*s*

Accept, adept, concept, crept, except, inept, intercept, kept, percept, precept, slept, stept, swept, transept, unkept, well-kept, wept, wind-swept, yclept

EPT
see

Pepys

EPYS
see
EEP-*S*

Cheque

EQUE
see
ECK

Adder, adorer, alter, amber, angel water, antler, archer, artificer, assayer, astrologer, babbler, backwater, badger, Baedeker, banker, banner, banter, barber, bather, bellwether, berserker, billposter, blather, blue-singer, boiler, bolster, boner, booster, bootlegger, bouncer, breakwater, broiler, bungstarter, bunker, butler, buyer, buzzer, caliber, camper, Cancer, canter, Casper, chamber, chandler, chapter, charger, Chaucer, checker, chiseler, choler, chooser, chorister, cipher, clabber, clapper, clinker, cloister, cobbler, conceiver, condoler, confer, conger, consumer, costumer, cowcatcher, coworker, creeper, cricketer, crosser, cruiser, dabster, dagger, dapper, daughter, decanter, deceiver, decipher, differ, dissenter, dodder, draper, drawer, dredger, dresser, dulcimer, duller, duster, eager, Easter, either, elder, embroider, encounter, err,

ER
see
ACKER
ACRE
ADER
AFTER
AGER
AILER
AITER
AKER
AMER
AMPER
ANDER
ANGER
APER
APPER
ARER
ARTER
ARTYR
ASHER
ASTER
ATER
ATRE

Esther, etcher, ether, exploiter, falter, farmer, farther, faster, father, feeler, fibber, fiber, filter, fire-eater, flivver, fodder, follower, forefather, forefinger, forerunner, former, foster, four poster, frankfurter, free-thinker, free trader, fuller, further, gambler, gangster, garner, gather, geyser, Gheber, gibber, golfer, grandfather, greater, greengrocer, grosser, gutter, halter, hammer, hanger, hanker, harder, hawker, hawser, headquarter, heather, heckler, heifer, helicopter, her, hill-climber, holster, hostler, huckster, hunger, idler, importer, improper, infer, inter, jabber, Jacob's ladder, jammer, jasper, jawbreaker, jaywalker, juggler, kilter, kosher, laborer, ladder, lamplighter, lancer, larder, larger, lather, laughter, launder, lawyer, leader, ledger, leper, lesser, lifer, lighter, linen duster, lobster, loiter, longer, loud speaker, lounger, Luther, madder, man-eater, maneuver, manner, manslaughter, marker, masher, meager, merger, Mesmer, milder, mineral water, minister, minster, miter, monger, monster, mossbunker, mouser, muffler, mummer, murder, necromancer, ne'er, neither, neuter, news-monger, nowhither, officer, oldster, onlooker, ostler, outer, oyster, pacer, panther, partner, passenger, paternoster, pauper, peddler, pepper, performer, pewter, pilfer, pitcher, planter, platter, player, plumber, plunder, plunger, poacher, Poet's Corner, pointer, porker,

ER

ATTER
ATYR
AUR
AVER
AYER
EATHER
EEPER
ELLER
ELTER
EMBER
EMER
ENDER
ENER
ENSER
ENTER
EPHYR
ERER
ERR
ESTER
ETER
ETHER
ETRE
ETTER
EUR
EVER
EWER
IAR
IBRE
ICKER
IDER
IDITY
IER
IFER
IGGER
ILDER
ILER

potato-masher, pouter, preacher, prefer, presbyter, primer, producer, prompter, proof-reader, propeller, proper, prosper, psalter, Ptolemy Soter, pucker, punster, purser, quarter, quicksilver, quitter, racer, rather, rathskeller, rattler, reconnoiter, redeemer, red pepper, reefer, refer, reflector, reformer, rejoiner, respecter, rhymster, ringleader, roadster, rooster, rope-ladder, rose water, roster, rougher, saber, saucer, saunter, scalper, scandal-monger, scavenger, scepter, scooter, scraper, scribbler, scriber, scupper, seeker, seersucker, seltzer, Sepher, sepulcher, Shalmaneser, sharpshooter, sherry cobbler, shockabsorber, shoplifter, shopper, shyer, shyster, silver, simper, slaughter, sleep-walker, slipper, smarter, smuggler, snubber, snuffer, soccer, sock-dologer, soda-water, somber, sooner, sou'wester, spanker, specter, spinster, sprinkler, stage-whisper, stagger, Star Chamber, star-gazer, steamboiler, stenographer, stepladder, stiffer, stomacher, stopper, stretcher, stroller, sucker, super, sundowner, supper, sutler, swagger, swashbuckler, sweater, sweeter, swindler, talebearer, tallow-chandler, Tam-o'-Shanter, tanker, tauter, teacher, teetotaler, temper, tempter, tether, thaler, Tiber, timer, tipster, together, toper, tougher, trader, transfer, transformer, traveler, trickster, trooper, trotter, tumbler, ulster, upholster, upper, user, usher, vacuum cleaner, Vancouver, verger, vesper,

ER

ILLER
IMBER
IMMER
INDER
INER
INGER
INKER
INNER
INTER
IPER
IPPER
IR
IRE
ISER
ISHER
ISTER
ITER
ITTER
IVER
IZER
OBBER
OBER
OCKER
OCRE
OER
OFFER
OGRE
OKER
OLDER
OLVER
OMBER
OMER
ONDER
ONER
OOMER
OONER

Vichy water, vintner, voucher, Wagner, waiter, warbler, warder, water, waver, way-farer, Webster, well-wisher, whaler, whimper, whisker, whisper, whiter, whither, wilder, wind-jammer, wine-bibber, wither, woodpecker, wrapper, wrecker, youngster

ER
OPHER
OPPER
ORDER
ORTER
OTHER
OULDER
OUNDER
OUR
OVER
OW*-*er*
OWDER
OWER
UBBER
UCRE
UDDER
UER
UIRE
UMBER
UMNER
UNDER
UR
URER
USTER
UTTER
UVRE
ing-ING
ly-E**

Camera, chimera, cholera, diptera, era, genera, Hera, lepidoptera, opera, Pera, Riviera, Sisera

ERA
see
A**

Conquerable, considerable, discoverable, imponderable, insuperable, intolerable, invulnerable, miserable, prefer-

ERABLE
see
ABLE

able, tolerable, unconquerable, venerable, vulnerable

ERABLE

Amperage, average, beverage, brokerage, leverage, peerage, steerage

ERAGE
see
AGE*

Collateral, consul-general, ephemeral, equilateral, fal-de-ral, federal, feral, funeral, general, lateral, liberal, literal, mackeral, mineral, numeral, quadrilateral, several, trilateral

ERAL
see
AL

Lateran, Lutheran, Teheran, veteran

ERAN
see
AN*

Exuberant, intolerant, itinerant, protuberant, tolerant

ERANT
see
ANT*

Adulterate, aerate, berate, commiserate, confederate, conglomerate, considerate, degenerate, desperate, enumerate, exaggerate, exasperate, exhilarate, exonerate, exuberate, federate, generate, illiterate, immoderate, incarcerate, incinerate, inconsiderate, intemperate, inveterate, iterate, lacerate, liberate, literate, macerate, moderate, numerate, obliterate, operate, preponderate, recuperate, refrigerate, reiterate, remunerate, reverberate, temperate, tolerate, transliterate, vituperate, vociferate

ERATE
see
ATE

Acerb, adverb, herb, kerb, potherb, **ERB**
proverb, reverb, Serb, superb, verb *see*
URB

Coerce, commerce, terce, sesterce **ERCE**
see
EARSE
ERSE
URSE

Perch **ERCH**
see
IRCH

Cowherd, halberd, herd, potsherd, **ERD**
shepherd, swineherd *see*
EARD
IRD
ORD**
URD

Adhere, ampere, Apollo Belvedere, **ERE***
atmosphere, austere, bathysphere, *see*
cashmere, cassimere, cohere, Guine- EER
vere, hemisphere, here, inhere, insin- IER
cere, interfere, mere, Paul Revere,
persevere, revere, sere, severe, sincere,
sphere, stratosphere

Anywhere, confrere, elsewhere, ere, **ERE****
everywhere, Folies Bergère, gruyère, *see*
nowhere, porte-cochère, somewhere, AIR
there, where ARE*
IARE
IERE

Were **ERE*****
see
IR

Doggerel, mackerel, pickerel

EREL
see
EL

Adherent, belligerent, coherent, different, incoherent, indifferent, inherent, irreverent, reverent

ERENT
see
ENT

Interferer, loiterer, philanderer, roysterer, sorcerer, wanderer

ERER
see
ER

Entereth, fluttereth, hindereth, lingereth, tendereth

ERETH
see
ETH

Serf

ERF
see
URF

Berg, erg, iceberg, Heidelberg, kilerg, Nuremberg, Venusberg

ERG
see
URG

Absterge, converge, deterge, diverge, emerge, merge, serge, submerge, verge

ERGE
see
IRGE
URGE

Clergy, energy

ERGY
see
E**

Algeria, bacteria, cafeteria, diphtheria, Egeria, hysteria, Iberia, Siberia

ERIA
see
IA

Aerial, immaterial, imperial, material, serial

ERIAL
see
AL
IAL

Atmospheric, choleric, climacteric, congeneric, esoteric, etheric, exoteric, generic, Homeric, mesmeric, neoteric, tumeric, spheric

ERIC
see
IC

Bijouterie, Conciergerie, eerie, Erie, Jacquerie, Janesserie, lingerie, menagerie, reverie

ERIE
see
IE*

Imperil, peril

ERIL
see
IL

Culverin, Erin, glycerin

ERIN
see
IN

Algerine, glycerine, pelerine, tangerine

ERINE
see
INE**

Bickering, burnt-offering, careering, covering, drink-offering, gathering, glistering, glittering, ingathering, loitering, long suffering, muttering, offering, sin-offering, smoldering, tapering, thank-offering, votive offering, wandering, whispering, wool-gathering, westering

ERING
see
ER-*ing*
ING

Ephemeris, Eris, sui generis

ERIS
see
IS*

Cherish, feverish, gibberish, impov-
erish, pantherish, perish, queerish

ERISH
see
ISH

Demerit, inherit, merit

ERIT
see
IT

Asperity, austerity, celerity, dex-
terity, insincerity, posterity, prosper-
ity, severity, sincerity, temerity, verity

ERITY
see
ITY

Clerk, beserk, hauberk, jerk, perk

ERK
see
IRK
URK

Merle

ERLE
see
EARL

Cleverly, casterly, elderly, formerly,
latterly, meagerly, motherly, northerly,
orderly, overly, properly, quarterly,
slenderly, soberly, southerly, tenderly,
Waverly, westerly

ERLY
see
E**
ER-*ly*

Berm, germ, isotherm, pachyderm,
sperm, term, therm

ERM
see
IRM

Altern, bittern, cavern, cistern,
cithern, concern, discern, eastern, ern,
fern, govern, Hohenzollern, intern,
jack-o'lantern, kern, lantern, leathern,
lectern, magic lantern, misgovern,
modern, northern, pattern, postern,

ERN
see
EARN
ERNE
OURN*
URN

silvern, slattern, southern, stern, sub-altern, tavern, tern, tree fern, western, zithern

ERN

Eternal, external, fraternal, infernal, internal, maternal, paternal, sempiternal, supernal, vernal

ERNAL
see
AL

Interne, Jules Verne, sauterne

ERNE
see
ERN

Bolero, cavalero, Cicero, hero, Nero, numero, pampero, Prospero, Rio de Janeiro, sombrero, Trocadero, zero

ERO
see
O*

Acheron, chaperon, Decameron, hanger-on, heron, Oberon, Percheron

ERON
see
ON

Adulterous, boisterous, cadaverous, cantankerous, dangerous, dexterous, generous, lecherous, numerous, obstreperous, oderiferous, onerous, pestiferous, ponderous, preposterous, prosperous, slanderous, somniferous, splendiferous, thunderous, viperous

EROUS
see
OUS

Excerpt

ERPT
see
URP-*ed*

Err

ERR
see
ER

Croix de guerre, nom de guerre, parterre, pied-à-terre

ERRE
see
AIR
ARE*

Berry, blackberry, blueberry, cherry, cranberry, elderberry, equerry, ferry, gooseberry, loganberry, merry, mulberry, raspberry, sherry, spiceberry, strawberry, Tom-and-Jerry

ERRY
see
ERY

Algiers, divers, headquarters, Ghebers, Seven Sleepers, Sicilian Vespers

ERS
see
ER-*s*

Adverse, asperse, converse, disperse, diverse, Erse, immerse, intersperse, inverse, obverse, perverse, reverse, terse, transverse, traverse, universe, verse

ERSE
see
EARSE
ERCE
URSE
ed-IRST
ORST

Erst

ERST
see
IRST

Advert, alert, assert, avert, concert, contravert, convert, covert, desert, dessert, disconcert, divert, Egbert, exert, expert, extravert, filbert, inert, insert, introvert, invert, malapert, overt, pert, pervert, re-assert, revert, sherbert, vert

ERT
see
IRT
UIRT
URT

Berth

ERTH
see
IRTH

Liberty, poverty, property

ERTY
see
E**

Cerberus, Hesperus

ERUS
see
US

Conserve, deserve, nerve, observe, preserve, reserve, serve, swerve, unnerve, unreserve, verve

ERVE
see
URVE

Adultery, anti-slavery, archery, artery, artillery, bakery, battery, blustery, brewery, bribery, buffoonery, cajolery, celery, cemetery, chancery, chandlery, chicanery, creamery, crockery, cutlery, deanery, debauchery, discovery, distillery, drapery, drudgery, effrontery, embroidery, emery, fakery, feathery, fernery, fiery, finery, fippery, fishery, flattery, flummery, foolery, forgery, frippery, gallery, grapery, greenery, grocery, gunnery, haberdashery, hatchery, hosiery, housewifery, imagery, ironmongery, jewellery, jittery, jugglery, knavery, lamasery, lathery, leathery, lottery, lubbery, machinery, mastery, millinery, misery, mockery, monastery, mummery, mystery, napery, nunnery, nursery, onery, pearl-fishery, peppery, perfumery, periphery, phylactery, pottery, presbytery, powdery, prudery, psaltery, quackery, query, raillery, recovery, refinery, revery, rockery, roguery, rogues gallery, rookery, scenery, self-

ERY
see
E**
ERRY
IVERY
ORY
OWERY
URY

mastery, shivery, showery, shrubbery, **ERY**
skulduggery, slavery, silvery, slippery,
soldiery, sorcery, spidery, surgery,
thievery, thuggery, tomfoolery, tot-
tery, tracery, treachery, trickery,
trumpery, upholstery, venery, very,
waggery, watery, whispering-gallery,
witchery

Beryl **ERYL**
see
IL

Aborigines, Achilles, Albigenses, **ES***
Anchises, Andes, Antilles, antipodes, *see*
Apelles, Archimedes, Ares, Aristides, ADES*
Aristophanes, Artaxerxes, auspices, ATES**
Averroës, Azores, Bacchantes, Benares, EASE
bay leaves, Des, Bootes, Buenos Ayres, EES
Celebes, Ceres, Cervantes, Corybantes, EIZE
crevasses, Damocles, Dark Ages, de- ESE
grees, Demosthenes, Dives, doges, IDES*
Dolores, Druses, Empedocles, Epi-
phanes, Erinyes, Euphrates, Ganges,
Graces, Hades, Heracles, Hercules,
Hermes, herpes, Holofernes, lares,
Lemures, Los Angeles, Manes, Me-
phistopheles, Mercedes, Middle Ages,
molasses, Moses, Oannes, oases, omnes,
open spaces, Orestes, penates, Pericles,
Pisces, Praxiteles, Procrustes, Sevres,
similes, Thales, Themistocles, Thersi-
tes, tresses, Ulysses, vortices, Xerxes,
Ximenes

Ducks-and-drakes, Fates, gules, Guy **ES****
Fawkes, Holmes, Medes, Naples, *see*

Rhodes, skittles, small clothes, stars **ES****
and stripes, steppes, Ten Lost Tribes,
Thebes, Wales, wolves

Yes   **ES*****
see
ESCE
ESS

Courtesan, diocesan, parmesan   **ESAN**
see
AN*

Acquiesce, coalesce, convalesce, ef-   **ESCE**
fervesce, effloresce, evanesce, intum- *see*
esce, opalesce   ES***
ESS

Burmese, Cantonese, Chinese, dio-   **ESE**
cese, Japanese, maltese, manganese, *see*
obese, Pekinese, Portuguese, Siamese, EAS**
Singhalese, Sudanese, these, Viennese, IECE
Veronese   IEZE
IS***
ISE***

Beset, boneset, reset   **ESET**
see
ET

Afresh, enmesh, flesh, fresh, gross-   **ESH**
flesh, horseflesh, mesh, refresh, thresh *see*

Amnesia, anæsthesia, freesia, mag-   **ESIA**
nesia, Polynesia, Rhodesia, silesia   *see*
IA

Anamnesis, antithesis, exegesis, Genesis, hypothesis, Lachesis, Nemesis, palingenesis, parenthesis, parthenogenesis, synthesis, telekinesis, thesis

ESIS
see
IS*

Desk, kneeling-desk, office desk

ESK
see
ESQUE

Arabesque, burlesque, grotesque, Moresque, Normanesque, picturesque, romanesque, statuesque

ESQUE
see
ESK

Abbess, abruptness, access, address, agelessness, aggressiveness, aloofness, antiqueness, artfulness, artless, awareness, bashfulness, bitterness, bless, bloodless, bootless, bottomless, boundlessness, brainless, burgess, buttress, calmness, caress, cheerfulness, chess, childishness, childless, closeness, clothespress, cloudless, compress, confess, congress, correctness, countless, cress, cypress, darkness, dauntless, deaconess, diffuseness, digress, dispossess, distress, dress, duchess, dulness, duress, eagerness, earnestness, effortless, egress, empress, enchantress, endless, ess, excess, exhaustless, expertness, express, eye-witness, fathomless, fastness, faultless, fearless, foolishness, footless, forgetfulness, forgiveness, formless, foulness, fruitless, fullness, goddess, godlessness, golden-tress, governess, groundless, guess, hairless, hardness, harness, heiress, helpless, hornless, hostess, huntress, idleness,

ESS
see
ELESS
ES**
ESCE
ESSE
ILESS
INESS
ed-EST

impress, ingress, jazzless, laundress, **ESS**
less, licentiousness, lightness, limitless,
lioness, listless, luckless, matchless,
mattress, meekness, mellowness, mess,
mistress, motionless, mulishness, nak-
edness, nameless, nearness, needless,
negress, ness, nothingness, numberless,
obligingness, obsess, odorless, ogress,
oneness, oppress, overdress, passive-
ness, pathless, peacefulness, peeress,
peerless, perfectness, piggishness, Pilgrim's Progress, poetess, pointless,
possess, powerless, preparedness, pre-
possess, press, priestess, princess, prior-
ess, process, profess, progress, prowess,
pythoness, Queen Bess, quenchless,
questionless, questless, quickness,
quietness, rankness, rashness, rayless,
readdress, recess, reckless, redness,
redress, regardless, regress, repress,
resistless, restless, retrogress, righte-
ousness, rudeness, ruthless, seamless,
seamstress, shadowless, shepherdess,
shiftless, shoreless, shrewdness, shy-
ness, sinless, sleepless, slothfulness,
slyness, sorceress, spaceless, spaceless-
ness, speechless, spotless, stainless,
stewardess, stillness, success, sugarless,
sullenness, sunless, supineness, sup-
press, sweetness, tactless, tenantless,
tenderness, thankless, thickness,
thoughtfulness, thoughtless, thriftless,
thusness, tigress, timeless, timeless-
ness, toothless, traitress, transgress,
treeless, undress, unless, uprightness,
upsidedownness, vagueness, voluptu-
ousness, waitress, wantonness, water-

cress, weakness, weightless, wickedness, wilderness, winepress, witless, witness, worthless, youthfulness

ESS

Finesse, largesse, noblesse

ESSE
see
ESS

Accession, cession, concession, confession, depression, digression, expression, impression, intercession, obsession, precession, procession, profession, progression, recession, regression, repression, retrocession, retrogression, session, succession, suppression, transgression

ESSION
see
ION

Acid test, addrest, alkahest, almagest, arrest, basest, behest, beholdest, bendest, best, bitterest, blendest, blessedest, blest, Budapest, cheapest, chest, chiefest, coarsest, congest, contest, coolest, crest, deprest, describest, despisest, detest, digest, dishonest, dispossest, divest, divinest, drest, driftest, earnest, enterest, Everest, exactest, forest, forlornest, frailest, fullest, genteelest, harvest, honest, horridest, id est, immodest, implorest, infest, inquirest, intensest, interest, invest, jest, keenest, laborest, lest, limberest, longest, manifest, mare's-nest, mayest, middle-west, minutest, modest, molest, nest, obscurest, opprest, palimpsest, pest, possest, prest, protest, purest, quietest, reforest, remotest, rest, returnest, rinderpest, robbest, second-

EST
see
EAST**
ESS-*ed*
IEST*
UEST

best, shreddest, sincerest, slickest, still- **EST**
est, stretchest, suggest, swiftest, temp-
est, test, thirstest, unblest, unmolest,
unrest, urgest, vaguest, vest, west,
widest, wildest, wottest, wrest, zest

Fiesta, podesta, siesta, Vesta, Zend **ESTA**
Avesta   *see*
                                        A**

Festal, pedestal, vestal   **ESTAL**
                                        see
                                        AL

Ester, fester, forester, jester, nor'- **ESTER**
wester, quester, rhymester, semester,   *see*
sequester, yester   ER

Nestle, pestle, trestle, wrestle   **ESTLE**
                                        see
                                        EL
                                        LE

Manifesto, presto   **ESTO**
                                        see
                                        O*

Amnesty, dishonesty, honesty, im-   **ESTY**
modesty, lese-majesty, majesty, mod-   *see*
esty, travesty, testy   E**

Cheesy, courtesy, heresy, poesy,   **ESY**
prophesy   *see*
                                        E**

Abet, aigret, alphabet, anchoret,   **ET**
asset, beget, bet, blanket, bonnet,   *see*
booklet, bouncing-Bet, brevet, Bridget, ACKET
brisket, brooklet, bucket, budget, buf- ANET

fet, bullet, cabaret, cadet, calumet, chaplet, circlet, claret, cloudlet, comet, cornet, corset, cosset, couplet, court-poet, covet, cresset, crotchet, curb-market, curvet, cygnet, deep-set, dragnet, dulcet, eaglet, egret, Emerald Tablet, emmet, epithet, facet, faucet, ferret, fish-net, flageolet, flibbertigib-bet, floweret, forget, freshet, fret, frisket, gadget, garnet, garret, gas-jet, gauntlet, get, gibbet, giblet, gimlet, goblet, gorget, gusset, hamlet, hatchet, helmet, hic jacet, hornet, inlet, inset, interpret, jennet, jet, junket, kismet, lancet, landaulet, latchet, leaflet, let, leveret, linnet, magnet, mallet, market, met, millet, minaret, moppet, mullet, musket, net, offset, onset, outlet, owlet, pallet, pamphlet, panne velvet, para-pet, pellet, pet, plummet, poet, poke bonnet, posset, privet, prophet, pullet, puppet, quartet, quintet, quodlibet, ratchet, regret, reset, ret, ricochet, ringlet, rivet, russet, scarlet, secret, set, sextet, sherbet, signet, singlet, sonnet, spinet, stet, stockinet, stockmarket, streamlet, sub-let, sunbonnet, sunset, tablet, tabouret, target, tea-set, Tebet, Thibet, thickset, tippet, toilet, To Let, Tophet, trinket, troutlet, turret, ultra-violet, upset, valet, varlet, velvet, videlicet, violet, wallet, wet, whet, wristlet, yet

ET

ASKET
EAT***
EBT
ELET
ENET
ESET
ETTE
ICKET
IDGET
IET
INET
IVET
OCKET
OMET
ONET
OSET
UET*
UGGET
ULET
UMPET
ed-ED

Centripetal, decretal, gun-metal, metal, petal

ETAL
see
AL

Etch, fetch, homestretch, ketch, outstretch, sketch, stretch, vetch, wretch

ETCH
see

Athlete, compete, complete, concrete, Crete, delete, deplete, effete, esthete, incomplete, mete, obsolete, Paraclete, replete, secrete

ETE*
see
EAT*
EET
UITE*

Tête à tête, fête, machete

ETE**
see
ATE

Altimeter, anemometer, barometer, cyclometer, Demeter, deter, diameter, gas-meter, heliometer, hydrometer, kilometer, meter, orometer, pedometer, perimeter, peter, pyrometer, saltpeter, speedometer, thermometer, trumpeter, variometer

ETER
see
ER

Abideth, affordeth, alloweth, Ashtoreth, beginneth, bestoweth, breaketh, chanceth, changeth, compriseth, dwelleth, Elizabeth, encompasseth, fleeth, flieth, gaveth, guideth, howleth, keepeth, lodgeth, loveth, Macbeth, maketh, Nazareth, observeth, seeth, Seth, shibboleth, sleepeth, slideth, taketh, useth, wakeneth, waneth, weepeth

ETH
see
AITH**
EATH**
ERETH
ILETH

Bell-wether, nether, tether, together, wether, whether

ETHER
see
EATHER
ER

Æsthetic, apathetic, arithmetic, **ETIC**
ascetic, athletic, cosmetic, emetic, *see*
energetic, frenetic, genetic, geodetic, IC
hermetic, homiletic, magnetic, noetic,
onomatopoetic, parenthetic, pathetic,
peripatetic, phonetic, phrenetic, poetic,
polysynthetic, prophetic, sympathetic,
synthetic

Leto, magneto, veto   **ETO**
                                          see
                                          O*

Breton, Eton, phaeton, simpleton,   **ETON**
skeleton   *see*
                                          ON

Kilometre, metre, saltpetre   **ETRE**
                                          see
                                          ETER

Chronometry, coquetry, geometry,   **ETRY**
marquetry, musketry, parquetry, po-   *see*
etry, psychometry, symmetry, trigo-   E**
nometry

Aigrette, anisette, barette, blan-   **ETTE**
quette, briquette, brochette, brunette,   *see*
chemisette, cigarette, collarette, co-   ET
quette, corvette, cravenette, croquette,
curette, dinette, epaulette, etiquette,
flannelette, fourchette, gazette, gris-
ette, historiette, kitchenette, Lafay-
ette, layette, leatherette, lorgnette,
lunette, maisonnette, Marie Antoin-
ette, midinette, mignonette, moquette,

novelette, oubliette, palette, parquette, **ETTE**
pipette, planchette, poussette, quar-
tette, quintette, rosette, roulette, satin-
ette, serviette, silhouette, soubrette,
statuette, suffragette, toilette, vedette,
vignette, vinaigrette, voiturette, wag-
onette

Begetter, better, dead letter, fetter, **ETTER**
getter, letter, red-letter, Roman letter, *see*
setter, typesetter, uncial letter, un- ER
fetter, wetter, whetter

Confetti, Rossetti, spaghetti **ETTI**
see
I**

Fettle, kettle, mettle, nettle, settle, **ETTLE**
tea-kettle *see*
EL
.LE

Allegretto, amoretto, falsetto, **ETTO**
ghetto, libretto, palmetto, Rigoletto, *see*
stiletto, terzetto, Tintoretto O*

Betty, jetty, petty, pretty **ETTY**
see
E**

Crotchety, fidgety, nicety, ninety, **ETY**
pernickety, rackety, rickety, safety, *see*
subtlety, surety, velvety E**

Epictetus, impetus, quietus **ETUS**
see
US

Feud **EUD**
see
UDE

Pseudo **EUDO**
see
O*

Athenaeum, Colosseum, Herculane- **EUM**
um, linoleum, lyceum, mausoleum, *see*
museum, odeum, petroleum, rheum, IUM
Te Deum OM

Amateur, bonheur, chauffeur, coif- **EUR**
feur, connoisseur, enterpreneur, fleur, *see*
grandeur, liqueur, masseur, monsieur, IR
raconteur, seigneur, sœur, voyageur OUR**
UR

Alpheus, Asmodeus, Briareus, cadu- **EUS**
ceus, coleus, hic liber est meus, Mor- *see*
pheus, nucleus, Orpheus, Peleus, Per- UCE
seus, Prometheus, Proteus, scarabæus, US
Smintheus, Theseus, Zeus

Berceuse, Betelgeuse, chartreuse, **EUSE**
danseuse, masseuse *see*
ERS
URS

Sleuth **EUTH**
see
UTH

Kislev **EV**
see

Coeval, medieval, primeval

EVAL
see
AL

Eve, Midsummer eve

EVE
see
EAVE
IEVE

Bevel, dishevel, level, revel, sea-level, spirit-level

EVEL
see
EL

Eleven, even, seven

EVEN
see
EN

Cantilever, dissever, ever, fever, for-ever, lever, never, retriever, sever, soever, whatever, whensoever, who-ever, whomsoever, whosoever

EVER
see
ER

Dare-devil, devil, evil, printer's devil, she-devil

EVIL
see
IL

Brevity, levity, longevity

EVITY
see
ITY

Bevy, chevy, levy

EVY
see
E**

Anew, askew, bedew, beefstew, be-shrew, bestrew, blew, brand-new, brew, corkscrew, crew, curfew, curlew, dew, drew, eschew, feverfew, few, Hebrew,

EW
see
AGUE***
IEW

hew, honey-dew, immew, Jew, knew, **EW**
merry-andrew, mew, mildew, nephew, o**
new, pew, phew, renew, screw, sew, ou*
shrew, sinew, skeleton crew, skew, u
slew, smew, spew, St. Andrew, St. Bar- ue*
tholomew, stew, strew, threw, thumb- *ed*-EWD
screw, unscrew, Wandering Jew, whew, s-ose**
withdrew, yew use*

Lewd, shrewd **EWD**
see
UDE

Bejewel, crewel, jewel, newel **EWEL**
see
EL

Ewer, fewer, hewer, reviewer, sewer, **EWER**
skewer *see*
ER

Hewn, rock-hewn, rough-hewn, **EWN**
sewn, strewn, unhewn *see*
OON

King's Mews, news **EWS**
see
EW-*s*

Newt **EWT**
see
OOT**

Chewy, dewy, mildewy, screwy, **EWY**
sinewy, skewy *see*
E**

Annex, apex, biconvex, circumflex,
codex, complex, convex, duplex, flex,
haruspex, ibex, ilex, index, inflex, mul-
tiplex, murex, perplex, pollex, pontifex,
reflex, rex, sex, silex, simplex, vertex,
vex, vortex

EX
see
ECK-*s*
ECT-*s*
EQUE-*s*
ed-EXT

Next, pretext, text, vex't, what-next

EXT
see
EX-*ed*

Abbey, Alderney, alley, attorney,
barley, bey, blarney, bluey, bogey,
bowling-alley, burley, chimney,
choosey, chop-suey, chutney, clayey,
cockney, convey, covey, courtsey,
darkey, dingey, disobey, Dombey,
donkey, dopey, fluey, flunkey, galley,
gin rickey, gluey, grey, Guernsey, gul-
ley, hackney, Hennessey, hey, jersey,
jitney, jockey, journey, key, Killarney,
lackey, lamprey, linsey-woolsey, malm-
sey, master-key, medley, monkey,
Monterey, motley, obey, Odyssey,
okey, Orkney, osprey, palfrey, parley,
parsley, pass-key, phoney, phooey,
Pompey, posey, pulley, purvey, Shel-
ley, shimmey, Sidney, skeleton-key,
surrey, survey, they, tourney, trey,
trolley, turkey, turnkey, valley, volley,
watchkey, Westminster Abbey, whey,
whimsey, whiskey, Wolsey

EY
see
A*
AY
E**
s-IES**

All-seeing Eye, buckeye, bull's eye,
cock-eye, evil-eye, eye, needle's eye,
ox-eye, sheep's eye, wall-eye

EYE
see
I*
IE**

Cortez, fez, oyez, Suez, Velasquez

EZ
see
EACH-*es*
OICE-*s*

Trapeze

EZE
see
EEZE
ESE

Intermezzo, mezzo

EZZO
see
O*

I SOUNDS

Alibi, alkali, alumni, Delphi, demi, **I***
Eli, fungi, genii, I, Magi, Malachi,   *see*
modus operandi, pi, rabbi, semi,   AI
Shang-ti, vox populi   EFY
            EYE
            IE**
            IFY
            IGH
            ISFY
            ULY**

Agni, Amalfi, Amenti, Ani, Assisi, **I****
bacardi, banditti, Bartholdi, beri-beri,   *see*
bhakti, Buonarotti, Cabiri, cadi, Capri,   ALI
chianti, Chili, conoscenti, Cotopaxi,   ATI
daiquiri, Disraeli, do-re-mi, droshki,   E*
effendi, ennui, Fascisti, Fiji, Firdausi,   EE
Fo-hi, frangipani, Gandi, Garibaldi,   ETTI
Gehazi, Gobi, Hadji, hari-kari, Hawaii,   IE*
Hopi, houri, Jami, khaki, kiwi, Lak-   IGREE
shmi, lapis lazuli, Leonardo da Vinci,   INI
Loki, Machiavelli, Mahdi, Maori,   IORI
Medici, Miami, Midi, mufti, Nagasaki,   ITI
Nazami, Nazi, obi, okapi, Parvati,   OLI
patchouli, peccavi, Pehlevi, peri, picca-   ONI
lilli, Pompeii, potpourri, quasi, Rishi,
Saadi, salmagundi, sans-souci, saki,
sakti, sbirri, scudi, ski, soldi, sperma-
ceti, sri, Sufi, Tauri, taxi, Tiki, Tishri,
Trimurti, tutti-frutti, Uffizi, Valmiki,

Vasari, Verdi, vermicelli, visconti, **I****
voici, Yogi

Abyssinia, acacia, Aglaia, Alexan- **IA**
dria, ambrosia, Andalusia, aphrodisia, *see*
apologia, Arabia, Arcadia, artemisia, A**
Assyria, Bessarabia, Bœotia, Bohemia, ALIA
Bolivia, braggadocia, Britannia, Cala- ANIA
bria, California, Cambodia, camellia, ARIA
Cappadocia, cassia, Circassia, claustro- ASIA
phobia, Columbia, cyclopedia, Cyn- EIA
thia, Czecho-Slovakia, dahlia, deutzia, ELIA
Dionysia, Discordia, dyspepsia, ency- ENIA
clopedia, Etruria, emphorbia, fuchsia, ENTIA
gilia, godetia, Hibernia, hydrophobia, ERIA
Hypatia, hypochrondia, India, in- ESIA
ertia, insignia, insomnia, intelligentsia, OLIA
Ischia, Ismailia, kleptomania, Lemuria, ONIA
loggia, Lucrezia Borgia, Malaysia, OPIA
Manchuria, memorabilia, Mesopota- ORIA
mia, militia, minutia, misericordia,
Moravia, neuralgia, nostalgia, Nubia,
Olympia, onomatopœia, paranoia, Pa-
tricia, Persia, Perugia, petunia, phantasmagoria, phobia, Phoenicia, Phry-
gia, pointsettia, Portia, Prussia, Py-
thia, raffia, rudbeckia, Russia, salvia,
Scandinavia, Scythia, sedilia, sepia,
sequoia, stadia, stevia, St. Sofia, sym-
posia, Syria, Thalia, tibia, Transcau-
casia, Trinosophia, via, via media,
Zenobia

Amiable, inexpiable, insatiable, in- **IABLE**
variable, justifiable, liable, pitiable, *see*
pliable, reliable, satiable, sociable, un- ABLE
deniable, variable EL
LE

Ammoniac, aphrodisiac, cardiac, celeriac, demoniac, elegiac, hypochondriac, kleptomaniac, maniac, pericardiac, symposiac, Syriac, theriac, Zodiac

IAC
see
AC

Iliad, jeremiad, myriad, naiad, Olympiad, Pleiad, triad

IAD
see
AD

Carriage, foliage, gun carriage, horseless carriage, marriage, verbiage

IAGE
see
AGE*

Jeremiah, Messiah, Mount Moriah, pariah, Zedekiah

IAH
see
AH

Actuarial, alluvial, ambrosial, antimonial, antisocial, Belial, bestial, biennial, burial, celestial, centennial, ceremonial, circumferential, circumstantial, colonial, coloquial, commercial, congenial, connubial, consequential, convivial, cordial, courtmartial, credential, crucial, decennial, deferential, denial, dial, differential, diluvial, entente cordial, equatorial, equinoctial, Escurial, essential, evidential, facial, filial, financial, finial, fluvial, glacial, impartial, imperial, inconsequential, industrial, inessential, inferential, influential, initial, jovial, labial, manorial, martial, matrimonial, memorial, menial, mercurial, non-essential, nuptial, official, palatial, parochial, partial, patrimonial, penitential, perennial, pestilential, phial, pluvial, post-pran-

IAL
see
AL
ERIAL
ICIAL
ORIAL

dial, potential, Prairial, prandial, pre-
glacial, presidential, primordial, pro-
verbial, providential, provincial, pru-
dential, racial, radial, residential, re-
trial, reverential, secretarial, self-
denial, social, spatial, special, substan-
tial, sundial, terrestrial, testimonial,
torrential, trial, triennial, trivial, uncial, uncongenial, unsocial, venial, vial

IAL

In memoriam, Miriam, Priam, Siam,
sweet-William

IAM
see
AM
EM

Amphibian, Andalusian, antedilu-
vian, antinomian, Arcadian, artesian,
Assyrian, Bacchanalian, bathycolpian,
beautician, Bodleian, Bohemian, Brob-
dingnagian, Carthusian, Castilian,
Christian, Cimmerian, Circassian, Cis-
tercian, Confucian, Corinthian, custo-
dian, Cyprian, Dickensian, diluvian,
Draconian, durian, Eleusinian, Ely-
sian, Ephesian, equestrian, Essenian,
Ethiopian, fringed-gentian, fustian,
guardian, Hanoverian, Hertzian, Hi-
bernian, Indian, Ionian, isthmian,
Itrurian, Justinian, Lilliputian, Luca-
dian, Lydian, Machiavellian, magian,
Manchurian, Merovingian, metaphysi-
cian, Midian, Midlothian, Norwegian,
Nubian, Olympian, Ossian, Parisian,
Parthian, pedestrian, Peloponnesian,
Persian, Perugian, Peruvian, Pierian,
plebian, Pomeranian, Pythian, Ra-
belaisian, reptilian, riparian, ruffian,

IAN
see
AN*
ARIAN
EDIAN
ICAN
ICIAN
IDIAN
ORIAN

salarian, Saturnalian, saurian, Shake-   **IAN**
sperian, Siberian, simian, Spenserian,
St. Sebastian, Stygian, Sumerian, Swa-
bian, Tasmanian, tertian, theologian,
Thespian, Titian, tragedian, Umbrian,
Uranian, Utopian, valerian, Venetian,
Wagnerian, Zoroastrian

Affiance, allegiance, alliance, appli-   **IANCE**
ance, brilliance, compliance, dalliance,   *see*
defiance, insouciance, invariance, lux-   ANCE
uriance, radiance, reliance, variance

Chateaubriand, viand   **IAND**
    see
    AND*

Brilliant, compliant, defiant, giant,   **IANT**
luxuriant, mediant, pliant, principiant,   *see*
radiant, reliant, suppliant, valiant,   ANT*
variant

Briar, familiar, friar, liar, peculiar,   **IAR**
sweetbriar, unfamiliar, Whitefriar   *see*
    AR*
    ER
    IRE

Tiara   **IARA**
    see
    A**

Billiard, galliard, poniard, Spaniard   **IARD**
    see
    ARD

Apiary, auxiliary, aviary, benefi-
ciary, breviary, diary, incendiary, in-
termediary, judiciary, pecuniary, peni-
tentiary, plenipotentiary, subsidiary,
tertiary

IARY
see
AIRY
E**
IE*
UARY

Alias, Ananias, bias, Deo gratias,
Elias, paterfamilias, Phidias, Tiresias,
Zacharias

IAS
see
AS*

Commissariat, fiat, lariat, proletar-
iat

IAT
see
AT*

Abbreviate, affiliate, alleviate, ap-
preciate, appropriate, associate, colle-
giate, conciliate, denunciate, depreci-
ate, deviate, dissociate, excruciate, ex-
patiate, expatriate, expediate, expiate,
expropriate, filiate, foliate, humiliate,
immediate, inappropriate, infuriate,
ingratiate, insatiate, intercollegiate,
intermediate, luxuriate, mediate, mis-
appropriate, negotiate, noviciate, ob-
viate, officiate, opiate, palliate, prin-
cipiate, propitiate, radiate, repatriate,
repudiate, retaliate, satiate, striate,
substantiate, transubstantiate, trifoli-
ate, vitiate

IATE
see
ATE
ITATE

Abbreviation, appreciation, aviation,
denunciation, expatriation, initiation,
negotiation, principiation, pronuncia-
tion, renunciation

IATION
see
ATION
ION

Ad lib., bib, Carib, corn-crib, crib, dib, drib, fib, glib, jib, nib, Ninib, rib, sahib, Sennacherib, sparerib, turbid, umbrella-rib

IB
see
UIB

Cannibal, Hannibal, intertribal, tribal

IBAL
see
AL

Dribble, fribble, nibble, quibble, scribble

IBBLE
see
EL
LE

Ascribe, bribe, circumscribe, describe, imbibe, inscribe, jibe, oversubscribe, prescribe, proscribe, scribe, subscribe, transcribe, tribe

IBE
see

Exhibit, inhibit, prohibit

IBIT
see
IT

Accessible, audible, Bible, collapsible, combustible, comprehensible, compressible, contemptible, convertible, corrigible, corruptible, credible, crucible, dirigible, discernible, divisible, edible, eligible, exhaustible, fallible, feasible, flexible, forcible, frangible, fusible, gullible, horrible, illegible, impassible, imperceptible, impossible, inaccessible, inaudible, incombustible, incompatible, incomprehensible, incontrovertible, inconvertible, incorrigible, incorruptible, incredible, indefensible, indestructible, inedible,

IBLE
see
EL
LE

inexhaustible, infallible, inflexible, insensible, intangible, intelligible, invincible, invisible, irascible, irresistible, irresponsible, legible, mandible, negligible, ostensible, partible, passible, perceptible, permissible, plausible, possible, reducible, refrangible, repressible, resistible, responsible, reversible, risible, sensible, susceptible, tangible, terrible, thurible, vendible, visible

IBLE

Audibly, forcibly, glibly, indelibly, invisibly, possibly, terribly, visibly

IBLY
see
E**

Calibre, fibre

IBRE
see
ER

Attribute, contribute, distribute, tribute

IBUTE
see
UTE

Accoustic, acrostic, agnostic, agrestic, akashic, alembic, allopathic, anelectric, anopisthographic, angelic, Antarctic, anthropographic, antiseptic, anti-toxic, Arabic, Arctic, asbestic, aspic, attic, authentic, azoic, baldric, barbaric, basic, benefic, bishopric, black magic, cambric, cataclysmic, cathartic, caustic, Celtic, cherubic, chic, chivalric, civic, classic, concentric, Coptic, cosmic, cryptic, cubic, cynic, decasyllabic, Delphic, diagnostic, diametric, domestic, eccentric, eclectic, ecliptic, egocentric, elliptic, empiric, endemic, eolithic, epic, epidemic,

IC
see
ACTIC
AIC
AMIC
ANIC
ANTIC
ASTIC
ATIC
ENIC
ERIC
ETIC
ICK
IFIC
INIC

ethic, eupeptic, eurythemic, evangelic, fabric, forensic, formic, frozen music, Gaelic, Gallic, garlic, geocentric, geodesic, geometric, gnostic, Gothic, graphic, gum arabic, hectic, heliocentric, hermeneutic, heroic, hieroglyphic, hierographic, homopathic, hydraulic, hydroelectric, iambic, Icelandic, idyllic, intrinsic, Ionic, Islamic, italic, karmic, lethargic, lyric, magic, majestic, malic, metallic, metamorphic, metric, mimic, monolithic, monosyllabic, mystic, mythic, natureopathic, neolithic, Nordic, obstetric, Olympic, optic, Orphic, orthopedic, orthorhombic, oxalic, palæstric, paleolithic, panegyric, patronymic, phallic, physic, picnic, picric, Pindaric, polytechnic, polytheistic, pragmatic, prognostic, prussic, psychiatric, psychic, psychoanalytic, public, Punic, pyrotechnic, relic, republic, rhombic, rubric, runic, rustic, salic, salicylic, sapphic, satiric, seismic, seraphic, Slavic, sic, skeptic, spic, stenographic, stoic, strategic, sulphuric, styptic, syllabic, symmetric, syndic, technic, telepathic, telestic, thalassic, therapeutic, thermometric, theurgic, tombic, toreutic, toxic, traffic, tunic, tyrannic, unauthentic, Vedic

IC

ISTIC
ITIC
ODIC
OGIC
OLIC
OMIC
ONIC
OPIC
ORIC
OTIC
ed-ICT
s-IX

Africa, America, angelica, arnica, Attica, basilica, Britannica, Corsica, harmonica, hepatica, Jamaica, japonica, majolica, materia medica, mica, nux vomica, pica, replica, sciatica, silica, veronica

ICA

see
A**

Delicacy, efficacy, indelicacy, in-   **ICACY**
tricacy   *see*
                                         ACY
                                         E**

Aeronautical, allegorical, anthropo-   **ICAL**
logical, artistical, biblical, biograph- *see*
ical, biological, canonical, chemical,   AL
chronological, clerical, comical, con-
ical, cosmical, cosmogonical, critical,
cylindrical, cynical, diabolical, ecclesi-
astical, emblematical, empirical, en-
cyclical, ethnological, etiological, ety-
mological, evangelical, farcial, finical,
genetical, geographical, grammatical,
heretical, hermeneutical, hierarchical,
historical, horological, hypercritical,
hypocritical, hypothetical, hysterical,
identical, illogical, inimical, ironical,
lackadaisical, logical, lyrical, magical,
majestical, medical, meteorological,
methodical, metrical, mimical, mor-
phological, musical, mystical, myth-
ological, nautical, nonsensical, numer-
ical, ontological, optical, paradoxical,
pathological, periodical, philosophical,
physical, piratical, poetical, pontifical,
practical, pragmatical, psychical, quiz-
zical, radical, rhetorical, sabbatical,
satirical, semi-tropical, skeptical, so-
phistical, spherical, stoical, surgical,
symbolical, symmetrical, technical,
technological, theatrical, theoretical,
tragical, tropical, typical, tyrannical,
unsophistical, vertical, vortical, whim-
sical

African, American, angelican, Mexican, pan-american, pelican, publican, republican, Vatican

ICAN
see
IAN

Applicant, communicant, insignificant, lubricant, mendicant, significant, supplicant

ICANT
see
ANT*

Abdicate, certificate, communicate, complicate, dedicate, delicate, domesticate, duplicate, eradicate, excommunicate, extricate, fabricate, fornicate, imbricate, implicate, indelicate, indicate, intoxicate, intricate, lubricate, masticate, pontificate, predicate, prevaricate, prognosticate, reduplicate, rusticate, sophisticate, supplicate, syndicate, vindicate

ICATE
see
ATE

Advice, allspice, beggar-lice, bice, device, dice, entice, field-mice, high-price, ice, interslice, low-price, mice, nice, not-nice, price, rice, sacrifice, slice, spice, splice, suffice, thrice, trice, twice, vice

ICE*
see
ISE**

Accomplice, apprentice, armistice, artifice, auspice, avarice, Beatrice, benefice, box-office, cantatrice, caprice, chalice, cicatrice, cornice, cowardice, crevice, dentifrice, hospice, injustice, justice, lattice, licorice, malice, malpractice, mounted-police, notice, novice, office, police, poultice, practice, precipice, prejudice, pumice, summer solstice, service, surplice, winter solstice

ICE**
see
IFICE
IS*
ISE****
ISS
ed-IST
s-IES**

Magnificent, munificent, reticent	**ICENT** _see_ ENT
Enrich, Greenwich, Ipswich, ostrich, rich, sandwich, which	**ICH** _see_ ICHE ITCH
Niche	**ICHE** _see_ ICH
Artificial, beneficial, judicial, official, prejudicial, sacrificial, superficial, unofficial	**ICIAL** _see_ IAL
Geometrician, magician, musician, optician, patrician, Phœnician, physician, politician, statistician, technician	**ICIAN** _see_ IAN
Fratricide, germicide, infanticide, matricide, parricide, regicide, suicide, vermicide	**ICIDE** _see_ IDE
Agnosticism, Catholicism, criticism, didacticism, empiricism, eroticism, fanaticism, gnosticism, mysticism, romanticism, witticism	**ICISM** _see_ ISM
Deficit, explicit, illicit, implicit, licit, solicit	**ICIT** _see_ IT
Authenticity, causticity, domesticity, duplicity, eccentricity, electricity, ellipticity, felicity, lubricity, periodicity, publicity, rusticity, sphericity, simplicity	**ICITY** _see_ E** ITY

Bailiwick, beggar-tick, Benedick, **ICK**
brick, broomstick, candlestick, chick, *see*
chopstick, click, cowlick, crick, derrick, IK
dirty trick, double-quick, drop-kick, *ed*-ICT
drumstick, fiddle-stick, flick, glass- *ly*-E**
brick, goldbrick, hayrick, Herrick, *s*-IX
homesick, joss-stick, kick, lick, limer-
ick, lipstick, maulstick, maverick,
Moby Dick, niblick, nick, pick, Pick-
wick, pinprick, polostick, prick, quick,
rick, rollick, seasick, sick, slapstick,
slick, St. Patrick, swizzle-stick, thick,
tick, toothpick, trick, walkingstick,
wick, yardstick, Yorick

Bicker, dicker, flicker, pricker, rag- **ICKER**
picker, slicker, snicker, sticker, thicker, *see*
wicker ER

Cricket, picket, thicket, ticket, **ICKET**
wicket *see*
ET

Fickle, mickle, pickle, prickle, sickle, **ICKLE**
tickle, trickle *see*
EL
LE

Finicky, panicky **ICKY**
see
E**

Auricle, canticle, chicle, chronicle, **ICLE**
conventicle, cubicle, cuticle, icicle, *see*
particle, pendicle, radicle, vehicle, EL
ventricle, versicle LE
YCLE

Calico, medico, Mexico, Pimlico, portico, Porto Rico, pro bono publico   **ICO**
see
O*

Harmonicon, Helicon, icon, irenicon, lexicon, Rubicon, silicon   **ICON**
see
ON

Academics, analytics, classics, dogmatics, dynamics, eclectics, empirics, ethics, genetics, kinetics, mathematics, metaphysics, metrics, physics, politics, psychics, statistics, tactics, thermodynamics, topics   **ICS**
see
IC-*s*

Addict, afflict, benedict, conflict, constrict, contradict, convict, depict, derelict, district, edit, evict, inflict, interdict, predict, relict, restrict, strict, verdict   **ICT**
see
IC-*ed*
ICK-*ed*
ed-ED

Benediction, diction, fiction, friction, interdiction, jurisdiction, malediction, prediction   **ICTION**
see
ION

Epicure, manicure, pedicure   **ICURE**
see
URE

Icy, impolicy, policy, spicy   **ICY**
see
E**

Acid, acrid, amid, Andromedid, aphid, avid, bi-cuspid, bid, candid, Cid, coverlid, David, did, Euclid, fervid, fetid, flaccid, florid, forbid, frigid, gelid, gravid, Haroun al-Rashid, hid,   **ID**
see
ALID
ED
EID

horrid, hybrid, ibid, id, insipid, in-
trepid, invalid, katydid, kid, Leonid,
lid, limpid, livid, lucid, lurid, Madrid,
masjid, mid, morbid, non-skid, orchid,
outbid, outdid, Ovid, pallid, pellucid,
placid, prussic acid, putrid, pyramid,
rabid, rancid, rapid, rid, rigid, sayid,
skid, slid, solid, sordid, splendid, stolid,
taurid, timid, torpid, torrid, turbid,
turgid, underbid, undid, valid, Valla-
dolid, vapid, viscid, vivid

ID
IED**
UID
UMID
UPID
YD

Bridal, cotidal, tidal, suicidal

IDAL
see
AL

Candidate, delapidate, elucidate, in-
timidate, invalidate, lapidate, liquid-
ate, validate

IDATE
see
ATE

Diddle, fiddle, griddle, middle, rid-
dle, twiddle, unriddle

IDDLE
see
EL

Abide, alongside, aside, astride,
autumn-tide, backslide, bedside, be-
side, betide, bona fide, bride, broad-
side, bromide, carbide, chide, coincide,
collide, confide, countryside, cyanide,
decide, deride, dioxide, divide, ebb-
tide, eventide, fireside, floodtide, gar-
den-side, glide, hayride, hide, hillside,
homicide, imbibe, ingleside, inside,
landslide, lopside, neap tide, noontide,
ocean-tide, outride, outside, over-ride,
oxhide, oxide, peroxide, preside, pride,
provide, rawhide, reside, ride, ringside,

IDE
see
EYE-*d*
ICIDE
IED*
UIDE
ed-ED
s-IDES**

roadside, seaside, set-aside, Shrovetide, side, slide, stand aside, stride, subside, sulphide, summertide, tide, wayside, Whitsuntide, wide, worldwide, yuletide
IDE

Accident, coincident, confident, incident, occident, over-confident, president, provident, resident, strident, trident
IDENT
see
ENT

Backslider, cider, circusrider, glider, outrider, outsider, provider, rider, roughrider, spider, wider
IDER
see
ER

Aristides, cantharides, caryatides, Eumenides, Eumolpides, Hebrides, Hesperides, Maimonides, Oceanides, Thucydides
IDES*
see
ES*

Besides, bestrides, coincides, Ides, Old Ironsides
IDES**
see
IDE-*S*

Abridge, auction bridge, bridge, cartridge, Coleridge, covered bridge, drawbridge, footbridge, low bridge, partridge, pepperidge, porridge, ridge, tollbridge
IDGE
see
AGE
EGE

Bridget, fidget, midget
IDGET
see
ET

Antemeridian, meridian, nullifidian, Numidian, ophidian, quotidian
IDIAN
see
IAN

Acidity, aridity, avidity, cupidity, fluidity, humidity, insipidity, intimity, intrepidity, lucidity, placidity, rapidity, sapidity, solidity, stupidity

IDITY
see
E**
ITY

Bridle, idle, sidle, unbridle

IDLE
see
EL
LE

Frigidly, idly, languidly, rigidly, timidly, vividly

IDLY
see
E**

Corridor, cuspidor, Fructidor, humidor, Messidor, Thermidor

IDOR
see
OR

Didst, midst

IDST
see

Width

IDTH
see

Bowie, brie, brownie, calorie, cap-à-pie, collie, coolie, coterie, dearie, Dixie, dominie, fantasie, gillie, girlie, kelpie, kiltie, lassie, lorrie, mashie, Mme. Curie, movie, nixie, organdie, parapluie, porgie, prairie, prima facie, rookie, sharpie, sortie, specie, talkie, Valkyrie

IE*
see
E**
ERIE
I**
S-EASE
E*-S
IES**

Belie, die, hie, huckleberry-pie, humble-pie, lie, magpie, mince-pie, necktie, pie, potpie, tie, untie, vie

IE**
see
EYE
I*

IE**
ed-IED*
s-ISE*

Altar-piece, fowling-piece, frontis-piece, itty-bitty piece, mantelpiece, masterpiece, mouthpiece, niece, piece, tailpiece

IECE
see
EASE**
ISE***

Allied, amplified, atrophied, certi-fied, citified, complied, countryfied, cried, crucified, defied, deified, denied, died, dried, espied, fortified, fried, glorified, gratified, hog-tied, implied, intensified, justified, lied, liquefied, magnified, mortified, multiplied, mum-mified, occupied, ossified, petrified, pied, pre-occupied, pried, purified, qualified, relied, replied, sanctified, satisfied, shied, spied, stupefied, sun-dried, supplied, tongue-tied, tried, un-occupied, unsatisfied, unversified, ver-sified

IED*
see
EYE-*d*
IDE
IE**-*d*

Ablebodied, astonied, buried, candid, dallied, ivied, levied, mutinied, pal-sied, parodied, serried, Siegfried, studied, taxied, travestied, varied, wearied

IED**
see
ED
ID

Bas-relief, belief, brief, chief, dis-belief, grief, handkerchief, kerchief, mischief, relief, thief, unbelief

IEF
see
EAF*
EEF
s-EAVE-*s*

Besiege, liege, siege

IEGE
see
IGE

Shriek

IEK
see
EAK*
EEK

Abdiel, Ariel, cocker-spaniel, Daniel, Gamaliel, oriel, spaniel, spiel, Uriel

IEL
see
EL

Afield, cornfield, field, infield, outfield, paddyfield, shield, stubblefield, wield, windshield, yield

IELD
see
ed-ED
EAL*-*ed*
EEL-*ed*

Carpe diem, per diem, requiem

IEM
see
EM

Alien, St. Julien, T'ien

IEN*
see
EAN**

Lien, mien

IEN**
see
EEN

Audience, clairaudience, conscience, convenience, experience, faience, inconvenience, inexperience, nescience, obedience, omniscience, patience, prescience, resilience, sapience, science, subservience

IENCE
see
ENCE

Ambient, ancient, client, convenient, deficient, desipient, ebullient, efficient, emollient, esurient, expedient, gradi-

IENT
see
ENT

ent, incipient, inconvenient, inexpedi- **IENT**
ent, ingredient, insufficient, lenient,
nescient, obedient, omniscient, Orient,
patient, percipient, proficient, pruri-
ent, recipient, reorient, resilient, sal-
ient, sapient, sentient, subservient,
sufficient

Angrier, atelier, barrier, bier, brazier, **IER***
brigadier, carrier, cashier, cavalier, *see*
chandelier, chiffonier, chillier, collier, ER
courier, courtier, croupier, crozier, EAR*
dossier, duskier, easier, fancier, farrier, ERE*
financier, fox terrier, frontier, glacier,
glazier, grenadier, heavier, hoosier,
lordlier, manlier, merrier, mightier,
Montpellier, moodier, osier, pannier,
pier, prettier, premier, rapier, ruddier,
soldier, sorrier, terrier, tier, toy soldier,
town crier, vizier, Whittier, Xavier

Amplifier, brier, flier, magnifier, **IER****
plier, purifier, sweet-brier *see*
IRE
S-IRES

Fierce, pierce, tierce **IERCE**
see

Arrière, boutonière, jardinière, por- **IERE**
tière *see*
ERE**

Apple pies, cries, dragon-flies, fire- **IES***
flies, flies, fortifies, lies, pies, plies, *see*
ratifies, skies, squash pies, supplies, IE**-s
tries, wailing-cries ISE*
Y-s

Absurdities, argosies, Aries, arteries, Caesar's Commentaries, cavities, centuries, charities, cities, comedies, congeries, courtesies, curiosities, darbies, dictionaries, doweries, duties, Early Nineties, East Indies, economies, eddies, effigies, Eleusinian Mysteries, exigencies, fairies, fallacies, fantasies, fillies, fisheries, flag-lilies, frailties, Furies, gullies, harpies, idolatries, miseries, monies, Notes and Queries, obsequies, oddities, orgies, pansies, peonies, pickaninnies, pigmies, pixies, ponies, quanderies, rareties, remedies, reveries, roaring forties, rubies, scurries, series, species, strawberries, superficies, superfluities, theories, trophies, Tuileries

IES**
see
E**-*s*
EEZE
EY**-*s*
ICE**-*s*
IE*-*s*
IS**

Airiest, driest, earliest, flabbiest, funniest, leakiest, lowliest, prettiest, ricketiest, rustiest, scantiest, sorriest, stateliest, swankiest, tidiest, trickiest, wittiest, worthiest

IEST*
see
EST
UEST

High-priest, priest

IEST**
see
EASE**-*d*
EAST*
ISTE

Diet, disquiet, quiet, Soviet

IET
see
ET

Anxiety, contrariety, gaiety, impiety, moiety, noteriety, piety, propriety, satiety, sobriety, society, variety

IETY
see
E**

Adieu, lieu, prie-dieu, purlieu, Richelieu	**IEU** *see* U
Achieve, believe, disbelieve, grieve, make-believe, relieve, reprieve, retrieve, St. Genevieve, thieve	**IEVE*** *see* EAVE EIVE S-IEVES
Sieve	**IEVE**** *see* IVE**
Forty Thieves, retrieves, thieves	**IEVES** *see* IEVE*-*s*
Interview, mountain-view, pre-view, purview, review, view	**IEW** *see* EW O**
Frieze	**IEZE** *see* EASE* EE-*s* ESE
Alif, aperitif, calif, Chateau d'If, if, khalif, motif	**IF** *see* IFE YPH
Alewife, bowie-knife, fife, housewife, inner-life, jack-knife, life, loosestrife, midwife, pocket-knife, rife, strife, wife, wild-life	**IFE** *see* S-IVE*-*s*

Fifer, lifer, Lucifer, thurifer

IFER
see
ER

Bailiff, biff, caitiff, Cardiff, cliff, hippogriff, jiff, mastiff, midriff, miff, Pecksniff, plaintiff, pontiff, sheriff, skiff, sniff, stiff, tariff, tiff, whiff

IFF
see
IF
IPH
YPH

Teneriffe

IFFE
see
IFF

Horrific, omnific, pacific, prolific, scientific, soporific, specific, sudorific, terrific, transpacific, unprolific

IFIC
see
IC

Edifice, orifice, sacrifice

IFICE
see
ICE**

Rifle, stifle, trifle

IFLE
see
EL
LE

Anguilliform, cruciform, cuneiform, oviform, triform, uniform, vermiform

IFORM
see
ORM

Adrift, chimney-swift, drift, gift, lift, makeshift, rift, shift, shoplift, sift, snowdrift, spendthrift, swift, thrift, uplift

IFT
see
ed-ED

Beautiful, bountiful, dutiful, fanciful, merciful, pitiful, plentiful, over-dutiful

IFUL
see
UL

Aerify, amplify, beautify, calcify, certify, clarify, classify, codify, crucify, deify, disqualify, diversify, dulcify, edify, electrify, falsify, fortify, fructify, gratify, horrify, identify, ignify, indemnify, intensify, justify, lapidify, lignify, liquify, magnify, modify, mollify, mortify, mummify, mystify, notify, nullify, ossify, pacify, personify, petrify, purify, qualify, ramify, ratify, rectify, requalify, revivify, salsify, sanctify, solidify, specify, speechify, stultify, terrify, testify, transmogrify, unify, verify, versify, vilify, vivify

IFY
see
I*
EFY
IGH
Y

Big, bigwig, brig, cat-rig, cig, dig, earwig, fig, gig, guinea-pig, jig, ladypig, nig, periwig, phennig, pig, prig, rig, scratch-wig, swig, thimblerig, thingumajig, trig, twig, whig, whirligig, wig

IG
see

Cardigan, hooligan, ptarmigan

IGAN
see
AN*

Frigate, fumigate, fustigate, instigate, investigate, irrigate, litigate, mitigate, navigate, obligate, profligate

IGATE
see
ATE

Prestige, vestige

IGE*
see
IEGE

Oblige

IGE**
see

Bigger, digger, gold-digger, jigger, nigger, outrigger, rigger, square-rigger, trigger

IGGER
see
ER

Higgle, jiggle, niggle, wiggle, wriggle

IGGLE
see
EL
LE

Anigh, high, knee-high, nigh, sigh, thigh, wellnigh

IGH
see
I*

Affright, after-sight, airtight, alight, all-right, arc-light, aright, beacon-light, bedight, benight, bight, birth-right, blight, bright, bull-fight, candle-light, copyright, daylight, delight, dimlight, downright, drop-light, eye-bright, eyesight, fight, flashlight, flight, floodlight, fly-by-night, footlight, fore-sight, fortnight, fright, frosty-night, gaslight, goodnight, headlight, hind-sight, honor-bright, insight, Isle of Wight, knight, light, limelight, lusty-knight, midnight, might, moonlight, night, outright, overnight, oversight, pilot-light, playwright, plight, prize-fight, purple-night, rapid-flight, red-light, right, rush-light, sea-fight, searchlight, second-sight, shining light, sidelight, sight, sit-tight, skylight, slight, spotlight, stagefright, starlight, sticktight, summer's night, sunlight,

IGHT
see
EIGHT**
ITE*
YTE
ed-ED

tail-light, taper-light, tight, tonight, **IGHT**
traffic-light, Twelfth-night, twilight,
upright, watertight, wheelwright,
wight, wright, yesternight

Almighty, blighty, flighty, high and **IGHTY**
mighty, highty-tighty, mighty, nighty *see*
E**

Enigma, sigma, stigma **IGMA**
see
A**

Align, assign, benign, condign, con- **IGN**
sign, design, ensign, malign, resign, *see*
sign, traffic-sign INE*
ed-IND*

Amigo, indigo, vertigo **IGO**
see
O*

Bigot, spigot **IGOT**
see
OT

Filigree, pedigree, perigee **IGREE**
see
EE

Effigy, prodigy **IGY**
see
E**

Batik, Bolshevik, mujik, sheik **IK**
see
EAK
IK

Paprika, swastika   **IKA**
                                                      see
                                                      A**

Alike, aspen-like, belike, bike, child-   **IKE**
like, dike, dislike, fanlike, ghostlike,   *see*
gnomelike, gooselike, hitch-hike,   AIK
homelike, hunger-strike, ladylike,
marline-spike, mike, pike, proboscis-
like, saintlike, sphinxlike, spike, sports-
manlike, statue-like, strike, suchlike,
swanlike, tike, trance-like, turnpike,
unlike, viselike, wandlike, war-like

Anvil, April, argil, Azrafil, basil,   **IL**
Boabdil, boll weevil, Brazil, cavil,   *see*
cheveril, civil, codicil, council, coutil,   ERIL
daffodil, distil, fibril, fossil, fulfil, fusil,   ERYL
instil, lentil, nil, nostril, pencil, Salsa-   EVIL
bil, slatepencil, stencil, sweetbasil, ten-   ILE**
dril, tonsil, tumbril, uncivil, until,   ILL
utensil, vigil, Virgil, Vril, weevil   ILLE
                                                      UIL
                                                      ed-ILD*

Jubilant, sibilant, vigilant   **ILANT**
                                                      see
                                                      ANT*

Dissimilar, similar   **ILAR**
                                                      see
                                                      AR*

Annihilate, dilate, jubilate, mutilate,   **ILATE**
ventilate   *see*
                                                      ATE

Filch, milch

ILCH
see

Brunhild, gild, regild

ILD*
see
IL-*ed*
UILD

Child, godchild, grandchild, mild, wild

ILD**
see
ILE*-*d*

Bewilder, builder, guilder

ILDER
see
ER

Anile, awhile, camomile, compile, crocodile, defile, erstwhile, exile, file, Gentile, juvenile, meanwhile, mile, Nile, pile, profile, reconcile, red-tile, reptile, revile, scissile, seldomwhile, senile, single-file, smile, statute mile, stile, tile, turnstile, vile, while, wile, woodpile

ILE*
see
ISLE
UILE
YLE
ed-ILD**

Anglophile, automobile, bastile, bibliophile, bissextile, Castile, cortile, docile, domicile, ductile, facile, febrile, fertile, flexile, fluviatile, fragile, futile, hostile, imbecile, immobile, mercantile, missile, mobile, pensile, prehensile, projectile, puerile, servile, sextile, sterile, subtile, tactile, tensile, textile, virile, versatile, volatile

ILE**
see
EAL*
EEL
IL

Campanile, facsimile, primummobile, simile

ILE***
see
E*

Compiler, tiler   **ILER**
see
ER

Merciless, penniless, pitiless   **ILESS**
see
ESS

Availeth, bewaileth, broileth, faileth,   **ILETH**
soileth   *see*
ETH

Bilge   **ILGE**
see

Pavilion, postilion, vermilion   **ILION**
see
ION

Ability, anility, applicability, com-   **ILITY**
patability, capability, civility, culpa-   *see*
bility, debility, dependability, disabil-   E**
ity, dividibility, durability, eligibility,
facility, fallibility, fertility, flexibility,
fraility, gentility, gullibility, immuta-
bility, impenetrability, inability, in-
civility, incompatibility, indefatigabil-
ity, indefectibility, indelibility, inev-
itability, infallibility, instability, in-
visibility, liability, mutability, negli-
gibility, nobility, notability, plausibil-
ity, possibility, probability, responsi-
bility, senility, servility, stability,
susceptibility, tangibility, tensibility,
utility, virility, visibility, volubility,
vulnerability

Asses' milk, bilk, buttermilk, ilk, milk, rawsilk, silk, skim milk

ILK
see

Ant-hill, bill, Bunker Hill, cambric-frill, chill, cranes-bill, dill, distill, door-sill, drill, duckbill, dunghill, fill, fire-drill, foothill, frill, fulfill, gill, goodwill, frill, gristmill, handbill, hill, hornbill, ill, ill-will, kill, mandrill, mill, mole-hill, pill, playbill, powder-mill, refill, rill, sandhill, sawmill, shrill, sill, skill, spill, spoonbill, standstill, still, stock-still, swill, thill, thrill, till, treadmill, trill, twill, uphill, whippoorwill, will, windmill, window-sill, Yggdrasill

ILL
see
IL
UILL
ed-ILD*
y-ILLY

Camilla, cedilla, chinchilla, Cinder-illa, flotilla, gorilla, guerilla, mantilla, Myrtilla, Priscilla, pulsatilla, sapodilla, sarsaparilla, scintilla, vanilla, villa

ILLA
see
A**

Bastille, chenille, dishabille, esca-drille, grille, Hotel de Ville, quadrille, Seville, soyez tranquille, vaudeville

ILLE
see
ILE**

Filler, miller, shriller, stiller, tiller, thriller

ILLER
see
ER

Billion, cotillion, million, pillion, trillion, vermillion

ILLION
see
ION

Armadillo, Murillo, negrillo, pecca-dillo

ILLO
see
O*

Billy, chilly, evilly, filly, hillbilly, hilly, Piccadilly, silly, stilly, willy nilly

ILLY
see
E**
ILL-*y*

Film, sound-film

ILM
see

Brickkiln, kiln, limekiln

ILN
see

Full-tilt, gilt, hilt, jilt, kilt, lilt, silt, spilt, stilt, tilt, wilt

ILT
see
UILT

Filth, spilth, tilth

ILTH
see

German silver, quicksilver, silver, solid silver

ILVER
see
ER

Bodily, busily, cannily, clammily, clumsily, craftily, daily, daintily, doily, dreamily, drearily, drowsily, easily, eerily, family, faultily, gaudily, gloomily, greedily, guiltily, homily, lazily, lily, luckily, lustily, merrily, mightily, moodily, pluckily, pondlily, primarily, scantily, shabbily, Sicily, speedily, spunkily, stealthily, temporarily, uncannily, unluckily, verily, voluntarily, waterlily, wily, wittily

ILY
see
E**
EE

Bedim, brim, broadbrim, cherubim, dim, Elohim, grim, him, interim, maxim, megrim, Mount Gerizim, passim, pilgrim, prim, Purim, rim,

IM
see
ATIM
ITHM

seraphim, skim, slim, swim, teraphim, **IM**
Thummim, trim, Urim, victim, whim   ONYM
 YMN
 YTHM

Bellissima, Cloaca Maxima, Fatima, **IMA**
lacrima, Lima, quadragesima, septua- *see*
gesima, sexagesima, Yima A**

Animal, decimal, infinitesimal, max- **IMAL**
imal, millesimal, primal *see*
 AL

Animate, antipenultimate, approxi- **IMATE**
mate, climate, decimate, estimate, in- *see*
animate, intimate, legitimate, over- ATE
estimate, penultimate, primate, proxi-
mate, reanimate, sublimate, ultimate

Limb **IMB***
 see

Climb **IMB****
 see

Limber, tall-timber, timber **IMBER**
 see
 ER

Nimble, thimble, wimble **IMBLE**
 see
 EL
 LE

Aforetime, bedtime, begrime, be- **IME***
time, cherry-time, chime, classtime, *see*
clime, crime, dime, grime, lifetime, YME

lilac-time, lime, mealtime, meantime, **IME***
ofttime, overtime, pantomime, pas-
time, prime, quicklime, ragtime, rime,
seedtime, slime, sometime, sparetime,
springtime, sublime, summer-time,
swingtime, time, wartime

Intime, maritime, mime, régime **IME****
see
EAM

Regimen, specimen **IMEN**
see
EN

Accompaniment, aliment, compli- **IMENT**
ment, condiment, crack regiment, *see*
detriment, embodiment, experiment, ENT
habiliment, impediment, liniment,
merriment, nutriment, orpiment, pre-
sentiment, raiment, regiment, re-em-
bodiment, rudiment, sediment, sentiment

Dimity, equanimity, magnanimity, **IMITY**
proximity, sublimity, unanimity *see*
E****
ITY

Dimmer, glimmer, shimmer, simmer, **IMMER**
slimmer *see*
ER

Centimo, duodecimo, Eskimo, for- **IMO**
tissimo, generalissimo, Geronimo, pia- *see*
nissimo, prestissimo, primo, proximo, O*
ultimo

Blimp, crimp, imp, limp, pimp, primp, scrimp, shrimp, simp, skimp

IMP
see
UIMP

Dimple, pimple, simple, wimple

IMPLE
see
EL
LE

Glimpse

IMPSE
see

A-cluckin' adrenalin, a-grin, akin, Aladdin, all in, antitoxin, assassin, a-throbbin', bareskin, basin, bearskin, begin, belaying pin, bewitchin', bin, bodkin, bowfin, Brahmin, break-in, buckskin, built-in, bulletin, bumpkin, buskin, cabin, calfskin, Capuchin, catkin, chagrin, chin, chinquapin, Chopin, clavecin, clothespin, cockrobin, coffin, cousin, creeping-in, cretin, cruisin', cryin', cumin, Darwin, dauphin, deerskin, din, doeskin, dolphin, Dublin, duckpin, dunlin, exceedin', Fagin, feelin', fetchin', fin, firkin, fit-in, florin, gelatin, gherkin, gin, goblin, griffin, grimalkin, grin, herein, highfalutin, hin, hobgoblin, in, insulin, interruptin', Jacobin, jasmin, jerkin, kaolin, khamsin, kin, king-pin, Kremlin, lambskin, linchpin, listen-in, logcabin, Lohengrin, lupin, mandarin, mannikin, margin, martin, matin, maudlin, Mazarin, mechlin, Merlin, metheglin, moccasin, moleskin, muezzin, muffin, muslin, napkin, nine-pin, nothin', nubbin, Odin, oilskin, origin,

IN
see
AMIN
ATIN
ELIN
ERIN
INN
OLIN
UIN
al-AL
ed-IND**
s-INS

paladin, paraffin, Pekin, Pepin, pepsin, **IN**
pidgin, pigskin, pin, pippin, poplin,
prevailin', protein, puffin, pumpkin,
push-in, rabbin, ragamuffin, raisin,
ramekin, Redskin, replevin, resin,
rolling-pin, round robin, running-in,
Ruskin, saccharin, safety-pin, Saladin,
Sanhedrin, scarf-pin, sculpin, sealskin,
sea-urchin, sheepskin, shin, sin, skin,
sloe gin, spadassin, spavin, spillikin,
spin, St. Swithin, tailspin, tannin, tar-
paulin, tellin', terrapin, therein, There-
min, thin, thole-pin, Tientsin, tiffin,
tocsin, toxin, tune-in, twin, underpin,
urchin, vermin, virgin, wanderin',
washbasin, welkin, wherein, win, with-
in, Yin

Ægina, Agrippina, ballerina, Caro- **INA**
lina, Catalina, cavatina, China, Cochin   *see*
China, concertina, czarina, lamina,   A**
Maria Farina, Medina, Messalina,
ocarina, Proserpina, regina, retina,
saltina, Salva Regina, stamina, vina

Aboriginal, cardinal, criminal, final, **INAL**
germinal, latitudinal, libidinal, longi-   *see*
tudinal, marginal, matutinal, nominal,   AL
original, paginal, Quirinal, subliminal,   IN-*al*
terminal, virginal

Culinary, extraordinary, imaginary, **INARY**
luminary, ordinary, preliminary, san-   *see*
guinary, seminary, veterinary   ARY

Assassinate, culminate, determinate, **INATE**
disseminate, dominate, eliminate, ex-   *see*
terminate, fascinate, fulminate, germi-   ATE

nate, hallucinate, illuminate, incrimi-
nate, indeterminate, insubordinate,
nominate, obstinate, originate, pere-
grinate, predominate, procrastinate,
recriminate, ruminate, subordinate,
terminate, vaccinate

INATE

Zinc

INC
see
INK

Black Prince, convince, evince,
mince, prince, province, quince, since,
wince

INCE
see
INT-*s*

Bullfinch, chaffinch, cinch, clinch,
finch, flinch, goldfinch, inch, pinch,
winch

INCH
see
YNCH

Distinct, extinct, indistinct, pre-
cinct, succinct

INCT
see
INK-*ed*

Behind, bind, blind, colorblind,
grind, humankind, kind, mankind,
master mind, mind, never-mind, pur-
blind, remind, rind, unkind, unwind,
wind, window-blind

IND*
see
IGN-*ed*
INE*-*d*

Etesian wind, night-wind, rescind,
second wind, tamarind, trade-wind,
west-wind, whirlwind, wind

IND**
see
IN-*ed*

Binder, blinder, cinder, cylinder,
grinder, hinder, path-finder, reminder,
stem-winder

INDER
see
ER

Brindle, dwindle, kindle, rekindle, spindle, swindle

INDLE
see
EL
LE

Airline, alkaline, Alpine, aniline, Apennine, aquiline, asinine, balloon vine, bovine, Brandywine, bread line, brine, canine, chalk-line, clothesline, coalmine, columbine, combine, concubine, confine, crystalline, decline, define, dine, disincline, divine, eglantine, enshrine, entwine, feline, fine, fishline, gadding vine, goldmine, grapevine, greedy-swine, headline, incline, intertwine, iodine, kine, leonine, line, lordly pine, lupine, mine, monkeyshine, moonshine, nine, opine, outline, Palatine, Palestine, pine, pitch-pine, plumbline, porcupine, port wine, quinine, ratline, recline, redwine, refine, repine, Rhine, rush line, saltmine, seabrine, sea-line, serpentine, shine, shoreline, shrine, side-line, sine, skyline, spine, streamline, strychnine, superfine, supine, swine, tapeline, thine, tine, trellised-vine, turbine, twine, undermine, valentine, vine, vulpine, water-line, whine, white wine, wine, woodbine

INE*
see
IGN
YNE
ed-IND*
s-INES

Adamantine, adrenaline, alexandrine, amaranthine, aquamarine, Argentine, atropine, Aventine, bandoline, Benedictine, benzine, brigantine, caprine, carmine, chlorine, clandestine, Constantine, crinoline, cuisine, destine,

INE**
see
AZINE
EAN
EEN
ENE

determine, discipline, doctrine, elephantine, engine, ermine, Euxine, Evangeline, famine, feminine, figurine, fluorine, gaberdine, gamine, gasoline, Ghibelline, grenadine, guillotine, heroine, horse marine, hyaline, illumine, imagine, incarnadine, intestine, jessamine, latrine, leporine, levantine, libertine, limousine, machine, margarine, marine, masculine, mazarine, medicine, mezzanine, muscadine, nectarine, opaline, ovine, palatine, paraffine, pelerine, peregrine, Philippine, Philistine, phocine, pilot-machine, porcine, praline, predestine, pristine, quarantine, rapine, ravine, routine, Sabine, saccharine, saline, Sibylline, Sistine, slot-machine, submarine, tambourine, tangerine, tourmaline, transpontine, ultramarine, undine, ursine, vaccine, vaseline, vitamine

INE**
ERINE
IENE
UIN
UINE

Continent, eminent, imminent, impertinent, incontinent, pertinent, preeminent, prominent

INENT
see
ENT

Ancient Mariner, diner, finer, fortyniner, liner, mariner, milliner, miner, moonshiner, ocean-liner, refiner, shiner, shriner

INER
see
ER

Bulkiness, business, cloudiness, coziness, dinginess, dowdiness, emptiness, fussiness, fustiness, ghastliness, giddiness, guiltiness, happiness, haughtiness, headiness, holiness, loneliness, loveliness, mightiness, mistiness, petti-

INESS
see
ES**
ESS

ness, readiness, silliness, steadiness, sultriness, surliness, tidiness, uneasiness, weariness, wordiness, worthiness

INESS

Bassinet, bobbinet, cabinet, clarinet, martinet, spinet

INET
see
ET

Absorbing, according, a-Maying, amazing, ambling, amusing, angling, anything, apronstring, a-wing, awning, baffling, bee-keeping, beetling, befitting, begrudging, belting, bing, blessing, bloodcurdling, blueing, bombing, boring, bowling, bowstring, boxing, bring, Browning, building, bungling, bunting, bustling, carding, carting, casing, ceiling, central-heating, chafing, charming, chattering, cling, clinging, closing, cod-fishing, coming, cotton-batting, crystal-gazing, cruising, cunning, curdling, damning, dancing, darling, dazzling, directing, dismantling, diverting, do-nothing, drawing, dressing, drifting, duckling, dumpling, during, dwelling, dying, easy-going, encircling, ending, Erl-king, etching, everlasting, face-lifting, far-reaching, far-seeing, farthing, fawning, feeling, flapping, fledgling, fleeting, flinching, fling, flouting, flowing, foregoing, foundling, fringing, frisking, gangling, glistening, glowing, going, goodbreeding, gosling, grilling, gurgling, gushing, hamstring, harrowing, hasty pudding, hazel-sapling, heat-lightning, heckling, hedging, herring, Highland fling, hik-

ING
see
ARING
ATING
EING
OMING
ER-*ing*
ly-E**
s-INGS

ing, hireling, hobnobbing, hooting,
howling, huddling, hustling, hymning,
ill-feeling, imposing, incoming, in-
dwelling, ingrowing, inkling, jarring,
jolting, jostling, juggling, key-ring,
kidding, kindling, king, Kipling, kneel-
ing, knitting, landscaping, lapwing,
lashing, lasting, latchstring, law-abid-
ing, leave-taking, libelling, lightning,
liking, lining, lodging, log-rolling, long-
ing, long-standing, longsuffering, lung-
ing, luring, lurking, lutestring, lying,
mainspring, marshaling, mass meeting,
matting, maying, mellowing, merry-
making, mining, moiling, mooring,
morning, motoring, mumbling, Nan-
king, necking, nestling, never-ending,
nothing, notwithstanding, nursling,
obliging, offing, offspring, oncoming,
opening, out-building, outlying, out-
pouring, outstanding, overlooking,
padding, painstaking, painting, paling,
parting, Peiping, pervading, pettifog-
ging, petting, piffling, playing, poor-
thing, prevailing, priming, princeling,
prize-ring, prompting, prying, pudding,
purling, ranking, rattling, reckoning,
redwing, rigging, ring, rising, ruching,
rustling, sacking, sapling, scantling,
screaming, sea-faring, sea-going, sea-
king, seal-ring, seasoning, seedling,
seething, self-denying, sewing, sham-
bling, shelving, shepherd-king, shock-
ing, shoestring, shortening, shrouding,
sidesplitting, sightseeing, signet-ring,
shilling, simpling, sing, singing, skulk-
ing, sling, smattering, snarling, sooth-

ing, spooning, spraying, spring, star- **ING**
gazing, starling, startling, sterling,
stilling, sting, stocking, string, strut-
ting, sucking, suckling, swaddling,
swelling, swing, swirling, swooping,
tantalizing, Tao-Teh-King, tap-danc-
ing, teeming, teething, thanksgiving,
thing, thorough-going, thronging, time-
serving, tingling, town-meeting, trek-
king, twinkling, ugly-duckling, under-
ling, underpinning, undying, unending,
unfeeling, unflinching, unknowing, un-
tiring, unveiling, upbuilding, uplifting,
upstanding, upswing, upyearning,
using, vanishing, varnishing, Viking,
wainscoting, waning, warning, waxing,
webbing, wedding, well-being, wend-
ing, whaling, whirling, whiting, wing,
winning, witling, worldling, wring,
writing, yawning, yearling, yearning

Astringe, binge, constringe, cringe, **INGE**
fringe, hinge, impinge, infringe, inter- *see*
tinge, singe, syringe, tinge, twinge,
unhinge

Finger, ginger, harbinger, lady- **INGER**
finger, linger, minnesinger, porringer, *see*
singer, slinger, wringer ER

Commingle, ingle, intermingle, jin- **INGLE**
gle, Kris Kringle, mingle, shingle, *see*
single, surcingle, tingle EL
LE

Bingo, dingo, flamingo, gringo, jingo, **INGO**
lingo, San Domingo *see*
O*

Apronstrings, armorial bearings, blessings, dwellings, innings, invisible wings, playthings, shillings, stockings, strings, things, wings

INGS
see
ING-*s*

Meringue

INGUE
see
ANG

Anno Domini, Benvenuto Cellini, contadini, Gemini, martini, Mussolini, Paganini, Puccini, Rimini, Rossini

INI
see
I**

Actinic, clinic

INIC
see
IC

Dominion, minion, opinion, pinion

INION
see
ION

Consanguinity, femininity, infinity, trinity, vicinity, virginity

INITY
see
E**
ITY

Bethink, blink, bobolink, brink, chewink, chink, clink, clovepink, drink, hoodwink, India-ink, interlink, jink, kink, link, mink, pen-and-ink, pink, prink, rink, rinky-dink, river-brink, shell pink, shrink, sink, slink, stink, think, wink

INK
see
ING
ed-INCT
s-INKS
INX
YNX

Blinker, diesinker, drinker, pinker, stinker, thinker, tinker

INKER
see
ER

Crinkle, periwinkle, Rip van Winkle, sprinkle, twinkle, wrinkle

INKLE
see
EL
LE

Cuff-links, golf-links, methinks

INKS
see
INK-*s*

Dinky, inky, kinky, pinky

INKY
see
E**

Inn, jinn, Tabard Inn, Wayside Inn

INN
see
IN

Dinner, inner, sinner, spinner, thinner, tinner, winner

INNER
see
ER

Finny, hinny, ninny, picaninny, shinny, tinny, whinny

INNY
see
E**

Albino, bambino, casino, domino, Filipino, maraschino, merino, Solferino

INO
see
O*

Bituminous, heinous, libidinous, luminous, mucilaginous, multitudinous, mutinous, ominous, platitudinous, resinous, ruinous, villainous, voluminous

INOUS
see
OUS

Asvins, fins, gherkins, ins, muggins, ninepins, nubbins, Redskins, shins, sins, skins, step-ins, Tom Collins, water-skins, wins

INS
see
IN-*s*

Rinse

INSE
see
INCE

Blueprint, cuckoopint, dint, finger-print, flint, footprint, glint, hint, hoof-print, imprint, lint, mezzotint, mint, peppermint, print, reprint, Septaugint, skinflint, sodamint, spearmint, splint, sprint, squint, stint, tint, varmint

INT
see
S-INCE

Inter, printer, splinter, sprinter, winter

INTER
see
ER

Absinth, Corinth, hyacinth, jacinth, labyrinth, plinth, terebinth

INTH
see

Faintly, quaintly, saintly

INTLY
see
E**

Chintz

INTZ
see
INT-S

Linus, minus, Ninus, Plotinus, Quirinus, sinus, Tarquinus, terminus

INUS
see
US

Jinx, minx, sphinx, Syrinx

INX
see
INK-S
YNX

Briny, destiny, hominy, ignominy, mutiny, Pliny, scrutiny, shiny, tiny

INY
see
E**

Adagio, addio, agio, arpeggio, Bellagio, Boccaccio, braggadocio, cheerio, Clio, Correggio, curio, ex-officio, finochio, Horatio, imbroglio, intaglio, internuncio, Io, nuncio, oratorio, patio, pistachio, Ponte Vecchio, presidio, punctilio, radio, ratio, Rio, Scipio, Scorpio, seraglio, solfeggio, studio, tertio, Tokio, trio

IO
see
ARIO
O*
OLIO

Hesiod, period

IOD
see
OD

Viol, vitriol

IOL
see
OL

Axiom, idiom

IOM
see
OM

Abjection, abortion, absorption, accordion, action, adhesion, adjunction, affection, air condition, Albion, Amphion, anthelion, ant lion, ascension, assertion, assumption, attention, battalion, benefaction, bisection, boon companion, bullion, carrion, caution, centurion, champion, circumscription, circumspection, coercion, Coeur de Lion, collection, collodion, companion, compulsion, conception, concoction, concretion, concussion, confection, congestion, conjunction, connection, contagion, contortion, contraction, contraption, convention, conversion,

ION
see
ASION
ATION
EGION
EON
ESSION
IATION
ICTION
ILION
ILLION
INION
ISION
ISSION
ITION

correction, corruption, counteraction, criterion, crucifixion, cushion, dandelion, deception, decoction, defection, dejection, description, Deucalion, dimension, discretion, discussion, disruption, distention, distortion, diversion, election, emotion, emulsion, enchiridion, Endymion, erection, exception, excursion, expansion, extension, extortion, extroversion, faction, fashion, film-version, fourth dimension, function, gammadion, ganglion, gumption, high tension, Hyperion, Ilion, inaction, inattention, incorruption, incursion, indigestion, indiscretion, induction, infraction, inhesion, injunction, inquisition, insertion, insurrection, intention, interjection, interruption, intervention, introspection, introversion, invention, inversion, Ion, irruption, Ixion, junction, lesion, lion, maladaption, mansion, Marmion, medallion, mention, mullion, objection, oblivion, old-fashion, onion, oppression, option, orchestrion, Orion, passion, pension, perception, percussion, perfection, perihelion, perversion, petrifaction, pincushion, portion, precaution, predilection, prelection, presumption, prevention, proportion, proscription, protection, putrefaction, Pygmalion, quaternion, question, rapscallion, reaction, recollection, redaction, redemption, reflection, reflexion, refraction, rejection, religion, repercussion, resumption, resurrection, revulsion, sanction, scion, scorpion, scul-

ION
ON
OSION
OTION
UCTION
UN
UNION
USION
UTION
al-AL
IONAL

lion, section, selection, stallion, stan- **ION**
chion, subjection, subscription, sugges-
tion, suspension, suspicion, tension,
traction, transaction, transfixion, unc-
tion, version, vivisection

Confessional, conventional, dimen- **IONAL**
sional, emotional, exceptional, frac-   *see*
tional, functional, intentional, inter-   AL
national, irrational, national, notional,
occasional, optional, precessional, pro-
fessional, proportional, rational, recessional, sectional, sensational, traditional, transitional, vocational

Anterior, behavior, excelsior, exte- **IOR**
rior, inferior, interior, junior, Melchior,   *see*
mother-superior, posterior, prior, sen-   OR
ior, superior, ulterior, warrior   ORE

A fortiori, a posteriori, a priori   **IORI**
                                            see
                                            I**

Adios, Helios   **IOS**
                                            see
                                            OS

Grandiose, otiose   **IOSE**
                                            see
                                            OSE

Chariot, cheviot, compatriot, idiot,   **IOT**
Judas Iscariot, patriot, riot   *see*
                                            OT

Abstemious, acrimonious, adscititious, adventitious, amphibious, anxious, atrocious, auspicious, bilious, bumptious, calumnious, capricious, captious, cautious, ceremonious, commodious, compendious, conscientious, conscious, contagious, contentious, copious, curious, delicious, delirious, disputatious, dubious, egregious, envious, expeditious, fastidious, felonious, ferocious, fictitious, flagitious, furious, glorious, gregarious, harmonious, hilarious, ignominious, impecunious, imperious, impervious, impious, inauspicious, industrious, infectious, ingenious, inglorious, inharmonious, injudicious, injurious, insidious, invidious, irreligious, judicious, laborious, licentious, lugubrious, luscious, luxurious, malicious, melodious, meretricious, meritorious, multifarious, mysterious, nefarious, notorious, noxious, nutritious, oblivious, obnoxious, obsequious, obvious, odious, officious, opprobrious, ostentatious, overcurious, parsimonious, penurious, perfidious, pernicious, pious, pluvious, precarious, precious, precocious, pretentious, previous, prodigious, propitious, punctilious, rebellious, religious, sacrilegious, salubrious, sanctimonious, scrumptious, seditious, self-conscious, serious, specious, spurious, studious, subconscious, supercilious, superstitious, surreptitious, suspicious, tedious, unceremonious, unconscious, uxorious, vainglorious, various, vexatious, vicarious, vicious, victorious

IOUS
see
ACIOUS
AMUS
EUS*
OUS
UOUS
US
ly-E**
OUSLY

Adeptship, apostleship, battleship, **IP**
buggy-whip, catnip, celery-tip, censor-   *see*
ship, championship, chip, clip, club-   *ed*-**IPT**
ship, companionship, cork-tip, court-   **YPT**
ship, cowslip, dictatorship, dip, drip,   **S**-**IPSE**
equip, fellowship, finger-tip, flip, gos-
sip, grip, guardianship, hare-lip, hard-
ship, hero-worship, hip, horsewhip,
kinship, ladyship, lightship, leadership,
lip, lordship, marksmanship, midship,
nip, outstrip, ownership, parsnip, part-
nership, penmanship, phantom-ship,
pillowslip, pleasure-trip, potato-chip,
quip, round trip, ruby-lip, sailingship,
scholarship, scrip, ship, showmanship,
sip, skip, slip, snip, strip, tallowdip,
tree-worship, trip, troop-ship, tulip,
turnip, warship, whaleship, whip, wor-
ship, zip

Assurbanipal, municipal, principal   **IPAL**
    see
    AL

Anticipate, dissipate, emancipate,   **IPATE**
participate   *see*
    ATE

Bagpipe, blowpipe, briar-pipe, cob-   **IPE**
pipe, gripe, guttersnipe, hornpipe,   *see*
organpipe, over-ripe, pipe, pitchpipe,   **YPE**
rareripe, reedpipe, ripe, sideswipe,
snipe, stovepipe, stripe, swipe, toma-
hawk-pipe, tripe, unripe, windpipe,
wipe

Juniper, pen-wiper, Pied Piper,   **IPER**
piper, sandpiper, sniper, swiper, viper   *see*
    ER

Caliph **IPH**
see
IFF

Disciple, multiple, participle, prin- **IPLE**
ciple, triple *see*
EL
LE

Big Dipper, clipper, dipper, flipper, **IPPER**
gallinipper, lady's-slipper, ripper, ship- *see*
per, skipper, slipper, tripper, worship- ER
per, zipper

Cripple, nipple, ripple, stipple, tipple **IPPLE**
see
EL
LE

Eclipse, ellipse **IPSE**
see
IP-*s*

Gipsy, tipsy **IPSY**
see
E**

Conscript, manuscript, nipt, nonde- **IPT**
script, postscript, script, transcript *see*
IP-*ed*
YPT
s-IPSE

Antique, bezique, cacique, clique, **IQUE**
critique, lyrique, Mozambique, oblique, *see*
perique, physique, pique, pneumatique, EAK*
pratique, technique, unique EEK

Astir, bestir, decemvir, elixir, Elze- **IR**
vir, emir, fakir, fir, Guadalquivir,   *see*
kaffir, Kashmir, Mimir, nadir, Ophir,   ARTYR
sir, souvenir, stir, tapir, triumvir,   ERE**
Vladimir, Ymir   IRR
  UR
  YRRH

Ça ira, Hegira, lira, Sapphira, **IRA**
Sephira   *see*
  A**

Conspiracy, piracy **IRACY**
  see
  ACY
  E**

Irate, pirate, triumvirate **IRATE**
  see
  ATE

Besmirch, birch, smirch **IRCH**
  see
  URCH

Arctic Circle, circle, encircle, semi- **IRCLE**
circle, sewing-circle   *see*
  EL
  LE

Bird, blackbird, catbird, gird, jail- **IRD**
bird, jaybird, lovebird, mockingbird,   *see*
night-bird, railbird, reedbird, secre-   ORD**
tary bird, third   IR-*ed*
  IRE-*d*

Admire, afire, aspire, attire, Ayrshire, **IRE**
back-fire, barb-wire, bonfire, campfire, *see*
conspire, cross-fire, crosswire, desire, ER
Devonshire, dire, empire, expire, fire, IAR
for-hire, grandsire, gunfire, haywire, IER***
hire, inspire, ire, live wire, mire, mis- OIR*
fire, perspire, pismire, quagmire, re- UIRE
spire, retire, samphire, sapphire, satire, YRE
shire, spare-tire, spitfire, suspire, tire, *ed*-EARD*
transpire, umpire, vampire, watch-fire, s-IRES
wildfire, wire

Dirge **IRGE**
see
OURGE

Dirk, irk, kirk, quirk, shirk, smirk **IRK**
see
ERK
ORK

Flower-girl, girl, old-girl, skirl, swirl, **IRL**
twirl, whirl *see*
EARL
URL
ed-ORLD

Affirm, confirm, firm, infirm, squirm **IRM**
see
ORM**

Andiron, castiron, Chiron, curling- **IRON**
iron, environ, flatiron, grappling-iron, *see*
gridiron, iron, midiron, pig-iron, sad- ON
iron, wrought-iron

Whirr	**IRR**
	see
	IR
First, thirst	**IRST**
	see
	ORST
	URST
Begirt, black shirt, dirt, flirt, girt, hobble-skirt, hoopskirt, outskirt, red shirt, seagirt, shirt, skirt, steel-girt, stuffed-shirt, undershirt	**IRT**
	see
	UIRT
	URT
Birth, firth, girth, mirth, rebirth	**IRTH**
	see
	ORTH**
Inquiry, miry, spiry, wiry	**IRY**
	see
	E**
Aegis, amaryllis, analepsis, analysis, Annus Mirabilis, Anubis, aphis, Apis, Artemis, Atlantis, Attis, axis, Bubastis, caddis, Chablis, Charybdis, Clovis, Colchis, crisis, De Profundis, Dis, Eblis, Eleusis, ephemeris, epidermis, Fenris, finis, hamamelis, Harmachis, houris, ibis, Iblis, ichthyornis, iris, Isis, Lake Moeris, laryngitis, mantis, marquis, Memphis, morris, myosotis, non compos mentis, Nunc Dimittis, ora pro nobis, orris, Osiris, parvis, pelvis, Phyllis, portcullis, proboscis, prognosis, Propontis, psycho-analysis, rara avis, sacred-ibis, Salamis, Salmacis, salpiglossis, Sardis, Semiramis,	**IS***
	see
	AIS
	ALIS
	ARIS
	ASIS
	ATIS
	ESIS
	ICE**
	ISE****
	ISS
	OLIS
	ONIS
	OPSIS
	OSIS
	UCE**

semper fidelis, Serapis, Sesostris, Smer- **IS***
dis, stephanotis, tennis, Thamyris,
Themis, thesis, Thetis, this, Tiflis,
Tigris, trellis, Tunis, Walpurgis

Chassis, his, is, 'tis, this-is **IS****
see
IZ
ACE-*s*
EACH-*s*

Ambergris, verdigris **IS*****
see
EESE**

Artisan, Nisan, non-partisan, parti- **ISAN**
san *see*
AN*

Disc **ISC**
see
ISK

Advise, anywise, apprise, arise, cate- **ISE***
chise, chastise, circumcise, coastwise, *see*
comprise, compromise, contrariwise, IZE
corner-wise, crosswise, demise, despise, EYE-*s*
devise, edgewise, enterprise, exercise, IE**-*s*
exorcise, franchise, improvise, incise, IES*
leastwise, lengthwise, likewise, mer-
chandise, moonrise, mortal-wise, no-
wise, otherwise, penny-wise, revise,
rise, slant-wise, suchwise, sunrise, su-
pervise, surmise, surprise, thuswise,
unwise, weatherwise, wise

Concise, Paradise, precise

ISE**
see
ICE*

Cerise, chemise, Heloise, marquise, valise

ISE***
see
EASE**
EESE**
ESE

Anise, mortise, practise, premise, promise, treatise

ISE****
see
ISS

Appetiser, despiser, Kaiser, miser, wiser

ISER
see
ER

Accomplish, admonish, apish, astonish, backshish, banish, blemish, bluefish, bookish, boorish, boyish, brackish, brandish, British, brutish, bulldoggish, burnish, butterdish, cat-fish, cattish, chafing-dish, churlish, cloddish, clownish, coltish, Cornish, crawfish, dervish, devilish, disrelish, elfish, embellish, English, establish, famish, fetish, finish, fish, Flemish, flourish, foolish, freakish, furbish, furnish, garish, garnish, girlish, goldfish, grayish, greenish, hashish, heathenish, hellish, hoggish, horseradish, hoydenish, impish, Irish, jelly-fish, Jewish, knavish, lavish, loutish, mannish, mawkish, minish, modish, monkish, Moorish, mulish, oafish, offish, ogreish, outlandish, paganish, parish, peevish, pilot-fish, pound-fool-

ISH
see
EESH
ERISH
OLISH
UISH
ly-E**

ish, priggish, prudish, publish, punish, **ISH**
radish, rakish, ravish, reddish, relish,
replenish, rubbish, sawfish, selfish,
sheepish, shellfish, shrewish, skirmish,
skittish, slavish, sluggish, snobbish,
Spanish, squeamish, starfish, stiffish,
sunfish, swish, swordfish, tarnish, Tar-
shish, ticklish, undiminish, vanish,
varnish, waggish, waspish, whirling
dervish, whitish, wish, womanish, Yid-
dish

Fisher, garnisher, kingfisher, pub- **ISHER**
lisher, well-wisher   *see*
                                   ER

Decision, derision, division, elision, **ISION**
envision, incision, indecision, precision, *see*
prevision, provision, revision, super- ION
vision, television, vision

Asterisk, basilisk, bisk, brisk, disk, **ISK**
frisk, obelisk, risk, tamarisk, whisk   *see*
                                        ISQUE

Frisky, risky, whisky   **ISKY**
                                        see
                                        E**

Aisle, blessed-isle, Carlisle, Emerald **ISLE**
Isle, fairy-isle, lisle, safety-isle, sea- *see*
swept-isle   ILE*

Actinism, altruism, analogism, an- **ISM**
thropomorphism, aphorism, asterism, *see*
atavism, baptism, barbarism, Bolshe- AISM
vism, Brahmanism, Buddhism, cate- ALISM
chism, chauvinism, chrism, collecti- ICISM
vism, conservatism, despotism, dyna- ONISM

mism, egoism, egotism, empiricism, **ISM**
epicurism, exorcism, Fascism, galvan- UISM
ism, gormandism, henotheism, heroism, YSM
hyperbolism, incendiarism, Islamism,
magnetism, mannerism, mechanism,
mesmerism, metabolism, micro-orga-
nism, modernism, monotheism, Nazism,
nepotism, nihilism, occultism, Ophism,
optimism, organism, ostracism, paci-
fism, paganism, pantheism, pedagog-
ism, pessimism, phallicism, polytheism,
prism, proletarianism, propagandism,
pugilism, purism, quietism, recidivism,
red-tapism, republicanism, rheuma-
tism, rowdyism, Sabæanism, sabba-
tism, Sadism, savagism, schism, Shiism,
sinapism, skepticism, solecism, som-
nambulism, sophism, Sufism, surreal-
ism, sybaritism, syllogism, symbolism,
theism, totemism, vandalism, voodoo-
ism, witticism

Benison, bison, caparison, compari-   **ISON**
son, garrison, imprison, jettison, Kyrie   *see*
eleison, liaison, orison, poison, prison,   ON
unison, venison

Crisp, lisp, will-o'-the-wisp, wisp   **ISP**
                                        see

Bisque, odalisque   **ISQUE**
                                        see
                                        ISK

Amiss, bliss, cumiss, dismiss, hiss,   **ISS**
kiss, miss, Swiss, remiss   *see*
                                        IS*
                                        YSS
                                        *ed-*IST

Admission, emission, intermission, mission, omission, permission, remission, submission, transmission

ISSION
see
ION

Fissue, issue, tissue

ISSUE
see
UE

Alarmist, alchemist, apiculturist, artist, atheist, atomist, atwist, autoist, balladist, banjoist, Baptist, bicyclist, bigamist, Bonapartist, caricaturist, cartoonist, chemist, cist, colonist, columnist, Communist, computist, conformist, consist, copyist, cubist, cyclist, deist, dentist, desist, druggist, egoist, egotist, equilibrist, enlist, eucharist, evangelist, exist, exorcist, fabulist, Fascist, fatalist, feminist, fist, florist, futurist, gist, glossarist, grist, herbalist, hist, hobbyist, homilist, humorist, insist, journalist, jurist, leftist, list, lobbyist, loyalist, Methodist, miniaturist, mist, moralist, motorist, naturalist, nihilist, non conformist, novelist, nudist, obscurantist, occultist, Oliver Twist, opportunist, optimist, optometrist, organist, orientalist, pacifist, palmist, parodist, Paulist, persist, pessimist, pharmaceutist, pharmacist, philatelist, physicist, physiognomist, physiologist, pianist, plagiarist, polytheist, propagandist, psalmist, psychist, pugilist, purist, pyramidologist, Quietist, realist, resist, revivalist, rhapsodist, rightist, ritualist, Romanist, royalist, Sadist, satirist, scientist, Scotch-mist,

IST*
see
OGIST
ONIST
UIST
YST*
ICE**-*ed*

shortist, soloist, somnambulist, sophist, **IST***
specialist, strategist, stylist, subsist,
surrealist, taxlist, thaumaturgist, the-
ist, theurgist, tourist, Trappist, twist,
violinist, vocalist, whist, wrist, wist

   Christ   **IST****
                                         see

   Ballista, genista, vista   **ISTA**
                                         see
                                         A**

   Artiste, batiste, modiste   **ISTE**
                                         see
                                     EAST*
                                     YST**

   Administer, barrister, blister, can-   **ISTER**
ister, minister, mister, register, sinister,   *see*
sister   ER

   Altruistic, anachronistic, animistic,   **ISTIC**
anomalistic, artistic, cabalistic, Cal-   *see*
vinistic, casuistic, characteristic, chre-   IC
mastistic, deistic, egoistic, egotistic,
Elohistic, euphuistic, fatalistic, inar-
tistic, Jehovistic, linguistic, militaris-
tic, modernistic, optimistic, panthe-
istic, pessimistic, phlogistic, realistic,
ritualistic, sadistic, spiritistic, statistic

   Bristle, epistle, gristle, peanut whis-   **ISTLE**
tle, thistle, whistle   *see*
                                         EL
                                         LE

Artistry, chemistry, ministry, palmistry, papistry, registry, sophistry

ISTRY
see
E**

Accredit, adit, admit, affidavit, audit, bandit, befit, benefit, bit, bottomless pit, bowsprit, chit, coalpit, cock-pit, comfit, commit, cubit, culprit, davit, debit, decline-it, decrepit, deposit, digit, discomfit, dispirit, emigravit, emit, exit, explicit, fit, flit, grit, habit, half-wit, hermit, hit, Holy Writ, howbeit, illicit, inhabit, intermit, ipsedixit, it, jack-in-the-pulpit, kit, knit, lamplit, licit, lickety-split, limit, lit, make-up kit, manumit, misfit, moonlit, nimble-wit, nit, nit-wit, no-hit, obit, omit, orbit, outfit, outwit, permit, pit, plaudit, posit, profit, prohibit, prosit, pulpit, pundit, rabbit, refit, remit, revisit, Sanskrit, sit, skit, slit, so-be-it, spirit, spit, split, sprit, starlit, stonepit, submit, summit, Tashmit, tidbit, tit, to wit, transit, twit, unfit, unit, visit, vomit, welsh-rabbit, whit, wit, writ

IT
see
EDIT
EIT**
ERIT
IBIT
ICIT
ITE**
UIT*
ed-ED
s-ITS

Amrita, per capita, Sita

ITA
see
A**

Charitable, habitable, hospitable, illimitable, indubitable, inevitable, inhospitable, inimitable, profitable, suitable, veritable

ITABLE
see
ABLE

Capital, hospital, marital, non-commital, orbital, recital, requital, vital

ITAL
see
AL

Cosmopolitan, metropolitan, Nea-
politan, puritan, Samaritan

ITAN
see
AN*

Annuitant, concomitant, exorbitant,
habitant, inhabitant, irritant, militant,
visitant

ITANT
see
ANT*

Agitate, cogitate, felicitate, gravi-
tate, gurgitate, hesitate, imitate, in-
capacitate, irritate, meditate, necessi-
tate, precipitate, premeditate, regurgi-
tate, rehabilitate, solicitate

ITATE
see
ATE
ed-ED

Auction pitch, backstitch, bewitch,
bitch, czarevitch, ditch, featherstitch,
flitch, hemstitch, hitch, itch, lock-
stitch, low pitch, pitch, stitch, switch,
twitch, whipstitch, witch

ITCH
see
ICH

Aconite, Adamite, aerolite, Amalek-
ite, Ammonite, anchorite, anthracite,
Aphrodite, appetite, apposite, Areopa-
pagite, ashy-white, backbite, bite,
blatherskite, bobwhite, box-kite, Ca-
naanite, Carmelite, cenobite, cite, con-
trite, cyanite, despite, dolomite, dyna-
mite, ebonite, Edomite, eremite, eru-
dite, excite, expedite, finite, frostbite,
Gilroy's kite, graphite, Hepplewhite,
hermaphrodite, hoplite, hyposulphite,
incite, incondite, indite, invite, Israel-
ite, Jacobite, kite, labradorite, lazulite,
lignite, lyddite, malachite, meteorite,
midshipmite, milkwhite, mite, Musco-
vite, Nazarite, niccolite, parasite, phos-
phite, plebiscite, polite, poor white,

ITE*
see
EIGHT**
IGHT
YTE

quite, recite, recondite, requite, rite, satellite, Semite, Sethite, Shiite, Shunammite, site, smite, socialite, spite, sprite, stalactite, stalagmite, suburbanite, sulphite, Sybarite, termite, thalmite, theodolite, trite, underwrite, unite, vulcanite, white, widow's mite, write **ITE***

Definite, exquisite, favorite, granite, indefinite, infinite, marguerite, opposite, perquisite, preterite, requisite **ITE**** *see* IT

Arbiter, ghost writer, Jupiter, liter, miter, niter, scimiter, typewriter, writer **ITER** *see* ER

Aerolith, blacksmith, crith, forthwith, frith, goldsmith, Judith, kith, Lilith, locksmith, megalith, Meredith, monolith, Neith, neolith, pith, silversmith, smith, Tanith, with, zenith **ITH** *see* YTH

Blithe, lithe, tithe, writhe **ITHE** *see* YTHE

Dither, nowhither, slither, thither, whither, wither, zither **ITHER** *see* ER

Logarithm **ITHM** *see* YTHM

Haiti, prakriti, Tahiti, wapiti **ITI** *see* I**

Critic, mephitic, parasitic, politic **ITIC**
see
IC

Abolition, admonition, air-condition, **ITION**
ambition, apparition, apposition, attri- *see*
tion, audition, coalition, coition, com- ION
petition, composition, condition, con-
trition, decomposition, disposition,
ebullition, edition, exhibition, expedi-
tion, exposition, extradition, fruition,
ignition, imposition, inhibition, Inquisition, intuition, juxtaposition, muni-
tion, nutrition, opposition, partition,
perdition, petition, position, predispo-
sition, premonition, prohibition, recog-
nition, recondition, rendition, repeti-
tion, requisition, sedition, special edition, superstition, supposition, tradi-
tion, tuition, volition

Auditive, competitive, fugitive, gen- **ITIVE**
itive, infinitive, inquisitive, partitive, *see*
primitive, prohibitive, punitive, sensi- IVE**
tive, transitive, volitive

Gitche Manito, incognito, mosquito, **ITO**
Quito *see*
O*

Auditor, city-editor, competitor, **ITOR**
creditor, depositor, inquisitor, janitor, *see*
monitor, progenitor, servitor, solicitor, OR
suitor, traitor, visitor

Calamitous, circuitous, felicitous, **ITOUS**
gratuitous, iniquitous, solicitous, ubiq- *see*
uitous OUS
US

Bitter, flitter, fritter, glitter, jitter, litter, outfitter, quitter, sitter, titter, transmitter, twitter

ITTER
see
ER

Belittle, brittle, lickspittle, little, spittle, tittle, vittle, whittle

ITTLE
see
EL
LE

Ditty, gritty, kitty, witty

ITTY
see
E**

Altitude, amplitude, aptitude, attitude, beatitude, certitude, decrepitude, exactitude, fortitude, gratitude, habitude, inaptitude, incertitude, ineptitude, infinitude, ingratitude, lassitude, latitude, longitude, magnitude, multitude, nigritude, platitude, plenitude, promptitude, rectitude, servitude, similitude, solicitude, solitude, turpitude, vicissitude, virisimilitude

ITUDE
see
UDE

Ad libitum, infinitum

ITUM
see
UM

Discomfiture, expenditure, forfeiture, furniture, garniture, geniture, investiture, portraiture, primogeniture

ITURE
see
URE

Emeritus, Hermaphroditus, St. Vitus, Tacitus, Theocritus, Titus, Unigenitus

ITUS
see
US

Constitute, destitute, institute, prostitute, substitute

ITUTE
see
UTE
ed-ED

Absurdity, alacrity, amity, anonymity, benignity, caducity, calamity, cavity, celebrity, chastity, city, comity, complexity, concavity, conformity, corporeity, credulity, deformity, density, depravity, dignity, enmity, enormity, entity, eternity, fatality, fecundity, fidelity, fraternity, frivolity, gravity, heredity, identity, immensity, indemnity, indignity, infidelity, infirmity, integrity, intensity, jollity, laity, laxity, maternity, necessity, nonconformity, nonentity, nudity, nullity, obesity, oddity, paucity, perplexity, perversity, pity, polity, probity, profundity, prolixity, propensity, quantity, Radio City, rotundity, salubrity, sanctity, sanity, scarcity, self-pity, solemnity, spontaneity, suavity, taciturnity, tensity, uniformity, university, varsity, velocity

ITY
see
ACITY
ALITY
ANITY
ARITY
E**
EITY
ENITY
ERITY
EVITY
ICITY
IDITY
ILITY
IMITY
INITY
IVITY
OCITY
ORITY
OSITY
UITY
UNITY
URITY

Fritz, seidlitz, sitz

ITZ
see

Howitzer, kibitzer

ITZER
see
ER

Alluvium, aquarium, atrium, bdellium, Belgium, Byzantium, calcium, chromium, compendium, cranium, decennium, delirium, delphinium, diluvium, effluvium, elysium, encomium, eulogium, euphorbium, exordium, geranium, gymnasium, harmonium, helium, herbarium, iridium, magnesium, medium, megatherium, millennium, nasturtium, odium, opium, opprobrium, osmium, palladium, pandemonium, peculium, pericranium, planetarium, polonium, potassium, premium, principium, proscenium, protevangelium, radium, rose-geranium, scholium, selenium, sodium, stadium, stramonium, symposium, tedium, trifolium, trillium, trivium, uranium

IUM
see
EUM
OM*
OME*
ORIUM
UM
UMN

Æsculapius, Apuleius, Aquarius, Athanasius, Boëthius, Cassius, Confucius, Dionysius, Erichthonius, expurgatorius, genius, Helvetius, Lucretius, Marcus Aurelius, Mencius, nisi prius, Pluvius, Polonius, Procopius, radius, Sagittarius, Sirius, Stradivarius, Suetonius, Tiberius, Titus Livius, Vesuvius

IUS
see
US

Arrival, carnival, festival, outrival, revival, rival, survival

IVAL
see
AL

Activate, cultivate, motivate, private, recidivate, titivate

IVATE
see
ATE

Alive, archive, arrive, beehive, chive, connive, contrive, deprive, dive, five, hive, revive, scared-alive, strive, survive, thrive

IVE*
see
YVE
S-IFE-S
IVES

Active, adhesive, aggressive, attentive, captive, cohesive, collective, compressive, consumptive, convective, convictive, cursive, decisive, defective, descriptive, destructive, detective, diminutive, directive, elective, endive, eruptive, executive, exhaustive, expansive, expensive, expressive, extensive, festive, forgive, furtive, give, housewive, impassive, inactive, incentive, inexpensive, inoffensive, instinctive, intensive, invective, inventive, irrespective, Khedive, live, massive, misgive, missive, objective, obstructive, offensive, ogive, olive, oppressive, outlive, passive, pendentive, pensive, perceptive, perspective, persuasive, pervasive, perversive, plaintive, presumptive, progressive, projective, prospective, qui vive, radioactive, receptive, reflective, respective, restive, retentive, retrogressive, secretive, selective, skive, sportive, suasive, subjective, submissive, substantive, subversive, suggestive, susceptive, vindictive, votive, wive

IVE*
see
ATIVE
IEVE**
ITIVE
OSIVE
OTIVE
USIVE

Drivel, shrivel, snivel, swivel

IVEL
see
EL
LE

Deliver, diver, driver, giver, law-giver, liver, purling-river, quiver, receiver, river, screw driver, slave-driver, shiver, sliver, waiver

IVER
see
ER

Delivery, livery

IVERY
see
E**

Archives, hives, housewives, pocket-knives

IVES
see
IVE*-*s*

Civet, privet, rivet, trivet

IVET
see
ET

Acclivity, activity, captivity, declivity, festivity, inactivity, nativity, objectivity, passivity, proclivity, receptivity, relativity, selectivity

IVITY
see
E**
ITY

Administratrix, affix, Aix, appendix, betwixt, calix, cicatrix, crucifix, felix, fix, infelix, intermix, janitrix, matrix, mix, nix, Phoenix, prefix, prolix, radix, semper felix, six, spadix, suffix, testatrix, transfix, Vercingetorix

IX
see
YX
IC-*s*
ICK-*s*
ed-IXT

Betwixt, 'twixt

IXT
see
IX-*ed*

Agassiz, biz, Cadiz, friz, Hafiz, phiz, rheumatiz, viz , whiz

IZ
see
IES**
IS**
IZZ
UIZ

Advertize, affinitize, anathematize, anglicize, apologize, apotheosize, assize, atomize, attitudinize, authorize, baptize, barbarize, botanize, capsize, cauterize, centralize, civilize, criticize, crystallize, demobilize, demoralize, deodorize, emphasize, energize, epitomize, eulogize, evangelize, extemporize, familiarize, fertilize, foreignize, fossilize, fraternize, galvanize, gormandize, headsize, hybridize, idolize, itemize, jeopardize, latinize, lionize, memorize, mercerize, mesmerize, minimize, mobilize, modernize, monopolize, neutralize, Nobel prize, organize, ostracize, overemphasize, oxidize, particularize, plagiarize, polarize, popularize, ˉprize, proselytize, pulverize, rhapsodize, recognize, satirize, scandalize, scrutinize, sensitize, size, solemnize, soliloquize, stabilize, sterilize, stigmatize, syllogize, sympathize, synchronize, temporize, terrorize, theorize, tranquilize, undersize, utilize, vaporize, victimize

IZE
see
ALIZE
ONIZE
EYE-*s*
IES*
ISE*
UISE*

Bedizen, citizen, denizen, wizen

IZEN
see
EN

Appetizer, atomizer, criticizer, fertilizer, organizer, vocalizer

IZER
see
ER

Fizz, gin fizz

IZZ
see
IZ

Drizzle, fizzle, frizzle, sizzle, swizzle **IZZLE**
see
EL
LE

O SOUNDS

Accelerando, akimbo, Alamo, Aleppo, alfresco, allegro, ambo, antipasto, Apollo, Aquilo, Ariosto, arroyo, auto, autogyro, banjo, Banquo, basso, basso-profundo, basso relievo, bayamo, bilbo, bravo, broncho, burro, Cairo, Cagliostro, calabozo, Callisto, Calypso, certo, chiaroscuro, chromo, Co.; Colombo, concerto, Consuelo, conto, corso, cui bono, de facto, Dido, ditto, dodo, Draco, dynamo, echo, ego, embryo, ergo, fiasco, Figaro, forego, fresco, fro, gaucho, gazebo, ginkgo, go, Gran Chaco, Guido, gusto, hidalgo, H_2O, Hoang-Ho, hobo, indigo, inferno, in toto, ipso facto, Jericho, Jethro, jocko, junco, Juno, kilo, kimono, lasso, let-go, libido, Lido, limbo, lo, Lorenzo, maestro, major-domo, Manchukuo, manifesto, mestizo, Michael Angelo, Monaco, Monte Carlo, Monte Cristo, Morocco, mulatto, Mumbo-Jumbo, Navajo, negro, no, octavo, oho, Orinoco, Palermo, papagayo, papyro, perfecto, Pernambuco, peso, photo, pico, Pizarro, placebo, Pluto, Po, poncho, pro, Prosilipo, proviso, pueblo, quarto, Quasimodo, rancho, recto, re-echo, righto, rococo, Salerno, salvo, San Diego, San Francisco, Sappho, Sargasso, secundo,

O*
see
ADO
AGO
ALO
ANGO
ANO
ANTO
AO
ARGO
ATO
EAU
EDO
EGO
ELLO
ENDO
ENTO
EO
ERO
ESTO
ETO
ETTO
ICO
ILLO
IMO
INGO
INO
IO
ITO
OE**

shako, Shinto, silo, sirocco, so, so and
so, so-ho, so-so, status quo, St. Elmo,
stucco, tabasco, tally-ho, tardo, taro,
Tasso, tempo, Terra del Fuego, testudo,
theorbo, to and fro, tobacco, torso,
tufo, tyro, undergo, Valparaiso, verso,
veto, Virgo, Yao, yo-ho, Zeno

O*
  OLO
  OSO
  OTTO
  OUGH*
  OW*
  OWE
  S-OSE*
   OWS

Ado, came-to, do, heave-to, hitherto,
how-d'ye-do, lean-to, outdo, overdo,
that-will-do, thereunto, to, to-do, two,
underdo, undo, unto, well-to-do, we-
two, who

O**
  see
  AGUE***
  EW
  IEW
  OE*
  OO
  OU*
  OUGH****
  OUX
  U
  UE*

Balboa, boa, cocoa, Genoa, goa,
proa, protozoa, Samoa, whoa

OA
  see
  A**

Accroach, approach, broach, coach,
cockroach, encroach, poach, reproach,
roach, slow coach, stage coach

OACH
  see
  OCHE

Abroad, broad, carload, corduroy-
road, crossroad, goad, highroad,
horned-toad, inroad, load, overload,
railroad, road, shipload, toad, tree
toad, unload, woad

OAD
  see
  ODE
  OW*-*ed*

Loaf, oaf

OAF
see
OPHE**

Bathcloak, Charter Oak, cloak, croak, holm-oak, live-oak, oak, scrub-oak, soak, uncloak, white-oak

OAK
see
OKE
S-OAX

Cannel coal, charcoal, coal, foal, goal, shoal

OAL
see
OL
OUL**

Foam, gloam, loam, roam, Siloam, sea-foam

OAM
see
OMB**
OME**

Bemoan, Darby and Joan, groan, loan, moan, roan

OAN
see
ONE*

Soap

OAP
see
OPE

Bezoar, boar, dripping-oar, hoar, muffled-oar, roar, soar, torrent's-roar, uproar, wild-boar

OAR
see
OOR*
ed-OARD
S-OR-*s*

Aboard, above board, all aboard, billboard, blackboard, board, bristol board, buckboard, cardboard, chequer-board, chess board, clapboard, cup-board, dashboard, hoard, inboard,

OARD
see
ORD*
OAR-*ed*
OR-*ed*

keyboard, lapboard, larboard, mop-
board, mortarboard, ouija-board, out-
board, overboard, pasteboard, running-
board, school-board, shipboard, shuffle-
board, sideboard, signboard, sounding-
board, starboard, switch-board

OARD

Boast, cinnamon toast, coast, corn-
roast, dry-toast, milktoast, pot-roast,
roast, toast

OAST
see
OST**
ed-ED

Afloat, bloat, blue-coat, boat, bum-
boat, canal boat, coat, cut-throat,
ferryboat, float, fur-coat, gloat, goat,
great-coat, gunboat, jolly-boat, life
boat, moat, motorboat, nanny-goat,
oat, overcoat, packet-boat, petticoat,
police boat, red coat, rowboat, sailboat,
scapegoat, shoat, speedboat, steam-
boat, surcoat, throat, topcoat, torpedo
boat, turncoat, U-boat, waistcoat,
whaleboat

OAT
see
OTE
s-OATS

Inchoate

OATE
see
ATE

Loath, oath

OATH
see
OTH*

Wild-oats

OATS
see
OAT-*s*

Blob, bob, cob, corncob, fob, gob, heart-throb, hob, hobnob, Jacob, job, knob, lob, mob, nabob, rob, slob, snob, sob, soft job, thingumbob, throb

OB*
see
AB**
UAB

Job

OB**
see
OBE

Approbate, probate, reprobate

OBATE
see
ATE

Dobber, jobber, robber, slobber

OBBER
see
ER

Cobble, gobble, hobble, wobble

OBBLE
see
EL
LE

Blobby, bobby, hobby, knobby, lobby

OBBY
see
E**

Disrobe, globe, lap-robe, lobe, microbe, nightrobe, probe, robe, wardrobe

OBE
see
OB**

October, sober

OBER
see
ER

Ennoble, ignoble, noble

OBLE
see
EL
LE

En bloc, havoc, langue d'Oc, Medoc, opodeldoc, roc, Tlaloc

OC
see
OCH

Bifocal, equivocal, focal, local, reciprocal, vocal

OCAL
see
AL

Allocate, dislocate, equivocate, invocate, locate, reciprocate, suffocate

OCATE
see
ATE

Antioch, Enoch, epoch, loch, Moloch, pibroch

OCH
see
OC
OCK

Troche

OCHE
see
OACH

Ochre

OCHRE
see
ER

Atrocity, ferocity, precocity, reciprocity, velocity

OCITY
see
E**
ITY

Alpenstock, bedrock, block, bock, bullock, burdock, buttock, cassock, chock-a-block, chopping-block, clock, cock, crock, deadlock, dock, fetlock, firelock, flintlock, flock, forelock, frock, game-cock, grandfather's clock, haddock, hammock, hassock, haycock,

OCK
see
OC
OCH
ed-OCT
s-OX

hemlock, hillock, hock, hollyhock, **OCK**
hummock, interlock, jabberwock,
joint-stock, knock, laughing-stock,
livestock, lock, lovelock, mattock,
minster-clock, mock, moss-grown-
rock, oarlock, o'clock, overstock, pad-
dock, padlock, peacock, pock, pollock,
poppy-cock, Plymouth Rock, Rappa-
hannock, rowlock, shaddock, sham-
rock, shell-shock, shock, shuttlecock,
Shylock, smock, sock, stock, stopcock,
stumbling-block, Tarpeian Rock, tick-
tock, town-clock, traprock, tussock,
unfrock, unlock, warlock, weathercock,
wedlock, white rock, woodcock

Knickerbocker, knocker, locker, **OCKER**
rocker, shilling shocker *see*
ER

Crocket, docket, locket, pickpocket, **OCKET**
pocket, rocket, sky-rocket, socket, *see*
sprocket ET

Mediocre **OCRE**
see
ER

Concoct, decoct **OCT**
see
OCK-*ed*

Crocus, focus, hocus-pocus, locus **OCUS**
see
US

Aaron's rod, Cape Cod, clod, coal-hod, cod, decapod, demigod, divining-rod, downtrod, dryshod, ephod, gastropod, God, goldenrod, Herod, hexapod, hod, land-o-Nod, lightning-rod, megapod, method, Nimrod, nod, Novgorod, od, pea-pod, platypod, plod, pod, prod, ramrod, rod, roughshod, sea-god, shod, slipshod, sod, sun-god, synod, tripod, trod, unshod, well-shod

OD
see
IOD
ODD
UAD

Bi-carbonate of soda, coda, pagoda, sal soda

ODA
see
A**

Odd

ODD
see
OD

Abode, à la mode, anode, bestrode, bode, cathode, code, commode, corrode, decode, discommode, episode, epode, erode, explode, forebode, incommode, lode, mode, monopode, node, ode, outmode, rode, strode

ODE
see
OAD
OW*-*ed*

Dislodge, dodge, hodge-podge, lodge

ODGE
see

Anodic, episodic, melodic, odic, parodic, periodic, prosodic, spasmodic

ODIC
see
IC

Coryphodon, glyptodon, mastodon

ODON
see
ON

Heterodox, orthodox

ODOX
see
OX

Anybody, body, chiropody, custody, disembody, embody, everybody, melody, monody, nobody, parody, prosody, psalmody, rhapsody, somebody, threnody, torpedo body

ODY
see
E**

Canoe, horseshoe, overshoe, shoe, snowshoe, Tippecanoe

OE*
see
O**
S-USE*

Aloe, Arapahoe, Crusoe, Defoe, doe, floe, foe, John Doe, mistletoe, oboe, pekoe, roe, shadroe, sloe, throe, tip-toe, toe, woe

OE**
see
O*
OW*
ed-OAD
OW*-*ed*
S-OSE

Poem, proem

OEM
see
EM

Boer, church-goer, doer, evil-doer, good-doer, o'er, shoer

OER
see
ER

Of, unheard of, thereof, whereof

OF
see
OVE**

Cast-off, cut-off, doff, far-off, kick-off, off, palm-off, ring-off, Romanoff, scoff, send-off, show-off, stand-off, take-off, tee-off, toff

OFF
see
OUGHT*****
ed-OFT

Coffer, offer, proffer, scoffer

OFFER
see
ER

Aloft, cockloft, croft, hayloft, how-oft, loft, Lowestoft, oft, soft

OFT
see
OFF-*ed*

Agog, backlog, befog, bog, bullfrog, clog, cog, cranberry bog, dog, egg-nog, firedog, flog, fog, frog, Gog, golliwog, grog, ground-hog, hedgehog, hog, hot dog, house-dog, incog., jog, knotty-log, lapdog, leapfrog, log, Magog, megafog, peat-bog, polly-wog, prairie-dog, river-hog, roadhog, sand-hog, sea-dog, sea-hog, spitz-dog, sundog, under-dog, watch-dog

OG
see
OGUE*

Saratoga, toga, yoga

OGA
see
A**

Abrogate, arrogate, interrogate, sur-rogate

OGATE
see
ATE

Doge, horologe, gamboge

OGE
see

Cyanogen, hydrogen, nitrogen, oxy-hydrogen

OGEN
see
EN

Boggle, goggle, horn-swoggle, joggle, woggle

OGGLE
see
EL
LE

Boggy, doggy, foggy, groggy, soggy **OGGY**
see
E**

Geologic, logic, pedagogic, philologic **OGIC**
see
IC

Anthologist, apologist, bacteriol- **OGIST**
ogist, biologist, craniologist, entomol- *see*
ogist, etymologist, fossilologist, geol- IST
ogist, graphologist, neurologist, ontol-
ogist, ornothologist, philologist, phre-
nologist, physiologist, psychologist,
sinologist, teratologist

Bologne, Bourgogne, eau de Cologne **OGNE**
see
ONE*

Ideogram, kilogram, monogram, **OGRAM**
parallelogram, program, radiogram, *see*
seismogram AM

Ogre **OGRE**
see
ER

Analogue, apologue, catalogue, Dec- **OGUE***
alogue, demagogue, dialogue, duo- *see*
logue, eclogue, epilogue, monologue, OG
mystagogue, pedagogue, prologue, pro-
rogue, sinologue, theologue, travelogue

Brogue, rogue, vogue **OGUE****
see

Amphilogy, analogy, eulogy, fogy, **OGY**
genealogy, logy, mineralogy, pedagogy, *see*
stogy, tetralogy, trilogy E**
OLOGY

Oh, Pharaoh, Shiloh	**OH** *see* O*
Kohl	**OHL** *see* OL
Demi-john, Prester John	**OHN** *see* ON
Hoi polloi, Borzoi, Tolstoi	**OI** *see* OY
Choice, invoice, joice, rejoice, voice	**OICE** *see* *ed*-OIST S-EZ
Alkaloid, aneroid, anthropoid, aster-oid, avoid, celluloid, deltoid, devoid, ichthyoid, mattoid, negroid, ornithoid, planetoid, rhomboid, spheroid, tab-loid, thyroid, typhoid, void	**OID** *see* OY-*ed*
Coif	**OIF** *see* OFF
Coign	**OIGN** *see* OIN
Boil, broil, cinquefoil, coil, despoil, embroil, foil, free-soil, fusel oil, hard-boil, midnight-oil, oil, panbroil, par-	**OIL** *see* OYLE

boil, quatrefoil, recoil, roil, salad-oil, **OIL**
soil, spark coil, spoil, subsoil, tinfoil,
toil, trefoil, turmoil, uncoil

Benzoin, coin, disjoin, enjoin, groin, **OIN**
heroin, join, loin, purloin, rejoin, sir-   *see*
loin, subjoin, tenderloin   OIGN

Heroine, Macedoine   **OINE**
see
INE

Anoint, appoint, dewpoint, disap-   **OINT**
point, fingerpoint, joint, needlepoint,   *see*
point, spear-point, standpoint, start-   *ed*-ED
ing-point, vanishing-point, viewpoint,
vowel point, West Point

Choir   **OIR***
see
IRE

Boudoir, memoir, peignoir, recevoir,   **OIR****
rouge et noir   *see*
AR*

Armoire, bête noire, Directoire, es-   **OIRE**
critoire, Grimoire, pourboire, reper-   *see*
toire   OIR**

Avoirdupois, chamois, Marguerite   **OIS**
de Valois, patois   *see*

Counterpoise, equipoise, noise, poise,   **OISE**
porpoise, tortoise, turquoise   *see*
OY-*s*

Foist, hoist, joist, moist

OIST
see
OICE-*d*

Adroit, exploit, maladroit, quoit

OIT
see

Amok, O.K., Ragnarok, Zadok

OK
see
OCK

Artichoke, awoke, bespoke, bloke, broke, choke, coke, convoke, downstroke, evoke, fog-smoke, invoke, joke, moke, poke, provoke, revoke, Roanoke, smoke, spoke, stoke, stroke, sunstroke, upstroke, woke, yoke

OKE
see
OAK
OLK
OQUE
en-OKEN
s-OAX

Bespoken, betoken, broken, Hoboken, outspoken, plainspoken, spoken, token, unspoken

OKEN
see
EN

Broker, choker, croker, joker, pawnbroker, poker, soker, stockbroker, stoker

OKER
see
ER

Alcohol, Bath kol, carol, consol, control, entresol, extol, fal-de-rol, frijol, gambol, horse-pistol, idol, lysol, menthol, old Sol, parasol, patrol, petrol, pistol, protocol, Sebastopol, self-control, symbol, systol, Tyrol

OL
see
IOL
OLE
ULL**
ed-OLD

Cupola, dongola, gondola, gorgonzola, Loyola, parabola, pergola, pianola, Pico della Mirandola, Romola, Savonarola, victrola, viola, Zola

OLA
see
A**

Chocolate, desolate, disconsolate, etiolate, inviolate, isolate, percolate, violate

OLATE
see
ATE

Age-old, behold, blindfold, bold, Childe Harold, Cloth of Gold, cold, cuckold, enfold, finegold, fold, foothold, foretold, fourfold, gold, hold, household, hundredfold, kobold, manifold, marigold, marsh marigold, mold, molten-gold, ninefold, old, scaffold, scold, sevenfold, sheepfold, sold, stonecold, stranglehold, stronghold, tenfold, thousandfold, threefold, threshold, told, unfold, untold, uphold, withhold, wold

OLD
see
OULD*
OL-*ed*
OLE-*d*
y-E**

Bolder, cigarette-holder, colder, folder, holder, landholder, older, shareholder, smolder

OLDER
see
ER

Air-hole, aureole, barberpole, barcarole, blowhole, bunghole, cajole, camisole, casserole, cigarette-hole, cole, condole, console, Creole, cubby-hole, dole, drole, girandole, glory-hole, groundmole, hole, keyhole, loophole, manhole, mole, North Pole, Old King Cole, oriole, parole, peephole, pigeonhole, pin-hole, pistole, pole, port-hole, ridge-pole, rigmarole, role, Seminole, sole, South Pole, tadpole, tent-pole, thole, totem-pole, whole

OLE*
see
OAL
OL
OLL*
OUL**
ed-OL-*ed*
OLD

Hyperbole, frijole

OLE**
see
E**

Indolent, insolent, malevolent, redo-   **OLENT**
lent, somnolent, violent   *see*
                                            ENT

Golf, werewolf, wolf   **OLF**
                                            see

Argoli, broccoli, Gallipoli, Rivoli,   **OLI**
tivoli   *see*
                                            I**

Anatolia,   magnolia,   melancholia,   **OLIA**
Mongolia   *see*
                                            IA

Alcoholic, bucolic, carbolic, catholic, **OLIC**
colic, diabolic, frolic, non-alcoholic,   *see*
parabolic, symbolic   IC

Semi-solid, solid, stolid   **OLID**
                                            see
                                            ID

Etiolin, lanolin, mandolin, violin   **OLIN**
                                            see
                                            IN

Folio, olio, portfolio   **OLIO**
                                            see
                                            IO

Acropolis, Annapolis, anolis, Heliop-   **OLIS**
olis, metropolis, necropolis, Persepolis   *see*
                                            IS*

Abolish, coolish, demolish, foolish,   **OLISH**
polish   *see*
                                            ISH

Country-folk, fisher-folk, folk, gen-
tle-folk, kinsfolk, yolk

OLK
see
OQUE
S-OAX

Boll, breakfast-roll, droll, enroll,
knoll, mossy-knoll, muster-roll, pay-
roll, roll, scroll, stroll, toll, troll, unroll

OLL*
see
OLE
OUL**

Doll, loll, moll, poll

OLL**
see

Collar, dollar, trade dollar

OLLAR
see
AR

Dolly, folly, holly, jolly, polly, sea
holly

OLLY
see
E**

Coco-bolo, Fra Diavolo, gigolo,
Marco Polo, piccolo, polo, solo, trem-
olo, water polo

OLO
see
O*

Anthology, apology, archæology,
astro-theology, biology, bryology,
Christology, chronology, cryptology,
dactylology, demonology, dermatol-
ogy, doxology, Egyptology, eschatol-
ogy, ethnology, etymology, geology,
glossology, graphology, hagiology, ho-
mology, horology, ichthyology, ideol-
ogy, lexicology, martyrology, meteor-
ology, metrology, morphology, myth-
ology, neology, nephology, nostology,
numerology, odontology, ontology,

OLOGY
see
OGY

oölogy, ornithology, orthology, osteol- **OLOGY**
ogy, pathology, penology, philology,
photology, phraseology, phrenology,
physiology, psychology, pyramidology,
seismology, sinology, tautology, tech-
nology, teleology, teratology, termi-
nology, theology, toxicology, zoölogy

Ben Bolt, bolt, colt, dolt, iron-bolt, **OLT**
jolt, king-bolt, micro-volt, molt, revolt, *see*
thunderbolt, volt

Absolute, dissolute, irresolute, reso- **OLUTE**
lute, volute *see*
UTE

Absolve, devolve, dissolve, evolve, **OLVE**
involve, resolve, revolve, solve *see*

Absolver, dissolver, resolver, re- **OLVER**
volver *see*
ER

Holy, melancholy, moly, monopoly, **OLY**
roly-poly, unholy *see*
E**

Accustom, besom, blossom, bore- **OM***
dom, bosom, bottom, buxom, carda- *see*
mom, carom, Christendom, Chrysos- EUM
tom, cockneydom, custom, Edom, em- IUM
bosom, envenom, Epsom, fathom, free- OME*
dom, from, hansom, heathendom, king- OSM
dom, lissom, maelstrom, martyrdom, UM
officialdom, Om, Peeping Tom, phan-
tom, Pithom, pogrom, random, ransom,
rock bottom, rush-bottom, serfdom,

Sodom, stardom, symptom, thralldom, tomtom, unbosom, venom, whilom, wisdom **OM***

Whom **OM*** *see* OOM

Aroma, coma, diploma, La Paloma, Oklahoma, pleroma, Point Loma, soma **OMA** *see* A***

Dragoman, Ottoman, toman, woman, yeoman **OMAN** *see* AN*

Aplomb, bomb, rhomb **OMB*** *see*

Catacomb, comb, coxcomb, curry-comb, hecatomb, honey-comb, tomb, uncomb, womb **OMB*** *see* UMB

Become, blithesome, burdensome, come, cumbersome, fearsome, four-some, frolicsome, gladsome, gruesome, handsome, income, irksome, lissome, loathsome, lonesome, meddlesome, mettlesome, noisome, outcome, over-come, quarrelsome, rollicksome, some, tiresome, toilsome, toothsome, trouble-some, venturesome, wearisome, well-come, wholesome, winsome **OME*** *see* IUM OM* UM UMN

Chrome, dome, gnome, hippodrome, home, metronome, monochrome, palin-drome, polychrome, Rome, St. Jerome, tome, vela-drome, Vendome **OME*** *see* OAM

Abdomen, cognomen, omen, women **OMEN**
see
EN

Astronomer, customer, Homer, in-comer, misnomer, newcomer, omer **OMER**
see
ER

Comet, Mahomet **OMET**
see
ET

Atomic, comic, economic, gastro-nomic, gnomic, serio-comic **OMIC**
see
IC

Blossoming, coming, homing, in-coming, on-coming, spring-blossoming, Wyoming **OMING**
see
ING

Chromo, Como, Ecce Homo, major-domo **OMO**
see
O*

Pomp, romp **OMP**
see
AMP**

Prompt **OMPT**
see

Anatomy, antinomy, economy, phle-botomy, physiognomy, zoötomy **OMY**
see
E**

Abandon, æon, Agamemnon, Ajalon, Anglo-Saxon, anon, antiphon, apron, Armageddon, Ascalon, Audubon, au-tomaton, Avalon, Avignon, Babylon, **ON**
see
AGON
AN**

backgammon, bacon, barbiton, baron, beckon, be-ribbon, blue-ribbon, bon-bon, bon-ton, bouillon, Bourbon, boustrophedon, caisson, call-upon, cannon, canon, canton, capon, carbon, carillon, carry on, cauldron, cedar of Lebanon, Celadon, Ceylon, chanson, Charon, chevron, chiffon, chiton, cinnamon, citron, colon, common, cordon, corydon, cotillon, cotton, coupon, crimson, crouton, damson, Demogorgon, Devon, dodecahedron, don, donjon, egg-on, eidolon, electron, emblazon, Emerson, epsilon, falcon, fanfaron, gallon, gibbon, gnomon, goings-on, gonfalon, Gorgon, grandson, griffon, gryphon, guerdon, guncotton, hanger-on, head-on, Hebron, horizon, Huron, jargon, Jupiter Ammon, klaxon, Kwannon, Lacedæmon, Laocōon, Lisbon, London, Mammon, marathon, matron, Memnon, mescal button, mignon, Milton, Mme. de Maintenon, Mormon, moron, Mother Shipton, myrmidon, neuron, Nippon, non, Oberon, on, pardon, parson, patron, pennon, person, phaëton, phenomenon, Phlegethon, piston, plastron, pompon, Poseidon, Princeton, pro and con, prolegomenon, python, rayon, reckon, rhododendron, ribbon, Rimmon, sabbaton, saffron, salmon, salon, Samson, Sanchoniathon, Sandalphon, Sargon, Saxon, semi-colon, sermon, sexton, Sheraton, Sidon, Simple Simon, simpleton, siphon, Solomon, Solon, son, soupçon, squadron, Stevenson, summon, talon, tampon, tarpon,

ON

ASON
AZON
EACON
EASON
ELON
EMON
EON
ERON
ETON
ICON
ION
IRON
ISON
ODON
OHN
ONE***
OPHON
UAN
UN
UTTON
YLON
YON
ed-UND

tendon, Tennyson, tetragrammaton, thereupon, torchon, Trianon, trilithon, triton, trogon, Typhon, uncommon, upon, wagon, wanton, Washington, weapon, welsh-mutton, whereon, yon, Yukon, zircon

ON

Arizona, Barcelona, Bellona, chincona, corona, Cremona, Crotona, Desdemona, Dodona, Latona, madrona, Pomona, Verona

ONA
see
A**

Ammonal, conditional, confessional, congressional, coronal, denominational, devotional, diagonal, dimensional, emotional, fourth dimensional, functional, gravitational, hexagonal, impersonal, international, meridional, national, notional, occasional, octagonal, optional, precessional, processional, prohibitional, rational, recessional, regional, seasonal, septentrional, sulphonal, traditional, unconditional, vegetational, veronal, visional

ONAL
see
AL

Dictionary, legionary, missionary, pulmonary, reactionary, revolutionary, stationary, visionary

ONARY
see
ARY

Donate, detonate, impersonate, intonate, passionate, pulmonate

ONATE
see
ATE

Once

ONCE*
see
UNCE

Ensconce, nonce, sconce | **ONCE****
see
ONSE

Conch | **ONCH**
see
ONK

Abscond, almond, baby bond, be- | **OND**
yond, blond, bond, correspond, de- | *see*
spond, diamond, fond, frond, Phara- | AND**
mond, pond, reedy-pond, respond,
Richmond, second, Slough of Despond,
split-second, Trebizond, vagabond

Anaconda, Gioconda, Golconda | **ONDA**
see
A**

Fonder, ponder, wonder, yonder | **ONDER**
see
ER

Alcyone, alone, anti-cyclone, atone, | **ONE***
backbone, baritone, barkstone, blood- | *see*
stone, bone, breast-bone, brimstone, | OWN*
brownstone, canzone, capstone, chap-
erone, cheekbone, cicerone, cobble-
stone, condone, cone, cornerstone,
crone, crossbone, curbstone, cyclone,
dethrone, dictaphone, doorstone,
drone, fir-cone, fishbone, foundation-
stone, freestone, frozen zone, funny-
bone, gramophone, graphophone,
gravestone, grindstone, half-tone,
headstone, hearthstone, herringbone,
holystone, hone, intone, jackstone,

jawbone, keystone, knucklebone, La-   **ONE***
drone, limestone, megaphone, memo-
rial-stone, microphone, milestone, mill-
stone, monotone, moonstone, neurone,
oilstone, outshone, overtone, ozone,
ozytone, padrone, paroxytone, philosopher's stone, phone, postpone, prone,
rawbone, rolling-stone, Rosetta stone,
sandstone, saxophone, scone, semitone,
shin-bone, shone, soapstone, stepping-
stone, stone, throne, tombstone, tone,
torrid-zone, tottering-throne, trom-
bone, undertone, whalebone, whet-
stone, xylophone, Yellowstone, zone

Agone, begone, bygone, gone, woe-   **ONE****
begone   *see*
                                         AWN

Done, none, one, outdone, overdone,   **ONE*****
someone, underdone, undone, welldone   *see*
                                         UN

Component, exponent, opponent   **ONENT**
                                         see
                                         ENT

Almoner, executioner, falconer, prac-   **ONER**
titioner, wagoner   *see*
                                         ER

Nones, sawbones   **ONES**
                                         see
                                         ONE-*s*

Baronet, bayonet, canzonet, clari-   **ONET**
onet, coronet   *see*
                                         ET

Honey, money, papermoney, pin-money

ONEY
see
EY

Age-long, along, among, belong, cradle-song, ding-dong, erelong, even-song, folksong, furlong, gong, head-long, headstrong, Hong Kong, livelong, long, mah-jong, oblong, oolong, ping-pong, prolong, prong, sarong, sidelong, singsong, siren's song, so-long, song, strong, swan song, thong, throng, tong, warsong, wrong

ONG
see
ONGUE
UNG

Sponge

ONGE
see
UNGE

Mother-tongue, ox-tongue, sacred tongue, silver tongue, tongue

ONGUE
see
ONG
UGN

Macaroni, Marconi, Zanoni, yoni

ONI
see
I**

Ammonia, begonia, Caledonia, Fran-conia, Harmonia, Macedonia, Pata-gonia, pneumonia

ONIA
see
IA

Bubonic, chronic, cyclonic, demonic, diatonic, electronic, harmonic, histri-onic, iconic, Ionic, ironic, laconic, mnemonic, moronic, Platonic, phil-harmonic, polyphonic, sardonic, Sla-vonic, symphonic, telephonic, Teu-tonic, tonic

ONIC
see
IC

Adonis, Coronis, Draconis	**ONIS** *see* IS*
Anachronism, antagonism, exhibitionism, hedonism, reactionism, synchronism, unionism	**ONISM** *see* ISM
Abolitionist, antagonist, cartoonist, hedonist, impressionist, protagonist	**ONIST** *see* IST
Agonize, canonize, carbonize, colonize, harmonize, lionize, patronize	**ONIZE** *see* IZE
Honk, monk	**ONK** *see* UNK
Commonly, matronly, only, wantonly	**ONLY** *see* E**
Belladonna, Madonna, primadonna, Vittoria Colonna	**ONNA** *see* A**
Carcassonne, Sorbonne	**ONNE** *see* ON
Absonous, anachronous, autochthonous, cacophonous, gluttonous, poisonous, synchronous	**ONOUS** *see* OUS

Blazonry, falconry, freemasonry, masonry, solid masonry

ONRY
see
E**

Response

ONSE
see
ONCE

Confront, dont, font, front, Helles-pont, shirtfront, water-front, wont

ONT
see
ANT**
UNT

Billionth, millionth, month, tril-lionth, twelfth-month

ONTH
see

Acrimony, agony, agrimony, ali-mony, antimony, antiphony, balcony, betony, bony, bryony, cacophony, ceremony, chalcedony, colony, crony, disharmony, ebony, euphony, felony, gluttony, harmony, hegemony, inhar-mony, irony, Mark Anthony, monot-ony, nudist colony, parsimony, patri-mony, peony, phony, pony, scammony, Shetland pony, testimony, theogony

ONY
see
E**

Anonym, caconym, pseudonym, synonym

ONYM
see
IM

Bonze, bronze

ONZE
see

Ballyhoo, bamboo, bazoo, boo, boo-hoo, Bronx-Zoo, cockatoo, coo-coo, cuckoo, goo-goo, halloo, hoodoo, hulla-balloo, igloo, kangaroo, karoo, moo,

OO
see
ABOO
O**

shampoo, shoo, skidoo, tattoo, tick-tack-too, too, toodle-oo, voodoo, Waterloo, Whangpoo, woo, yoo-hoo, zoo

OO
OUGH****
U

Boob

OOB
see
UBE

Brooch, hooch, mooch, scooch

OOCH
see

Basswood, blueblood, boxwood, briarwood, brushwood, camphorwood, candlewood, childhood, cottonwood, cypress wood, deadwood, dogwood, driftwood, firewood, good, gopher wood, greenwood, hardihood, holyrood, hood, ironwood, kindling-wood, knighthood, likelihood, livelihood, logwood, matchwood, misunderstood, monkhood, motherhood, neighborhood, no good, priesthood, Red Riding Hood, redwood, Robin Hood, rosewood, sandal-wood, satinwood, selfhood, stood, teakwood, understood, Wedgwood, wildwood, withstood, wood

OOD*
see
OULD

Blood, blueblood, cold blood, flood

OOD**
see
UD

Brood, food, mood, rood, snood, solid food

OOD***
see
UDE

Broody, goody, moody, woody

OODY
see
E**

Aloof, bombproof, bulletproof, dis-proof, fireproof, foolproof, galley-proof, gas-proof, high-proof, hoof, proof, rain-proof, reproof, roof, shadoof, spoof, waterproof, woof

OOF
see

Scrooge, stooge

OOGE
see
UGE

Pooh-pooh

OOH
see
OO

Betook, book, brook, buttonhook, cook, crook, doomsday book, fishhook, forsook, guide-book, hook, Holy Book, ingle-nook, log-book, look, minnowy-brook, mistook, murmuring-brook, nook, nuthook, outlook, overlook, pocketbook, pothook, prayerbook, psalm-book, Sandy Hook, school book, scrapbook, shepherd's crook, shook, sketch book, story-book, tenterhook, textbook, took, undertook, unhook, visitor's book

OOK*
see

Nansook, spook

OOK**
see
UKE

Gadzooks

OOKS
see

April-fool, campstool, cool, cotton-wool, drool, ducking-stool, faldstool, finishing-school, fool, footstool, Liver-pool, millpool, mineral wool, pool, rock

OOL
see
OUL***
ULE

wool, school, spool, stool, Sunday
school, swimming-pool, toadstool, tool,
whirlpool, wool

OOL

Ante-room, bloom, book room, boom,
bridegroom, broadloom, broom, club
room, doom, elbow-room, foredoom,
gloom, greenroom, grillroom, groom,
guest-room, heirloom, jib-boom, keep-
ing-room, loom, messroom, mushroom,
show-room, smoke-room, spare-room,
stateroom, store-room, taproom, wait-
ing-room, zoom

OOM
see
OM**
OMB***
UME

Bloomer, roomer

OOMER
see
ER

Afternoon, anæmic-moon, aswoon,
baboon, balloon, bassoon, boon, buf-
foon, cartoon, cocoon, coon, croon,
curved-moon, doubloon, dragoon, eft-
soon, festoon, forenoon, galloon, half-
moon, harpoon, harvest moon, honey-
moon, hunter's moon, lagoon, lampoon,
loon, macaroon, maroon, monsoon,
moon, mushroon, new moon, noon,
octoroon, pale-moon, Pantaloon, pica-
roon, platoon, poltroon, pontoon,
quadroon, raccoon, Rangoon, rigadoon,
saloon, sandal-shoon, shalloon, shoon,
silverspoon, simoon, soon, spittoon,
spoon, swoon, teaspoon, typhoon,
woodenspoon, zoon

OON
see
EWN
UNE

Crooner, honeymooner, schooner,
spooner

OONER
see
ER

Coop, droop, goop, hen-coop, hoop, loop, nincompoop, poop, scoop, scroop, sloop, snoop, stoop, swoop, troop, war-hoop, whoop

OOP
see
OUP
OUPE**
UPE

Barndoor, door, floor, indoor, next-door, stage-door, threshing-floor, trap-door, waxed-floor

OOR*
see
OR

Blackamoor, boor, Kohinoor, land-poor, moor, poor, spoor

OOR**
see
URE

Burnoose, caboose, calaboose, choose, goose, loose, mongoose, moose, Mother Goose, noose, papoose, unloose, va-moose

OOSE
see
UCE*
USE*

Tarboosh

OOSH
see

Boost, roost

OOST
see

Afoot, alumroot, arrowroot, bandi-coot, barefoot, bitter-root, bloodroot, boot, cahoot, calamus-root, cheroot, coot, crowfoot, cube root, eryngo root, flagroot, flatfoot, forefoot, hoot, hot-foot, lightfoot, loot, moot, offshoot, overshoot, presser foot, pussyfoot, root, scoot, shoot, snakeroot, snoot, soot, splayfoot, square root, taproot, tenderfoot, toot, underfoot, uproot, webfoot

OOT
see
UIT**
UT*
ed-ED

Booth, buck-tooth, eye-tooth, for-sooth, smooth, sooth, tooth, walrus-tooth

OOTH
see
OUTH*

Booty, snooty, sooty

OOTY
see
E**

Behoove, groove

OOVE
see
OVE***

Booze, ooze, snooze

OOZE
see
USE*

Æsop, archbishop, bishop, bucket-shop, chimney-top, chop, cop, crop, Cyclop, develop, dewdrop, drop, ear-drop, eavesdrop, flop, forest-top, gal-lop, grogshop, gumdrop, hop, house-top, hyssop, lollypop, lop, milksop, mop, Mrs. Malaprop, non-stop, organ-stop, orlop, overdevelop, overtop, pawnshop, pegtop, plop, pop, pork-chop, prop, raindrop, scallop, shallop, shop, shortstop, slip slop, slop, snow-drop, stop, strop, sweatshop, sweetsop, swop, teardrop, tip-top, top, tree-top, trollop, wallop, whop, wild-hyssop, workshop

OP
see
AP**
UP
ed-OPT
s-OPS

Copal, episcopal, opal

OPAL
see
AL

Allopath, homeopath, neuropath, osteopath   **OPATH** *see* ATH

Antelope, bellrope, Cape of Good Hope, chromoscope, cope, cymoscope, dope, electroscope, elope, envelope, grope, guyrope, heliotrope, hope, horoscope, interlope, kaleidoscope, kinetoscope, microscope, mirrorscope, misanthrope, mope, moviescope, myope, ope, periscope, pope, pyrope, rope, scope, slope, stanhope, spectroscope, syncope, telescope, tight-rope, trope, wire-rope   **OPE*** *see* OAP

Calliope, Merope, Parthenope, Penelope   **OPE**** *see* E*

Catastrophe   **OPHE*** *see* E*

Antistrophe, strophe   **OPHE**** *see* OAF

Gopher, philosopher, St. Christopher   **OPHER** *see* ER

Bellerophon, colophon, Zenophon   **OPHON** *see* ON

Anthroposophy, atrophy, philosophy, theosophy, trophy   **OPHY** *see* E**

Cornucopia, Ethiopia, Utopia   **OPIA**
see
IA

Canopic, Ethiopic, kaleidoscopic, **OPIC**
microscopic, myopic, philanthropic, *see*
telescopic, topic, tropic   IC

Chopper, clodhopper, copper, corn- **OPPER**
popper, cropper, grasshopper, hopper, *see*
topper, whopper, woodchopper   ER

Choppy, floppy, poppy, sloppy, **OPPY**
soppy   *see*
E**

Cecrops, Cheops, cyclops, Ops, Pe- **OPS**
lops   *see*
OP-*s*

Copse   **OPSE**
see
OPE-*s*

Ampelopsis, calliopsis, coreopsis, **OPSIS**
synopsis, thanatopsis   *see*
IS*

Adopt, coöpt, Copt, epopt, opt   **OPT**
see
OP-*ed*

Canopus, magnum opus, octopus, **OPUS**
opus, Rhodopus   *see*
US

Baroque, toque **OQUE**
see
OKE

Colloquy, obloquy, soliloquy **OQUY**
see
E**

Abettor, abhor, ancestor, anchor, **OR**
antecessor, arbor, armor, Asia Minor, *see*
author, bachelor, boa-constrictor, cam- ACTOR
phor, candor, cantor, captor, carbure- ADOR
tor, Castor, censor, chancellor, clangor, AMOR
color, condor, conductor, confessor, ATOR
councilor, counselor, conveyor, de- AUR
meanor, discolor, doctor, done for, ECTOR
donor, dor, endeavor, Endor, ephor, IDOR
error, father-confessor, favor, fervor, IOR
flavor, for, governor, Hathor, honor, ITOR
horror, humor, ichor, impostor, in- OAR
structor, inventor, labor, languor, liquor, OOR*
lor', louis d'or, Luxor, major, manor, ORE
mayor, mentor, metaphor, meteor, OUR**
milor, minor, mirror, misdemeanor, UTOR
motor, Mount Tabor, neighbor, Nes- *ed*-OARD
tor, non-conductor, nor, odor, off-color, ORD*
oppressor, or, pallor, parlor, pastor, *s*-ORES
phosphor, preceptor, predecessor, pre- ORS
sentor, proctor, professor, proprietor,
protestor, purveyor, rancor, razor,
rector, reflector, rigor, rumor, sailor,
savor, sculptor, sector, señor, sheet
anchor, social error, splendor, sponsor,
squalor, straw-color, stupor, successor,
succor, suitor, supervisor, surveyor,
survivor, technicolor, tenor, terror,
Thor, tor, tormentor, tremor, tricolor,

Tudor, unlooked-for, Ursa Major, Ursa Minor, valor, vapor, vendor, victor, vigor, visor, watercolor, Windsor

OR

Agora, amphora, angora, aurora, carnivora, Cora, Diaspora, fedora, flora, Leonora, mandragora, Marmora, Pandora, plethora, signora, sora

ORA
see
A**

Anchorage, borage, forage, harborage, storage

ORAGE
see
AGE

Balmoral, caporal, chloral, choral, coral, corporal, floral, immoral, littoral, moral, oral, pastoral, pectoral, temporal

ORAL
see
AL

Anaxagoras, Pythagoras

ORAS
see
AS

Ameliorate, commemorate, corporate, corroborate, deteriorate, directorate, elaborate, evaporate, expectorate, incorporate, invigorate, meliorate, pastorate, perforate, perorate, protectorate, reinvigorate

ORATE
see
ATE

Absorb, orb, resorb, sorb

ORB
see

Divorce, enforce, force, perforce, reinforce, tour de force

ORCE
see
ORSE*

Blowtorch, porch, scorch, torch

ORCH
see

Accord, afford, broadsword, chord, clavichord, concord, cord, discord, ford, harpsichord, Hartford, hexachord, lord, monochord, Norwegian fiord, overlord, Oxford, record, sword, war-lord, whip-cord

ORD*
see
OARD
ORDE
ORE-*d*
ed-ED

By-word, catchword, crossword, foreword, one-word, password, watch-word, word

ORD**
see
EARD*
ERD
IRD
URD

Horde

ORDE
see
ORD

Border, corder, disorder, order, re-corder

ORDER
see
ER

Adore, afore, alongshore, ashore, battledore, before, bore, chain-store, chore, coldsore, commodore, core, de-plore, drug-store, encore, evermore, explore, folk-lore, fore, foreshore, four-score, furore, furthermore, galore, gore, hellebore, heretofore, ignore, implore, inshore, lore, more, nevermore, off-shore, ore, pebbled-shore, pinafore, pore, restore, score, semaphore, shore, Singapore, snore, sophomore, sore, spore, stevedore, store, sycamore, Ta-gore, Terpsichore, therefore, threescore, tore, underscore, wherefore, whore, wore, yore

ORE
see
IOR
OAR
OOR*
OR
OUR**
ed-OARD
ORD*
s-ORES

Ad valorem, theorem **OREM**
see
EM

Swedenborg **ORG**
see

Disgorge, drop-forge, St. George, **ORGE**
gorge *see*

Morgue **ORGUE**
see

Gloria, noria, phantasmagoria, Victoria **ORIA**
see
IA

Armorial, consistorial, dictatorial, **ORIAL**
editorial, gladiatorial, gubernatorial, *see*
immemorial, inspectorial, memorial, IAL
phantasmagorial, pictorial, piscatorial,
purgatorial, sartorial, senatorial, sensorial, territorial, tonsorial

Dorian, gregorian, historian, salutatorian, stentorian, valedictorian **ORIAN**
see
IAN

Allegoric, Amoric, amphoric, boric, **ORIC**
caloric, Doric, historic, paregoric, plethoric, prehistoric, rhetoric, toric *see*
IC

Anteriority, authority, inferiority, **ORITY**
majority, minority, priority, sonority, *see*
sorority, superiority E**
ITY

Auditorium, emporium, moratorium, sanatorium, scriptorium

ORIUM
see
IUM

Cork, fork, New York, pitchfork, pork, stork, tuning fork, York

ORK*
see

All-work, basketwork, brickwork, butcher-work, clock-work, earthwork, fancywork, field-work, framework, fretwork, frostwork, groundwork, guesswork, handiwork, hard work, needlework, network, open-work, overwork, schoolwork, scrollwork, stonework, trellis-work, trestlework, waxwork, welfare work, wickerwork, work

ORK**
see
ERK

Schorl, whorl

ORL
see
URL

Netherworld, underworld, upperworld, world

ORLD
see
IRL-*ed*
URL-*ed*

Barnstorm, chloroform, conform, deform, dust-storm, form, inform, iodoform, misinform, norm, perform, platform, reform, sandstorm, sea-storm, snowstorm, thought-form, thunderstorm, transform

ORM
see
ARM**
IFORM

Angleworm, armyworm, bookworm, earthworm, glow-worm, grubworm, inchworm, silkworm

ORM**
see
ERM
IRM

Formal, informal, normal, subnormal, supernormal

ORMAL
see
AL

Acorn, adorn, barleycorn, baseborn, bicorn, bighorn, blackthorn, born, broomcorn, buckthorn, bugle-horn, Cape Horn, Capricorn, careworn, corn, drinking-horn, earthborn, firstborn, foghorn, footworn, forsworn, freeborn, goat's horn, greenhorn, hartshorn, hawthorn, horn, inborn, Leghorn, longhorn, lorn, manor born, morn, newborn, Norn, outworn, overworn, popcorn, powder horn, pronghorn, ram's horn, saxhorn, scorn, seaborn, shoehorn, shopworn, shorn, shorthorn, staghorn, stubborn, suborn, sweetcorn, sworn, thorn, twice-born, unborn, unicorn, unshorn, water-born, war-torn, wayworn, worn

ORN
see
ARN**
OURN

Amorous, carnivorous, dolorous, glamorous, humorous, languorous, malodorous, odorous, omnivorous, phosphorous, porous, rancorous, rigorous, sonorous, stertorous, vigorous

OROUS
see
OUS

Dorp, thorp

ORP
see
ARP**

Corpse

ORPSE
see
ORP-*s*

Lorry, sorry, worry

ORRY
see
E**

Scissors **ORS**
see
OR-*s*

Clotheshorse, cockhorse, gorse, **ORSE**
hobby-horse, horse, indorse, Norse, *see*
race-horse, remorse, rockinghorse, saw- ORCE
horse, seahorse, stalking-horse, stud- OURCE
horse, worse

Worst **ORST**
see
ERST
URST

Abort, assort, bellwort, cavort, co- **ORT**
hort, colewort, comfort, comport, con- *see*
sort, contort, davenport, deport, dis- ART**
comfort, disport, distort, effort, escort, OURT
exhort, export, extort, field-sport, fig- UART
wort, fort, gipsywort, import, liver- *ed*-ED
wort, mugwort, passport, port, pur-
port, report, resort, retort, ribwort,
seaport, short, snort, sort, spiderwort,
sport, support, transport, what sort

Immortal, mortal, portal **ORTAL**
see
AL

Ottoman Porte, Sublime Porte **ORTE**
see
ORT

Exporter, importer, porter, reporter, **ORTER**
shorter, sorter, supporter *see*
ER

Forth, go-forth, henceforth, Kenil- **ORTH**
worth, north, thenceforth, Words- *see*
worth, worth ARTH
OURTH

Decorum, forum, pons asinorum, **ORUM**
quorum, Roman Forum, sanctum *see*
sanctorum UM

Apollodorus, Bosphorus, chorus, hel- **ORUS**
leborus, Horus, phosphorus *see*
US

Accessory, allegory, armory, audi- **ORY**
tory, category, chicory, compulsory, *see*
cursory, desultory, directory, dormi- ATORY
tory, dory, evocatory, factory, fish- E**
story, ghost-story, glory, gory, hickory,
history, illusory, introductory, inven-
tory, invocatory, ivory, lory, memory,
morning-glory, non-compulsory, offer-
tory, Old Glory, olfactory, peremp-
tory, perfunctory, pillory, porphory,
pre-inventory, priory, promissory,
promontory, rectory, refectory, refrac-
tory, repository, satisfactory, savory,
sensory, short-story, story, succory,
territory, theory, tory, transitory,
vainglory, valedictory, vapory, victory

Abydos, Anteros, Argos, asbestos, **OS**
Atropos, Barbados, bathos, Bucepha- *see*
los, caballeros, chaos, Chronos, cosmos, IOS
dithyrambos, Encelados, Eos, epos, OSS
Eros, Galapagos, Hyksos, Hypnos,
Lemnos, Lesbos, logos, Minos, Mount
Athos, naos, Ninon de l'Enclos, Om-

phalos, os, Parthenos, pathos, Patmos,   **OS**
Patroclos, Pergamos, pharos, Psycho-
pompos, pueblos, reredos, rhinoceros,
Samos, S.O.S., Tantalos, Tenedos,
thanatos, thermos, Triptolemos

Amorosa, Formosa, Mater Dolorosa,   **OSA**
mimosa, scabiosa, sub rosa, via dolorosa   *see*
         A**

Adipose, albuminose, appose, aquose,   **OSE***
arose, bellicose, bottlenose, cellulose,   *see*
chose, close, comatose, compose, crys-   IOSE
talose, damask rose, decompose, de-   O*-*es*
pose, disclose, dispose, dose, equipose,   OE**-*s*
expose, frostnipt-nose, foreclose, glu-   OTHE-*s*
cose, hooknose, hose, impose, inclose,   OW*-*s*
interpose, jocose, juxtapose, lachry-   OWS
mose, metamorphose, morose, Nivose,   OZE
nose, oppose, overdose, overexpose,
plumose, Pluviose, pope's nose, pose,
predispose, presuppose, primrose, pro-
pose, prose, pruinose, purpose, repose,
Roman nose, rose, scapose, 'spose,
suppose, tea-rose, those, transpose,
tuberose, unclose, Ventose, verbose,
wildrose

Lose, whose   **OSE****
       see
       USE

Closet, marmoset   **OSET**
       see
       ET

Bosh, cohosh, galosh, gosh, josh, kibosh, mackintosh, Oshkosh, slosh

OSH
see
ASH**
UASH

Corrosion, erosion, explosion

OSION
see
ION

Apodosis, apotheosis, diagnosis, hypnosis, kenosis, metamorphosis, metempsychosis, necrosis, prognosis, psychoneurosis, psychosis, sorosis, tuberculosis

OSIS
see
IS*

Anfractuosity, aquosity, curiosity, generosity, gibbosity, impetuosity, jocosity, luminosity, monstrosity, nebulosity, pomposity, ponderosity, sabulosity, sinuosity, tortuosity, verbosity, virtuosity

OSITY
see
ITY

Corrosive, erosive, explosive

OSIVE
see
IVE

Bosk, kiosk

OSK
see
OSQUE

Macrocosm, microcosm

OSM
see
OM*

Amoroso, capriccioso, gracioso, Orlando Furioso, so-so, virtuoso, whoso

OSO
see
O*

Kiosque, mosque   **OSQUE**
                                                  see
                                                  OSK

Across, albatross, boss, bugloss,   **OSS**
Charing-Cross, criss-cross, cross, dou-   *see*
ble-cross, dross, emboss, engross, Flor-   AUCE
ida moss, floss, gloss, golden-cross,   OS
gross, hoss, iron cross, joss, loss, moss,   OSSE
peat-moss, Red Cross, Southern Cross,
toss

Fosse, lacrosse, posse   **OSSE**
                                                  see
                                                  OSS

Bossy, flossy, glossy, mossy   **OSSY**
                                                  see
                                                  E**

Accost, Bifrost, cost, defrost, em-   **OST***
bost, frost, hoarfrost, Jack Frost, long-   *see*
lost, lost, Pentecost   AUST
                                                  ed-ED

Almost, easternmost, foremost,   **OST****
ghost, hindermost, host, impost, in-   *see*
most, innermost, middlemost, mile-   OAST
post, most, nethermost, northernmost,
outpost, parcel post, post, provost,
signpost, southernmost, topmost, up-
permost, utmost, westernmost, whip-
ping-post

Apostle, jostle, throstle   **OSTLE**
                                                  see
                                                  EL
                                                  LE

Closure, composure, disclosure, en-   **OSURE**
closure, exposure, foreclosure, inclo-   *see*
sure, overexposure, underexposure   URE

Argosy, nosy, posy, prosy, rosy   **OSY**
                                              see
                                           E**

Euphrosyne, Mnemosyne   **OSYNE**
                                              see
                                           E*

All-hot, allot, apricot, ballot, begot,   **OT***
bergamot, bloodshot, blot, bowknot,   *see*
bowshot, buckshot, Camelot, carrot,   ACHT
coffee-pot, co-pilot, cot, despot, diglot,   AT**
divot, dot, dryrot, earshot, ergot,   ATT
fagot, fairy-grot, fleshpot, flowerpot,   IGOT
forget-me-not, forgot, foxtrot, gallipot,   IOT
Gordian-knot, got, grapeshot, grot,   OTT
harlot, helot, hot, hotspot, Hotten-   OTTE
tot, ingot, jackpot, jogtrot, jot,
knot, lot, loveknot, maggot, marmot,
marplot, mascot, monoglot, not, pale-
tot, parrot, pilot, piping hot, pivot,
plot, polyglot, pot, redhot, reef-knot,
rot, ryot, sabot, Scot, shot, slingshot,
slipknot, slot, snapshot, sot, spot, tea-
pot, tender spot, tommyrot, topknot,
tot, touch-me-not, trot, turbot, turkey-
trot, try-pot, unguent-pot, upshot,
wainscot, wateringpot, whatnot, wild-
carrot, wot, zealot

Argot, bon mot, depot, Huguenot,   **OT****
jabot, matelot, Pierrot, robot, tarot   *see*
                                           O*

Dakota, iota, Minnesota, quota, **OTA**
rota   *see*
    A**

Dotage, flotage, sabotage˙   **OTAGE**
    see
    AGE

Annotate, connotate, rotate   **OTATE**
    see
    ATE

Blotch, botch, crotch, hopscotch, **OTCH**
hot-Scotch, notch, Scotch, splotch, *see*
top-notch   ATCH**

Anecdote, antidote, banknote, ca- **OTE**
pote, chorus-note, connote, cote, coy- *see*
ote, creosote, demote, denote, devote, OAT
dote, dovecote, footnote, keynote, mis- s-OATS
quote, mote, note, quote, promote,
redingote, remote, rote, sheepcote,
smote, straw vote, table d'hote, tote,
treasury note, vote, wrote

Both, quoth, Sabbaoth, sloth, Suc- **OTH***
coth   *see*
    OATH
    OWTH

Ashtaroth, azoth, behemoth, beroth, **OTH****
betroth, broadcloth, broth, cheese- *see*
cloth, cloth, fishbroth, froth, Goth,
mammoth, moth, neckcloth, oilcloth,
sackcloth, Sephiroth, Thoth, troth,
Visigoth, wroth

Clothe

OTHE
see
OATH

Another, bother, brother, foster-mother, grandmother, half-brother, mother, other, pother, smother, step-mother, tother

OTHER
see
ER

Chaotic, demotic, despotic, epizoötic, exotic, hypnotic, idiotic, narcotic, neurotic, patriotic, quixotic

OTIC
see
IC

Commotion, devotion, emotion, lo-comotion, lotion, love potion, motion, notion, perpetual motion, potion, pro-motion, slow-motion

OTION
see
ION

Automotive, locomotive, motive, promotive

OTIVE
see
IVE

Boycott, Scott

OTT
see
OT
OTTE

Calotte, charlotte, cocotte, gavotte, sans culotte, Wyandotte

OTTE
see
OT
OTT

Bluebottle, bottle, mottle, throttle, smelling-bottle

OTTLE
see
EL
LE

Blotto, Giotto, grotto, lotto, motto, **OTTO**
Otto, risotto, sotto　　　　　　　*see*
　　　　　　　　　　　　　　　　　o*

Anjou, bayou, bijou, caribou, frou- **OU***
frou, loup garou, marabou, sou, you　*see*
　　　　　　　　　　　　　　　　　UE*

Thou　　　　　　　　　　　　　**OU****
　　　　　　　　　　　　　　　　see
　　　　　　　　　　　　　　　　OUGH
　　　　　　　　　　　　　　　　OW**

Doubt, misdoubt, redoubt　　　　**OUBT**
　　　　　　　　　　　　　　　　see
　　　　　　　　　　　　　　　　OUT

Caoutchouc　　　　　　　　　　**OUC**
　　　　　　　　　　　　　　　　see
　　　　　　　　　　　　　　　　OOK*

Avouch, bridal-couch, couch, crouch, **OUCH***
game-pouch, grouch, ouch, pouch, *see*
slouch, vouch

Retouch, touch　　　　　　　　**OUCH****
　　　　　　　　　　　　　　　　see
　　　　　　　　　　　　　　　　UCH*

Barouche, cartouche, douche, Scara- **OUCHE**
mouche　　　　　　　　　　　　*see*

Aloud, becloud, cloud, enshroud, **OUD**
loud, overcloud, overloud, proud, *see*
purse-proud, shroud, stroud, thunder- OWD
cloud　　　　　　　　　　　　　OW**-*ed*

Rouge **OUGE**
see

Although, borough, dough, furlough, **OUGH***
though, thorough *see*
O*

Acacia-bough, apple-bough, bough, **OUGH****
Golden Bough, plough, slough, sough *see*
OW**
S-OUSE**

Enough, rough, slough, tough **OUGH*****
see
UFF

Through **OUGH******
see
U

Cough, hiccough, trough **OUGH*******
see
OFF

Afterthought, besought, bethought, **OUGHT**
bought, brought, drought, forethought, *see*
fought, inwrought, methought, nought, AUGHT*
ought, sought, take thought, thought, AUT*
unsought, well-fought, wrought

Bedouin **OUIN**
see
UIN

Saint Louis **OUIS**
see
E**

Afoul, befoul, foul   **OUL***
                                                see
                                                OWL

Over-soul, soul   **OUL****
                                                see
                                                OL

Ghoul, Stamboul   **OUL*****
                                                see
                                                ULE

Mould   **OULD***
                                                see
                                                OLD

Could, should, would   **OULD****
                                                see
                                                OOD

Boulder, shoulder   **OULDER**
                                                see
                                                ER

Noun, pronoun   **OUN**
                                                see
                                                OWN**

Announce, bounce, cherrybounce,   **OUNCE**
denounce, flounce, jounce, ounce,   *see*
pounce, pronounce, renounce, trounce

Abound, aground, around, astound,   **OUND**
background, blood-hound, bound,   *see*
camping-ground, compound, dumb-   OWN**-*ed*
found, expound, found, greyhound,   *ed*-ED
harehound, hidebound, homeward-

bound, horehound, hound, impound, ironbound, merry-go-round, mound, musclebound, outward bound, playground, pound, profound, propound, rebound, redound, resound, round, sleuth-hound, snowbound, sound, spellbound, staghound, stamping-ground, surround, underground, vantage-ground, whimpering-hound, wound

OUND

Bounder, flounder, founder, grounder, rounder

OUNDER
see
ER

Coffee-grounds, fish pounds, zounds

OUNDS
see
OUND-*s*

Young

OUNG
see
UNG

Lounge

OUNGE
see

Account, amount, catamount, count, discount, dismount, fount, miscount, mount, paramount, recount, surmount, tantamount, viscount

OUNT
see

Bounty, county, mounty

OUNTY
see
E**

Croup, group, pea-soup, recoup, thick soup, soup, troup

OUP*
see
OOP
OUPE**
UPE

Coup **OUP****
see
OU
UE

Cantaloupe **OUPE***
see
OPE

Troupe **OUPE****
see
OUP
UPE

Amour, armour, belabour, colour, **OUR**
détour, devour, dour, downpour, fa- *see*
vour, flavour, flour, four, giaour, glam- EUR
our, half-hour, honour, hour, ill-favour, OAR
labour, our, outpour, paramour, par- OR
lour, Pompadour, pour, rumour, sav- OWER
iour, scour, sour, splendour, succour, URE
tambour, tour, troubadour, vigour,
your

Resource, source **OURCE**
see
OURSE

Gourd **OURD**
see
URD

Scourge **OURGE**
see
ERGE
IRGE
URGE

Adjourn, bourn, sojourn   **OURN***
                                            see
                                            URN

Mourn   **OURN****
                                            see
                                            ORN

All fours, hours, ours, velours, yours   **OURS**
                                            see
                                            OUR-*s*

Bourse, concourse, course, discourse,   **OURSE**
intercourse, of-course, race-course, re-   *see*
course, water-course   ORSE
                                            OURCE

Court, divorce court, police court,   **OURT**
Supreme Court   *see*
                                            ORT

Fourth   **OURTH**
                                            see
                                            ORTH

Ambidextrous, analogous, andro-   **OUS***
gynous, anepigraphous, anonymous,   *see*
barbarous, bibulous, blasphemous,   ALOUS
bulbous, callous, chivalrous, cumbrous,   EOUS
declivous, desirous, diaphanous, dis-   EROUS
astrous, enormous, famous, frivolous,   INOUS
gibbous, gluttonous, hazardous, homol-   IOUS
ogous, idolatrous, infamous, joyous,   ITOUS
lithophagous, ludicrous, magnanimous,   ONOUS
mischievous, molluscous, momentous,   OROUS
monstrous, multifidous, murmurous,   ULOUS
nervous, nitrous, nubilous, ominous,   UOUS

parlous, pendulous, perilous, pompous, portentous, posthumous, prognathous, pusillanimous, rapturous, raucous, ravenous, rigorous, riotous, scurrilous, stupendous, sulphurous, synonymous, torturous, tremendous, troublous, tyrannous, unanimous, venomous, venous, venturous, viscous, wondrous

OUS*
US
ly-E**
OUSLY

Entre nous, rendevous

OUS**
see
U

Almshouse, blue-titmouse, bughouse, chapterhouse, chophouse, coach-house, custom-house, dormouse, douse, farmhouse, flitter-mouse, full-house, greenhouse, grouse, hot house, house, lighthouse, log-house, louse, meeting-house, mouse, penthouse, playhouse, poorhouse, power-house, rough-house, roundhouse, schoolhouse, shrew-mouse, souse, state house, storehouse, summerhouse, titmouse, wheel-house, White House, workhouse

OUSE*
see

Arouse, blouse, carouse, espouse, rouse, spouse

OUSE**
see
OUGH**-*s*
OWSE

Assiduously, continuously, copiously, curiously, furiously, instantaneously, joyously, previously, simultaneously, viciously

OUSLY
see
E**
IOUS-*ly*
OUS-*ly*

Joust, oust, roust   **OUST**
                                              see

About, blow-out, bout, boyscout,   **OUT***
clout, cut-out, devout, dugout, eke out,   *see*
fingerling trout, flatten-out, flout, gad-   AUT**
about, gout, hereabout, in and out,   OUBT
knockout, knout, layout, long-drawn-
out, lookout, lout, out, out and out,
pig's-snout, pout, right-about, root-
out, roundabout, rout, salmon trout,
scout, set-out, shout, snout, spout,
sprout, stout, thereabout, throughout,
tout, trout, try-out, turn-out, walkout,
wash-out, waterspout, whereabout,
without, worn-out

Mahout, marabout, surtout   **OUT****
                                              see
                                              OOT**

Passe partout, ragout   **OUT*****
                                              see
                                              OU*

Route   **OUTE**
                                              see
                                              OUT*

Couth, Plymouth, uncouth, ver-   **OUTH***
mouth, Yarmouth, youth   *see*
                                              UTH

Drouth, mouth, south   **OUTH****
                                              see

Billet-doux, Sioux **OUX**
see
O**

Approval, disapproval, oval, removal **OVAL**
see
AL

Innovate, ovate, renovate **OVATE**
see
ATE

Alcove, clove, cove, drove, grove, **OVE***
hove, interwove, Jove, mangrove, rove, *see*
shrove, stove, strove, throve, treasure AUVE
trove, trove, wove

Above, belove, boxing-glove, dove, **OVE****
foxglove, glove, kid-glove, ringdove, *see*
self-love, shove, turtledove, unglove OF

Approve, disapprove, disprove, im- **OVE*****
prove, move, prove, remove, reprove *see*
OOVE

Grovel, hovel, novel, shovel **OVEL**
see
EL
LE

Beethoven, cloven, disproven, inter- **OVEN**
woven, oven, proven, sloven, woven *see*
EN

Clover, cover, discover, four-leaved **OVER**
clover, hang-over, Hanover, hover, *see*
lover, moreover, over, Passover, plover, ER

popover, recover, rover, runover, stop-over, turnover, uncover, undercover

OVER

After-glow, aglow, backflow, barge-tow, bellow, below, bestow, billow, blow, borrow, bungalow, burrow, cross-bow, crow, dormer-window, elbow, fan window, fiddlebow, flow, follow, fore-shadow, furbelow, Glasgow, glow, goodmorrow, grass-widow, hedge-row, inflow, Jim Crow, know, low, meadow, minnow, morrow, mow, outgrow, over-flow, overshadow, overthrow, peach-blow, peepshow, pillow, plow, pussy-willow, rainbow, roadshow, rose-win-dow, row, rum-row, saddlebow, scare-crow, shadow, show, show window, slow, snow, sorrow, stone's-throw, stow, throw, tomorrow, tow, undertow, widow, willow, window, winnow

OW*
  see
  ALLOW
  ARROW
  EAU
  ELLOW
  OE**
  OUGH*
  OWE
  URROW
  ed-OAD
  ODE
  er-ER
  OUR*
  ly-E**
  OWLY
  ś-OSE*
  OZE

Allow, anyhow, avow, bow, bow-wow, brow, Chinese-chow, chowchow, cow, dhow, disavow, endow, enow, ere now, eyebrow, for-now, Hankow, high-brow, how, kowtow, Moscow, Nankow, now, plow, pow-wow, row, scow, snow-plow, somehow, sow, trow, vow, wow

OW**
  see
  AU***
  OU**
  OUGH**
  ed-OUD
  OWD
  ś-OUSE**

Crowd, overcrowd

OWD
  see
  OUD

Chowder, gunpowder, powder

OWDER
  see
  ER

Crowdy, dowdy, howdy, rowdy

OWDY
see
E**

Owe

OWE
see
O*

Bowel, dowel, paper-towel, roller-towel, towel, trowel, vowel

OWEL
see
EL

Borrower, bower, candlepower, cauli-flower, cornflower, cower, dower, em-bower, empower, flower, gilliflower, glower, horsepower, Leaning Tower, left-bower, lotus-flower, lower, may-flower, Mouse Tower, overpower, ower, passion flower, power, right-bower, shower, sunflower, tower, wallflower, watchtower, widower, wood-flower

OWER
see
ER
OUR*
OW*-*er*

Bowery, flowery, lowery

OWERY
see
ERY

Bowl, finger-bowl, pipe-bowl, wassail bowl

OWL*
see
OUL**

Cowl, fowl, growl, howl, jowl, night-owl, prowl, river-fowl, scowl, screech-owl, sea-fowl, water-fowl, yowl

OWL**
see
OUL*

Lowly, narrowly, slowly

OWLY
see
E**

Blown, disown, flown, fullblown, fullgrown, grown, highflown, known, mown, new-mown, outgrown, overblown, overthrown, own, self-sown, shown, sown, strown, thrown, unblown, unknown, unsown, well-known

OWN*
see
OAN
ONE*

A-down, brown, Cape Town, Chinatown, clown, comedown, crown, down, downtown, dressing-gown, drown, frown, gown, knock-down, let-down, low-down, marked-down, nightgown, plank down, renown, shakedown, showdown, shutdown, sit-down, Southdown, sun-down, swan's-down, thistledown, thrown-down, touch-down, town, tumbledown, uncrown, upsidedown, uptown

OWN**
see
OUN
ed-OUND

Bellows, gallows, overgrows, whoknows

OWS
see
OSE*
OW*-*s*

Browse, drowse

OWSE
see
OUSE**
OW**-*s*

Growth, overgrowth, undergrowth

OWTH
see
OATH
OTH*

Billowy, shadowy, willowy

OWY
see
E**

Ballot-box, bandbox, box, chatter-box, cowpox, deposit box, ditty-box, equinox, fox, letterbox, musicbox, muskox, Nox, ox, paddlebox, Pandora's box, paradox, pepperbox, phlox, pillbox, prowling-fox, rosewood box, saltbox, shooting-box, smallpox, snuffbox, soapbox, spitbox, strongbox, tinderbox

OX
see
OCK-*s*
ODOX

Doxy, foxy, heterodoxy, orthodoxy, proxy

OXY
see
E**

Ahoy, alloy, altar boy, annoy, babyboy, boy, bus boy, cabin-boy, charpoy, cloy, convoy, corduroy, coy, decoy, destroy, employ, enjoy, envoy, errandboy, hautboy, Helen of Troy, highboy, joy, killjoy, lowboy, newsboy, old boy, overjoy, playboy, Rob Roy, savoy, sepoy, ship-ahoy, teapoy, tomboy, toy, viceroy

OY
see
UOY
ed-OID
s-OISE

Loyal, pennyroyal, royal, unloyal

OYAL
see
AL

Lloyd, sloyd

OYD
see
OID

Gargoyle, Hoyle

OYLE
see
OIL

Bulldoze, doze, froze

OZE
see
OSE*
OW*-*s*

U SOUNDS

Babu, Bantu, bhikshu, Danu, emu, fichu, gnu, Hindu, Honolulu, impromptu, I.O.U., Jehu, ju-jitsu, juju, Khosru, Khufu, menu, Meru, Mu, Nu, ormolu, pari passu, parvenu, perdu, Peru, poilu, Shu, Timbuktu, Vishnu, zebu, Zulu

U

see
AGUE**
EW
IEU
IEW
INUE
O**
OO
OU
OUGH****
UE*
URU
UT**
S-EW-*S*
  OOSE**
  OOZE
  OSE**
  OUS**
  UISE**
  USE*

Aqua, Chatauqua, Gargantua, Joshua, Nicaragua, Padua, Papua

UA

see
A**

Equable, invaluable, valuable

UABLE

see
ABLE

Quad, squad

UAD
see
OD

Dissuade, overpersuade, persuade

UADE
see
ADE*
EDE**

Quaff

UAFF
see
AFE**

Agglutinative language, assuage, language

UAGE
see
AGE*

Actual, annual, bi-annual, bilingual, casual, co-equal, contextual, continual, conventual, dual, effectual, eventual, gradual, habitual, homo-sexual, individual, ineffectual, intellectual, lingual, manual, mutual, perpetual, punctual, residual, ritual, sensual, sexual, spiritual, unusual, usual, victual, virtual, visual

UAL
see
AL
ly-UALLY

Casually, eventually, habitually, mutually, perpetually, punctually, spiritually, unusually, usually, virtually

UALLY
see
ALLY
E**

Qualm

UALM
see
ALM

Assuan, Don Juan, gargantuan, San Juan

UAN
see
AN**

Nuance, piquance, pursuance **UANCE**
see
ANCE

Piquant, pursuant, truant **UANT**
see
ANT

Blackguard, bodyguard, coastguard, **UARD**
guard, lifeguard, mud-guard, safe- *see*
guard, vanguard ARD

Quarry **UARRY**
see
ORY

Mary Stuart, quart **UART**
see
ART**
ORT

Quartz **UARTZ**
see
ORT-*s*

Actuary, antiquary, electuary, es- **UARY**
tuary, February, January, mortuary, *see*
obituary, ossuary, reliquary, residuary, AIRY
sanctuary, statuary, voluptuary ARY
E**

Crookneck-squash, quash, mus- **UASH**
quash, squash *see*
ASH**

Kumquat **UAT**
see
AT**

Accentuate, actuate, adequate, anti-quate, attenuate, devaluate, evacuate, evaluate, extenuate, fluctuate, gradu-ate, inadequate, individuate, infatuate, insinuate, perpetuate, postgraduate, punctuate, sinuate, situate, superannu-ate, undergraduate

UATE
see
ATE

Suave, Zouave

UAVE
see

Cawquaw, musquaw, squaw

UAW
see
AW

Paraguay, quay, Uruguay

UAY
see
AY

Bathtub, Beelzebub, club, cub, dub, grub, hubbub, Indian club, pub, rub, rub-a-dub, scrub, shrub, sillabub, slub, snub, strawberry shrub, stub, sub, tub, yacht club

UB
see

Blubber, India-rubber, landlubber, rubber, snubber

UBBER
see
ER

Chubby, fubby, grubby, hubby, nubby, scrubby, snubby, tubby

UBBY
see
E**

Cube, inner-tube, jujube, rube, speaking-tube, tube

UBE
see

Dissoluble, double, insoluble, redouble, resoluble, rouble, soluble, trouble, voluble

UBLE
see
EL
LE

Adduce, Bruce, conduce, deuce, educe, induce, introduce, lettuce, produce, puce, reduce, reproduce, seduce, spruce, superinduce, traduce, truce

UCE
see
EUS
OOSE*
UICE

Forasmuch, inasmuch, much, nonsuch, overmuch, such

UCH*
see
OUCH**
UTCH

Eunuch, Pentateuch

UCH**
see
UKE

Ruche

UCHE
see

Amuck, awestruck, bestruck, buck, Calmuck, Canuck, chuck, cluck, duck, Friar Tuck, goodluck, horror-struck, luck, moonstruck, muck, muscovy duck, pluck, pot-luck, Puck, roebuck, sawbuck, shuck, struck, stuck, suck, tuck, truck, woodchuck

UCK
see
OK

Buckle, chuckle, honeysuckle, knuckle, muckle, shoebuckle, suckle

UCKLE
see
EL
LE

Lucre **UCRE**
see
ER

Abduct, conduct, construct, duct, **UCT**
induct, instruct, misconduct, obstruct, *see*
product, reconstruct, safe conduct, via- EDUCT
duct

Auction, deduction, destruction, in- **UCTION**
struction, obstruction, overproduction, *see*
production, reduction, reproduction, ION
ruction, seduction, suction

Bestud, bud, collar-stud, cud, dud, **UD**
mud, rosebud, scud, spud, stud, Tal- *see*
mud, thud OOD**

Rudder, shudder, udder **UDDER**
see
ER

Befuddle, fuddle, huddle, muddle, **UDDLE**
puddle *see*
EL
LE

Allude, collude, conclude, crude, **UDE**
delude, desuetude, dude, elude, etude, *see*
exclude, exude, include, inquietude, EUD
interlude, intrude, mansuetude, nude, ITUDE
obtrude, preclude, prelude, protrude, OOD***
prude, quietude, rude, seclude IEW-*ed*
UE*-*ed*
S-UDES

Begrudge, budge, drudge, fudge, grudge, judge, misjudge, nudge, sludge, smudge, trudge

UDGE
see

Soapsuds

UDS
see
UD-*s*

Accrue, argue, avenue, barbecue, blue, clue, construe, continue, cue, curlycue, due, ensue, flue, glue, hue, imbue, ingenue, marble-statue, misconstrue, out-argue, overdue, pursue, queue, rescue, retinue, revenue, revue, ring-true, robin's egg blue, rue, sky-blue, slue, statue, subdue, sue, true, true-blue, undervalue, undue, untrue, value, vendue, virtue

UE*
see
AGUE***
ISSUE
U
ed-EWD
UDE
s-EW-*s*
UISE**
USE

Fatigue, intrigue, overfatigue

UE**
see
AGUE**

Cruel, duel, fuel, gruel, Pantagruel, Samuel, sequel

UEL
see
EL

Guelph

UELPH
see

Affluence, congruence, consequence, effluence, eloquence, sequence

UENCE
see
ENCE

Minuend

UEND
see
END

Abluent, affluent, confluent, constituent, delinquent, effluent, eloquent, fluent, frequent, grandiloquent, inconsequent, influent, infrequent, refluent, sequent, subsequent, unguent

UENT
see
ENT

Beleaguer, chequer, exchequer, lacquer, pursuer

UER
see
ER

Quern

UERN
see
ERN

Bequest, conquest, follow-guest, guest, inquest, quest, request

UEST
see
EAST**

Banquet, bluet, cruet, duet, minuet, paroquet, piquet

UET*
see
ET

Croquet, parquet, sobriquet, tourniquet

UET**
see
A*

Bluff, buff, cuff, dandruff, duff, fisticuff, fluff, gruff, guff, handcuff, herbal snuff, huff, luff, Macduff, muff, plumduff, puff, rebuff, ruff, scruff, scuff, snuff, sob-stuff, stuff

UFF
see
OUGH**
ed-UFT

Candytuft, puft, tuft

UFT
see
UFF-*ed*

Bug, chug-chug, drug, dug, firebug, fire-plug, hearth-rug, hug, humbug,

UG
see

jug, lady-bug, lightning-bug, lug, **UG**
mealy-bug, mug, plug, potato-bug,
pug, rug, shrug, slug, smug, snug,
spark-plug, thug, tug, vinegar jug,
wicker-jug

Kali Yuga, Satya Yuga **UGA**
see
A**

Centrifugal, frugal, fugal, Portugal **UGAL**
see
AL

Deluge, huge, refuge, subterfuge **UGE**
see

Drugget, nugget **UGGET**
see
ET

Juggle, smuggle, snuggle, struggle **UGGLE**
see
EL
LE

Buggy, muggy, puggy, sluggy **UGGY**
see
E**

Impugn, oppugn **UGN**
see
UNG

Alleluia **UIA**
see
IA

Squib

UIB
see
IB

Juice, fruitjuice, grapejuice, sluice, tomato-juice

UICE
see
USE**

Druid, fluid, languid, liquid, quid, squid, tertian quid

UID
see
ID

Guide, misguide

UIDE
see
IDE

Guayaquil, jonquil, tranquil

UIL
see
IL

Build, guild, upbuild

UILD
see
ILD*
ILL-*ed*

Beguile, guile

UILE
see
ILE*

Goose-quill, quill, squill

UILL
see
ILL

Bedquilt, built, clipper-built, guilt, quilt

UILT
see
ILT
ed-ED

Guimp

UIMP
see
IMP

Algonquin, Bedouin, beguin, bruin, harlequin, lambrequin, mannequin, palanquin, penguin, ruin, sequin, Tarquin

UIN
see
IN
UINE

Equine, genuine, sanguine

UINE
see
INE**

Acquire, esquire, inquire, quire, require, squire

UIRE
see
IRE

Quirt, squirt

UIRT
see
IRT
URT

Disguise, guise

UISE*
see
IZE

Bruise, cruise

UISE**
see
USE

Anguish, bluish, cliquish, distinguish, extinguish, languish, relinquish, roguish

UISH
see
ISH

Altruism, truism, ventriloquism

UISM
see
ISM

Altruist, casuist, linguist, ventrilo- **UIST**
quist   *see*
                                              IST

Acquit, biscuit, circuit, conduit,   **UIT***
Jesuit, pilot-biscuit, quit, short-circuit   *see*
                                              IT

Breadfruit, bruit, dress-suit, follow **UIT****
suit, fruit, grapefruit, lawsuit, pursuit,   *see*
recruit, suit, unionsuit   UTE

Mesquite, suite, tout de suite   **UITE***
                                              see
                                              EAT*

Quite, requite   **UITE****
                                              see
                                              ITE*

Ambiguity, annuity, antiquity, con-   **UITY**
gruity, equity, gratuity, incongruity,   *see*
inequity, ingenuity, iniquity, longin-   E**
quity, obliquity, perpetuity, perspicu-   ITY
ity, propinquity, superfluity, tenuity,
ubiquity

Quiz   **UIZ**
                                              see
                                              IZ

Habakkuk, Kalmuk, Marduk, Sa-   **UK**
rouk, Volapuk   *see*
                                              UCH**
                                              UKE

Archduke, cuke, duke, fluke, Luke, **UKE**
Mameluke, peruke, rebuke   *see*
   OOK**
   UK

Annul, artful, awful, baleful, bane- **UL**
ful, bashful, brimful, bulbul, caracul,   *see*
careful, cheerful, consul, cupful, de-   IFUL
lightful, distrustful, doleful, doubtful,   ULL*
Elul, eyeful, faithful, fateful, fitful, for-
getful, fretful, graceful, grateful, harm-
ful, heartful, heedful, hurtful, ireful,
lawful, lustful, masterful, mindful,
mirthful, Mogul, mournful, mouthful,
needful, pailful, painful, plateful, play-
ful, powerful, prayerful, proconsul,
purposeful, regretful, remorseful, re-
proachful, resentful, restful, revenge-
ful, rueful, shameful, shovelful, sloth-
ful, sorrowful, tearful, thankful, thim-
bleful, thoughtful, tuneful, unfaithful,
ungrateful, unmirthful, useful, venge-
ful, wakeful, watchful, wilful, wishful,
wistful, woeful, wonderful, worshipful,
wrathful, wrongful, youthful

Calendula, Caligula, campanula, co- **ULA**
matula, copula, fibula, formula, Gula,   *see*
hula-hula, incunabula, nebula, penin-   A**
sula, scapula, spatula, spicula, St. Ur-
sula, tarantula

Angular, binocular, cellular, circular, **ULAR**
corpuscular, funicular, granular, glob-   *see*
ular, insular, irregular, jocular, jugu-   AR
lar, lenticular, lobular, lunular, molec-
ular, monocular, muscular, nebular,

oracular, orbicular, particular, peninsular, perpendicular, popular, rectangular, regular, secular, semi-circular, singular, spectacular, triangular, tubular, unpopular, valvular, vascular, vehicular, vernacular

ULAR

Articulate, calculate, circulate, coagulate, confabulate, congratulate, consulate, ejaculate, emulate, expostulate, formulate, granulate, immaculate, inarticulate, inoculate, insulate, jaculate, manipulate, matriculate, miscalculate, modulate, osculate, peculate, perambulate, populate, postulate, recapitulate, regulate, simulate, speculate, stimulate, stipulate, strangulate, tabulate, ululate, undulate

ULATE
see
ATE

Bulb, electric-light bulb, gladiola bulb, rubber-bulb

ULB
see

Mulch

ULCH
see

Animacule, capsule, cellule, corpuscule, crepuscule, ferrule, footrule, globule, golden-rule, granule, lobule, minuscule, misrule, module, molecule, mule, nodule, over-rule, plumbrule, pule, pustule, reticule, ridicule, rule, schedule, sumpter-mule, tule, vestibule, yule

ULE
see
OOL
OUL***

Corpulent, fraudulent, opulent, succulent, truculent, turbulent, virulent

ULENT
see
ENT

Amulet, Capulet, epaulet, rivulet **ULET**
see
ET

Engulf, gulf **ULF**
see

Bulgar, vulgar **ULGAR**
see
AR

Bulge, divulge, effulge, indulge, pro- **ULGE**
mulge *see*

Fulgent, effulgent, indulgent, over- **ULGENT**
indulgent *see*
ENT

Bulk, hulk, skulk, sulk **ULK**
see

Bulky, sulky **ULKY**
see
E**

Armfull, bull, chestfull, chock-full, **ULL**
cull, dull, full, gull, hull, jaw-full, jig- *see*
full, lull, mull, null numskull, pull, OL
scull, sea-gull, skull, you'll UL

Tulle **ULLE**
see
ULE

Bully, carefully, dully, fully, gully, **ULLY**
ruefully, spitefully, sully, truthfully, *see*
untruthfully, wilfully E**

Credulous, cumulous, fabulous, garrulous, homunculous, incredulous, meticulous, miraculous, nebulous, pendulous, populous, querulous, ridiculous, scrupulous, tremulous, tumulous, unscrupulous

ULOUS
see
OUS
US

Gulp, pulp

ULP
see

Pulse, impulse, repulse

ULSE
see
ULT-*s*

Adult, antepenult, catapult, consult, cult, difficult, exult, insult, occult, penult, result, semi-occult, tumult

ULT
see
ed-ED
s-ULSE

Difficulty, faculty, faulty

ULTY
see
E**

Calculus, convolvulus, ranunculus, Romulus, stimulus, tumulus

ULUS
see
US

Duly, patchouly, truly, unruly

ULY*
see
E**

July

ULY**
see
I*
Y

Addendum, adytum, alarum, album, **UM**
alburnum, alum, annum, antidotum, *see*
arboretum, asylum, bay rum, begum, ANUM
bum, bunkum, candelabrum, capsicum, ATUM
cerebrum, chewing-gum, chrysanthe- AUM
mum, chum, colchicum, conundrum, EUM
corrigendum, curriculum, date-plum, ITUM
doldrum, drum, E pluribus unum, er- IUM
gastulum, factotum, Fatum, fe-fi-fo- OM*
fum, fulcrum, glum, gum, gypsum, OME*
harum-scarum, hokum, hoodlum, hor- ORUM
rendum, hum, humdrum, index rerum, OMB
interregnum, kettledrum, Khartum, UUM
labarum, laburnum, lignum, magnum,
maximum, memorandum, minimum,
modicum, momentum, mum, nostrum,
oakum, opossum, pabulum, panjan-
drum, pax vobiscum, pendulum, pep-
lum, per-annum, platinum, plectrum,
plum, quantum, referendum, regnum,
rostrum, rum, sanctum, scrum, scum,
scutum, sedum, serum, simulacrum,
sistrum, slum, sorghum, spectrum,
strum, sugar-plum, sum, summum
bonum, sweet alyssum, tantrum, Tar-
gum, thrum, tintinnabulum, Tum,
unguentum, unum, vade-mecum, vel-
lum, viaticum, wampum, yum-yum

Montezuma, Numa, puma, Satsuma, **UMA**
Uma *see*
A**

Hanuman, human, inhuman, super- **UMAN**
human *see*
AN*

Benumb, crumb, dumb, numb, plumb, succumb, thumb, Tom Thumb

UMB
see
OMB**

Cucumber, cumber, encumber, lumber, number, slumber, outnumber

UMBER
see
ER

Bumble, crumble, fumble, grumble, humble, jumble, mumble, rumble, stumble, tumble

UMBLE
see
EL
LE

Gumbo, jumbo, Mumbo Jumbo

UMBO
see
O*

Penumbra, umbra

UMBRA
see
A**

Assume, brume, consume, costume, exhume, flume, fume, illume, legume, nom de plume, perfume, plume, presume, resume, quivering-plume, subsume, volume

UME
see
OOM

Acumen, albumen, bitumen, catechumen

UMEN
see
EN

Argument, document, emolument, instrument, integument, monument, wind-instrument

UMENT
see
ENT

Humid, tumid

UMID
see
ID

Drummer, hummer, Indian-summer, midsummer, mummer
UMMER
see
ER

Chummy, dummy, gummy, mummy, thingummy, tummy
UMMY
see
E**

Autumn, column, fluted column
UMN
see
UM

Air-pump, bump, chump, clump, dump, frump, hump, jump, lump, mugwump, plump, pump, rump, slump, stump, thump, trump
UMP
see
S-UMPS

Crumpet, trumpet, strumpet
UMPET
see
ET

Galumph, humph, triumph
UMPH
see

Dumps, mumps
UMPS
see
UMP-*s*

Air-gun, begun, Bull Run, bun, dun, fun, gun, homespun, hot-cross-bun, Hun, injun, machine gun, Maxim-gun, nun, out-run, over-run, popgun, pun, rising-sun, run, shotgun, spun, sun, tun
UN
see
ION
ON
ONE**

Arjuna, Fortuna, lacuna, luna, tuna, una, Varuna, vicuna
UNA
see
A**

Quidnunc

UNC
see
UNK

Dunce

UNCE
see
ONCE*

Bunch, crunch, hunch, lunch, munch, Planter's punch, punch, quick-lunch, scrunch

UNCH
see

Adjunct, defunct

UNCT
see

Bund, fecund, fund, furibund, gerund, jocund, moribund, orotund, refund, rotund, sinking-fund, Sigismund

UND
see

Asunder, blunder, sunder, thunder, under

UNDER
see
ER

Foundry, laundry, sundry

UNDRY
see
E**

Bay of Fundy, Burgundy, maundy, Mrs. Grundy

UNDY
see
E**

Commune, demilune, dune, fortune, good-fortune, immune, importune, jejune, June, misfortune, Neptune, opportune, picayune, prune, rune, sandy-dune, triune, tune

UNE
see
EWN
OON

Bung, clung, dung, far-flung, flag-strung, flung, high-strung, hung, lung, moss-hung, rung, slung, sprung, strung, stung, sung, swung, underhung, un-hung, unstrung, unsung, wide-flung, wrung

UNG
see
ONG**

Expunge, lunge, plunge

UNGE
see
ONGE

Bunion, communion, non-union, re-union, union

UNION
see
ION

Community, immunity, impunity, opportunity, unity

UNITY
see
E**
ITY

Bunk, chipmunk, chunk, drunk, dunk, flunk, funk, hunk, junk, plunk, punk, Saratoga trunk, shrunk, skunk, slunk, spunk, stunk, sunk, tree-trunk, trunk

UNK
see

Funnel, runnel, tunnel

UNNEL
see
EL

Bunny, funny, gunny, sunny

UNNY
see
E**

Blunt, brunt, hunt, punt, runt, shunt, stunt

UNT
see
ONT*

Cluny, luny, puny

UNY
see
E**

Ambiguous, anfractuous, arduous, congruous, conspicuous, contemptuous, contiguous, continuous, deciduous, fatuous, flexuous, impetuous, incestuous, incongruous, inconspicuous, indeciduous, ingenuous, insinuous, mellifluous, presumptuous, promiscuous, sensuous, sinuous, strenuous, sumptuous, superfluous, supersensuous, tempestuous, tumultuous, tenuous, tortuous, unctuous, vacuous, virtuous, voluptuous

UOUS
see
OUS
US

Breeches-buoy, buoy, life-buoy

UOY
see
OY

Acorn-cup, buttercup, check-up, chirrup, clean-up, close-up, cup, dried-up, drinkingcup, flare-up, frame-up, get-up, gold-cup, grown-up, hang-up, het-up, hiccup, holdup, hook-up, ketchup, keyed-up, kick-up, larrup, let-up, line-up, lockup, loving-cup, make-up, painted-cup, pent-up, pick-me-up, pickup, puffed-up, pup, round-up, scup, set-up, seven-up, shake-up, shut up, smash-up, speed-up, standing-up, step-up, stirrup, stirrup-cup, stuck-up, sup, syrup, teacup, toss-up, up, up and up, well-brought-up, wind-up

UP
see
OP

Dupe, Guadalupe **UPE**
see
OOP

Cupid, stupid **UPID**
see
ID

Abrupt, bankrupt, corrupt, disrupt, **UPT**
erupt, interrupt *see*

Ashur, augur, Baldur, concur, Côte **UR**
d'Azur, cur, demur, fur, incur, King *see*
Arthur, larkspur, lemur, murmur, Nip- ERE***
pur, Nishapur, non sequitur, occur, EUR
recur, slur, spur, sulphur, Ur, Vidur, URE
Yom Kippur URR
ed-URD
s-URS

Angostura, Asura, aura, camera- **URA**
obscura, coloratura, datura, Estrema- *see*
dura A**

Augural, conjectural, guttural, in- **URAL**
augural, intramural, mural, natural, *see*
plural, preternatural, rural, scriptural, AL
structural, subnatural, supernatural,
unnatural, Ural

Accurate, commensurate, curate, in- **URATE**
accurate, inaugurate, incommensurate, *see*
obdurate, saturate, triturate ATE

Blurb, curb, disturb, perturb, sub- **URB**
urb, uncurb *see*
ERB

Church, lurch

URCH
see
EARCH
ERCH
IRCH

Absurd, curd, Kurd, surd

URD
see
EARD*
ERD
URE-*d*

Curdle, hurdle

URDLE
see
EL
LE

Hurdy-gurdy, sturdy

URDY
see
E**

Abjure, adventure, agriculture, allure, aperture, assure, azure, brochure, capture, censure, cincture, cocksure, coiffure, conjure, culture, cure, debenture, demure, departure, disfigure, embouchure, embrasure, endure, enrapture, ensure, failure, faith-cure, figure, fissure, fixture, floriculture, gesture, gravure, high-pressure, horticulture, imposture, impure, indenture, injure, insecure, insure, inure, jointure, juncture, lay figure, lecture, leisure, lowpressure, lure, manufacture, manure, mind cure, misadventure, mixture, moisture, mure, nurture, obscure, overture, pasture, pelure, peradventure,

URE
see
ASURE
ATURE
EUR
ICURE
ITURE
OOR**
OSURE
OUR**
ed-ERD
IRD
ORD**
URD

perjure, photogravure, picture, portraiture, posture, prefecture, prefigure,
premature, pressure, procedure, pro-
cure, puncture, pure, quadrature, rap-
ture, reassure, reinsure, Scripture, se-
cure, seizure, sepulture, sinecure, struc-
ture, sure, suture, tenure, texture,
tincture, tonsure, torture, transfigure,
venture, verdure, vesture, vulture, wax
figure, you're

URE

Treasurer, usurer

URER
see
ER

Surf, turf

URF
see
ERF

Gettysburg, Strasburg, Vicksburg

URG
see
ERG

Demi-urge, inner urge, Panurge,
purge, scourge, splurge, spurge, surge,
thaumaturge, urge

URGE
see
ERGE
IRGE

Dramaturgy, liturgy, metallurgy,
thaumaturgy, theurgy

URGY
see
E**

Futurity, impurity, insecurity, ma-
turity, obscurity, purity, security, semi-
obscurity

URITY
see
E**
ITY

Lurk, murk, Turk	**URK** *see* ERK IRK
Churl, curl, furl, hurl, purl, unfurl	**URL** *see* EARL IRL ORL *ed*-ORLD
Curly, burly, hurly-burly, surly	**URLY** *see* E**
Auburn, burn, churn, lecturn, mortuary-urn, nocturn, overturn, return, Saturn, spurn, sunburn, taciturn, turn, Tyburn, upturn, urn	**URN** *see* EARN OURN*
Diurnal, journal, nocturnal	**URNAL** *see* AL
Burnt, sunburnt	**URNT** *see*
Usurp	**URP** *see* *ed*-ERPT
Aaron Burr, blurr, burr, purr	**URR** *see* UR
Burrow, furrow	**URROW** *see* OW*

Curry, flurry, furry, hurry, scurry **URRY**
see
E**

Accurse, curse, cut-purse, disburse, **URSE**
impurse, nurse, purse, reimburse, shep- *see*
herd's-purse, wet-nurse EARSE
ERCE
ed-ED

Accurst, burst, cloudburst, curst, **URST**
durst, nurst, outburst, sunburst *see*
IRST
ed-ED

Blurt, curt, Frankfurt, hurt, spurt, **URT**
yurt *see*
ERT
IRT
UIRT

Hurtle, mockturtle, snapping turtle, **URTLE**
turtle *see*
EL
LE

Guru **URU**
see
U

Arcturus, Epicurus, Eurus **URUS**
see
AURUS
US

A-curve, curve, incurve **URVE**
see
ERVE

Augury, bury, Canterbury, century,
conjury, fury, injury, jury, luxury,
Mercury, penury, perjury, tilbury,
treasury, usury

URY
see
E**

Abacus, Academus, acanthus, Æolus,
agnus, ailanthus, Albertus Magnus,
alumnus, amaranthus, angelus, animus,
ankus, Antæus, arbutus, Augustus,
Autolycus, Avernus, Bacchus, bacillus,
Belus, bogus, bolus, bonus, Brutus,
bus, cactus, Cadmus, Catullus, Cau-
casus, caucus, Celsus, census, cholera-
morbus, cirrus, citrus, colossus, Co-
lumbus, Comus, consensus, conspectus,
Copernicus, Coriolanus, corpus, Crœ-
sus, Cronus, cultus, cuniculus, cyprus,
Cyrus, demiurgus, dianthus, Diodorus,
discobolus, discus, Duns Scotus, En-
celadus, Ephesus, Erasmus, Erebus,
eucalyptus, exodus, faunus, fungus,
habeas corpus, Halicarnassus, helian-
thus, Hephæstus, Herodotus, hibiscus,
humus, Hyacinthus, Hymettus, Iam-
blicus, Icarus, ictus, ignis-fatuus, impetus, incubus, isthmus, Janus, Jesus,
Josephus, Judas Maccabæus, litmus,
Leviticus, lotus, Lucullus, magnus,
maybush, Menelaus, mittimus, modus,
Momus, mucus, narcissus, nautilus,
negus, Nicodemus, Nilus, nimbus,
Ninus, nisus, nonplus, obolus, Oceanus,
Œdipus, Olympus, omnibus, onus,
opus, ornithorhynchus, Paracelsus, pa-
radus, Parnassus, Patroclus, Pegasus,
Peloponnesus, Pentelicus, Phœbus,
platypus, plexus, plus, polyanthus,

US
see
AGUS
ALUS
AMPUS
AMUS
ATUS
AURUS
EOUS
ERUS
ETUS
EUS*
INOUS
INUS
IOUS
ITOUS
ITUS
IUS
OCUS
OPUS
ORUS
OUS
ULOUS
ULUS
URUS
USS
YLUS
YRUS

Polygnotus, Polyphemus, Pontus, Pri- **US**
apus, prospectus, pus, Pyrrhus, raucus,
rebus, Remus, Rhadamanthus, rhom-
bus, rumpus, sanctus, Silenus, Sil-
vanus, Sisyphus, solus, Somnus, status,
strophanthus, stylus, surplus, syllabus,
Tacitus, Tarsus, Tartarus, tetanus,
thaumaturgus, Theophrastus, thesaurus, thus, thyrsus, Trismegistus,
uræus, Uranus, Ursus, U.S., us, Venus,
versus, virus, walrus, Xanthus

Anchusa. Arethusa, Medusa, Susa **USA**
see
A**

Carousal, causal, espousal, perusal, **USAL**
refusal *see*
AL

Abstruse, abuse, accuse, amuse, **USE**
bemuse, confuse, diffuse, disuse, Druse, *see*
effuse, enthuse, exclude, excuse, fuse, OOSE*
hypotenuse, infuse, interfuse, misuse, OSE**
muse, obtuse, peruse, profuse, recluse, UISE**
refuse, ruse, suffuse, transfuse, use, EW-*s*
Vauclause OE*-*s*
U-*s*
UE*-*s*

Ambush, blush, brush, bulrush, **USH**
bush, crush, flush, gush, hush, inrush, *see*
lush, mush, onrush, plush, push, rush,
sagebrush, scrubbing-brush, shad-bush,
slush, spicebush, steeple-bush, thrush,
toothbrush, tush

Allusion, conclusion, confusion, delusion, disillusion, exclusion, fusion, illusion, inclusion, infusion, intrusion, obtrusion, profusion

USION
see
ION

Conclusive, delusive, elusive, exclusive, illusive, inclusive, intrusive, obtrusive, unobtrusive, preclusive

USIVE
see
IVE

Dusk, husk, mollusk, musk, rusk, tusk

USK
see
USQUE

Cusp

USP
see

Brusque

USQUE
see
USK

Blunderbuss, buss, cuss, discuss, fuss, muss, percuss, puss, sour puss, truss

USS
see
US

Adjust, anti-rust, august, brickdust, bust, combust, crust, disgust, distrust, dust, entrust, gold-dust, gust, incrust, intrust, just, locust, lust, mistrust, must, piecrust, portrait-bust, readjust, robust, rust, sawdust, star-dust, thrust, trust, unjust, wanderlust

UST
see

Adjuster, baluster, bluster, buster, cluster, duster, filibuster, fluster, luster, muster

USTER
see
ER

Bustle, hustle, rustle

USTLE
see
EL
LE

Crusty, dusty, fusty, gusty, lusty, musty, rusty, trusty

USTY
see
E**
UST-*y*

Abut, betelnut, brazil-nut, brut, but, butternut, catgut, chestnut, chut, clear-cut, cocoanut, Connecticut, cross-cut, cut, doughnut, gamut, halibut, hut, jut, Lilliput, Mut, nut, output, put, peanut, rebut, rut, sackbut, scut, short-cut, shut, slut, smut, strut, tut, uncut, walnut, woodcut

UT*
see
OOT*

Début

UT**
see
U

Brutal, refutal

UTAL
see
AL

Clutch, crutch, Dutch, hutch, smutch

UTCH
see
UCH*

Acute, astute, brute, Canute, chute, commute, compute, confute, cute, deaf-mute, dilute, dispute, disrepute, electrocute, execute, flute, hirsute, jute, lute, minute, mute, parachute, persecute, pollute, prosecute, refute, repute, salute, transmute, tribute, Ute

UTE
see

Azimuth, bismuth, Ruth, truth, untruth, vermuth

UTH
see
EUTH
OOTH
OUTH*

Ablution, circumlocution, constitution, contribution, dissolution, distribution, elocution, evolution, involution, locution, persecution, pollution, prosecution, restitution, retribution, revolution, solution

UTION
see
ION

Contributor, distributor, executor, interlocutor, persecutor, prosecutor, tutor

UTOR
see
OR

Mutt, putt

UTT
see
UT*

Butter, clutter, cutter, flutter, gutter, mutter, peanut butter, putter, revenue cutter, shutter, sputter, stonecutter, stutter, utter

UTTER
see
ER

Button, glutton, mutton

UTTON
see
ON

Nutty, putty, smutty

UTTY
see
E**

Beauty, deputy, duty

UTY
see
E**

Meum et tuum, residuum, vacuum   **UUM**
                                   see
                                   UM

Chef d'œuvre, Louvre, manœuvre   **UVRE**
                                   see
                                   ER

Afflux, conflux, crux, efflux, fiat lux,   **UX**
flux, influx, Ku Klux, Pollux, reflux   *see*
                                          UCK-*s*
                                          UCT-*s*

Buy, guy   **UY**
             see
             Y

Santa Cruz, St. Jean de Luz, Tam-   **UZ**
muz, Uz, Vera Cruz   *see*
                       OOZE

Guzzle, muzzle, nuzzle, puzzle   **UZZLE**
                                   see
                                   EL
                                   LE

Y SOUNDS

Apply, awry, blackfly, blue-sky, butterfly, by, by and by, cry, damsel fly, dragonfly, dry, espy, firefly, fly, fry, gad-fly, go-by, hereby, housefly, imply, lullaby, mayfly, mid-sky, mis-apply, multiply, my, nearby, occupy, outcry, passerby, Paul Pry, ply, pre-occupy, pry, reply, satisfy, shoo-fly, shy, sky, sly, small fry, spanish fly, spry, spy, stand-by, sty, supply, thereby, thy, try, war-cry, whereby, why, wry

Y
  see
  EFY
  EYE
  I*
  IFY
  IGH
  ULY**
  UY
  YE*

Cherimoya, Libya, Maitreya, Surya

YA
  see
  A**

Dryad, dyad, hamadryad

YAD
  see
  AD

Triptych

YCH
  see
  ECK

Bicycle, cycle, kilocycle, megacycle, Metonic Cycle, motorcycle, tricycle

YCLE
  see
  EL
  LE

Jamshyd	**YD** *see* EED
Clepsydra, hydra	**YDRA** *see* A**
Aye, bye, dye, eye, goodbye, lye, rye, tye	**YE*** *see* I** Y
Ye	**YE*** *see* E*
Oxygen	**YGEN** *see* EN
Dyke, tyke, Vandyke	**YKE** *see* IKE
Beryl, dactyl, idyl, methyl, sibyl	**YL** *see* EL
Adactyle, hypostyle, peristyle, pro-style, style	**YLE** *see* ILE*
Babylon, pylon	**YLON** *see* ON

Sylph **YLPH**
see

Rhyme, thyme **YME**
see
IME*

Hymn **YMN**
see
IM

Lymph, nymph, woodnymph **YMPH**
see

Lynch **YNCH**
see
INCH

Anodyne, auld lang syne, dyne, het- **YNE**
erodyne
see
INE*

Larynx, lynx, pharynx **YNX**
see
INX

Amphictyon, amphitryon, Apollyon, **YON**
canyon, halcyon
see
ON

Gyp, polyp **YP**
see
IP

Archetype, daguerreotype, linotype, **YPE**
monotype, prototype, stereotype, tin-
type, type
see
IPE

Anaglyph, glyph, hieroglyph, tri-glyph

YPH
see
IF

Apocalypse

YPSE
see
IP-*S*

Crypt, Egypt

YPT
see
IPT

Martyr, satyr, zephyr

YR
see
AR*
ER

Byre, gyre, lyre, pyre, Tyre

YRE
see
IRE

Myrrh

YRRH
see
IR

Papyrus, zephyrus

YRUS
see
US

Abysm, cataclysm, paroxysm

YSM
see
ISM

Chlamys

YS
see
IS*

Abyss **YSS**
see
IS*

Amethyst, analyst, catalyst, cyst, **YST**
tryst *see*

Acolyte, neophyte, proselyte, troglo- **YTE**
dyte *see*
IGHT
ITE*

Myth **YTH**
see
ITH

Scythe **YTHE**
see
ITHE

Rhythm **YTHM**
see
IM

Gyve **YVE**
see
IVE*

Onyx, oryx, Pnyx, pyx, sardonyx **YX**
see
IX